PORTRAIT OF VILLAGE LIFE

Also by Keith Nethercoate-Bryant

Articles for *The Villager*. *1983-2006*

Submarine Memories. Laceys 1995

More Submarine Memories. Laceys 1997

Shoreham-by-Sea Past and Present
  (with E. Colquhoun). Sutton 1997

Death Escape: HMS Perseus
  (contributor). Finatec. Cephalonia 2001

18th Century Windmills of Brighton. University of Sussex

Even More Submarine Memories. Laceys 2005

Keith Nethercoate-Bryant

Photograph by courtesy of Gerald Thompson, Steyning Herald

Portrait
of
Village Life

Beeding, Bramber
and Botolphs
in Sussex

Keith Nethercoate-Bryant

Collated and edited, with an introduction,
by
Peter Thorogood

Bramber Press
2011

Portrait of Village Life has been sponsored by Peter Thorogood MBE FSA, and comprises a collection of articles by Keith Nethercoate-Bryant printed in *The Villager*, the parish magazine of Upper Beeding and Bramber with Botolphs in Sussex between April 1983 and March 2005. Peter Thorogood has collated and edited the collection, to which he has added over a hundred illustrations and an extensive reference section, together with a biographical introduction.

A CIP catalogue record for this book is available from the British Museum.
ISBN 978-1-905206-03-2

Copyright © Bramber Press 2011

Picture editing and graphics by Tony Ketteman
Final formatting of the complete text for printing by Alan Durden

All enquries to:
Bramber Press, St. Mary's House, Bramber, West Sussex BN44 3WE
Tel: 01903 816205 www.bramberpress.co.uk

Front cover: Painting of Bramber tollhouse by C. Cowper 1887
(Thorogood-Linton Collection)
Photograph by Peter Merrick

Back cover photograph of Keith Nethercoate-Bryant
by courtesy of West Sussex County Times

Printed and bound by CPI Group (UK) Ltd, Croydon, CR0 4YY

In memory of my wife Margaret
for her patience and friendship

'My long experience of life tells me that the more one knows
about the past, the clearer the picture is of the future.'

'Without knowledge of past happenings many of the awful mistakes
of earlier generations will be carried into the future.'

'I class myself as an inquirer.
I hate to leave puzzles and mysteries unsolved.'

'History is a treasure hunt, a detective story with exciting clues.'

Keith Nethercoate-Bryant

Contents

Preface

The editing and preparation for publication of a writer's work carries with it a tremendous responsibility and the added obligation of being true to the original as is humanly possible. Whilst after four years of painstaking work I am only too aware of the first of these requirements, I have made every effort to honour the second. The initial impetus comes from a real admiration for one's author, followed by a growing awareness of, in his case, his historical intention, and always with deference to his wishes. One has to take into account the remorseless monthly deadlines that beset the author, thinking up yet another new theme and never knowing the extent of the research required in the time available. I can only admire Keith's tenacity, his sense of purpose, his enthusiasm for history and, above all, his innate love of the community in which he chose to live and subsequently write about.

My first task was to track down a complete set of his articles (including the repeated ones) covering some twenty years. Whilst our archive at St. Mary's House, Bramber, had a near-complete set, I was pleased to be able to discover the errant numbers either from Keith himself or from the collection donated by him to the Steyning Museum.

The first volume began its life in April 1983 and thus included only nine monthly issues; thereafter, volumes appeared in twelve monthly articles. Each volume was numbered in Roman numerals, which I have replaced with Arabic numerals as a better working arrangement and which also makes things easier for the reader. For example, Vol. XVIII No.2 becomes simply 18.2. I have also adopted this method of numbering in the indexes at the end of the book.

In time I began to realise that page numbering of articles should be secondary since each article, which had its own volume numbering, was limited to a single page in the original A5 format of the magazine itself. The only instance in the whole book where page numbers are listed is in the 'Contents' page.

In places, discrepancies occur in titles and volume numbers; the Steyning Museum list and that held in the St. Mary's Bramber Archive differs in some instances. This confusion is more apparent in the later issues of *The Villager*, when a handful of reprints started to appear with different titles.

Eventually I abandoned the idea of grouping the articles under subject and opted for the chronological approach, so the idea to include the date of each article, giving the effect of a monthly diary, succeeded in lending a sense of immediacy to the text, though I am guilty of deleting one or two colloquialisms where the text was weakened by their inclusion.

I have also reduced the prolific use of capitals. For example, 'church' would refer to any church, and 'Church' to a specific church or, as in 'The Church', the institution itself. In the context of this book, I have taken the local use of 'Beeding' to mean 'Upper Beeding'. 'Lower Beeding' is rarely mentioned but, when it is, I have used its full name.

Regarding dates, I have chosen to use the more contemporary fashion, eliminating the apostrophe as in 'the 1860s' and the full-stop in 'c1860'.

Where they occur, most of Keith's parentheses and asides have been relegated to the ends of the articles. I have also added, where relevant, references to similar themes dealt with in later pieces.

In the latter years, there were many repeated articles. Thus only a handful of new ones appear in this book, quite a number of which are reworkings of earlier themes. Soon I realised that the more enquiring reader might also wonder why, for example, 10.9 and 22.4 are missing, so a list of repeated articles omitted from the text had to be compiled. After October 2004, no new articles by Keith appeared.

My work was made easier once I had built up a viable indexing system, which enabled me to track down and check other references to the topic in hand. In view of the vast number of these references, this became an almost insuperable task. I felt like Sysiphus, endlessly rolling his great boulder up the hill and never reaching the top. A variety of lists began to proliferate: lists of people, lists of places, lists of pursuits, alphabetical lists, and chronological lists.

I have not attempted to include any editorial comment, but I will be pleased to receive further information the reader may consider of use in the preparation of any future edition of this book, or be told of any errors, factual or otherwise.

My choice of illustrations was made easier in the early part of the book since the articles in the main were about specific buildings, streets, rivers, bridges, historical figures, and village people. Many articles were more abstract, dealing with such topics as beating the bounds of the villages, taxes and tolls, customs and pursuits, and so on, and have no companion illustrations.

The quality of the illustrations may vary according to the condition of the originals. Though I have been mostly fortunate in my searches, some useful archival material has been taken from ancient photographs, inferior photocopies and even faded newspaper articles. Occasionally, I have chosen an illustration for its special interest rather than its intrinsic merit.

Following the demise of *The Villager*, a monthly magazine under the name of *The New Adur Herald* continued to publish repeats of Keith's articles either whole or in part. From this publication I have, in Appendix One, introduced three articles, one entitled *The Dead of Bramber*, which includes useful information on burials in the churchyard. The decline and fall of *The Villager* is graphically described in *Farewell to the Parish Magazine* and *The End of the Road*.

Finally, though this book is intended to be my tribute to Keith's writing, I think I may be allowed to consider its editorship as my own special contribution to the history of the community in which I also live.

Portrait of Village Life is not merely a straightforward compilation of Keith's monthly articles. It is the bringing-together in book form of an invaluable body of personal research by a gifted local historian.

Peter Thorogood

Editor's Acknowledgements

The following have provided me
with invaluable advice, information and permissions:

The Beeding and Bramber Local History Society
The President and Fellows of Magdalen College Oxford
The Nethercoate-Bryant family archive
The Steyning Museum
Sussex Archaeological Collections, Lewes

And in particular I wish to thank:

Sister Mary Andrew, The Towers Convent, Upper Beeding
Dr. Peter Brandon FSA, Sussex author and historian
Dr. Robin Darwall-Smith FSA FRHistS, Archivist, Magdalen College,
    Oxford
Gillian Fox, former Chairman, Bramber Parish Council
Roger Linton MBE, Curator, St, Mary's House and Gardens, Bramber
Dr Dudley Moore, archaeologist and Key-keeper, Bramber Castle (for
    English Heritage)
Robin Myers MBE FSA, Archivist Emeritus, The Worshipful Company
    of Stationers
Pat Nightingale, Secretary and honorary archivist, Beeding and Bramber
    Local History Society
Dr. Janet Pennington, Sussex author and historian
David Thompson, researcher and archivist, Steyning Museum
Chris Tod, Curator, Steyning Museum

During the preparation of this collection of articles by Keith Nethercoate-Bryant I have also drawn on the Thorogood-Linton collections of the St. Mary's House Library and Archive. In particular, I have been enormously grateful for the advice and skills of my friends and colleagues of the Bramber Press: Alan Durden (administrator, St. Mary's House), and archivists to St. Mary's House, Tony Ketteman and Diana Durden, who all, variously in their diligent preparation, proof-reading and computer-formatting of the text, have given me, through their expertise, the encouragement to complete the task of collating and editing what I believe to be a valuable work of reference which gathers together many sources of local knowledge for the benefit of present and future scholars of Sussex local history.

Peter Thorogood
St. Mary's House
Bramber

Keith Nethercoate-Bryant as I Know Him
by
Peter Thorogood

Over the years I have had the privilege of conversing with Keith Nethercoate-Bryant on countless occasions. This has given me a unique opportunity to piece together the facts of his life and to discover in him someone who has given more than his fair share of devotion to his community and its history.

The Parish Councillor

Keith's public achievements are well documented. For 25 years a member of the Beeding Parish Council and seven years its chairman, he was also a Trustee of the Yobe (Somalia) Project, commissioning Chairman of the Botolph's Burial Board, co-founder of the Beeding and Bramber Local History Society, founding Chairman of the Gatwick Submarine Archive, and President of the Gatwick Submariners Association.

Such an incomplete list as this does not take more than a few seconds to read, but it covers a lifetime of service. Among his many activities, he became heavily involved in the campaign in 1980 to build a bypass for Steyning, Beeding and Bramber, saving the villages from damage caused by the thundering of heavy traffic through their high streets. For the opening, he chose to have no celebrities, but to invite the children of the three villages to open the bypass themselves.

As Chairman of the 'Twin Aid' Yobe Project, Keith joined forces with Mrs. Gill Fox, Chairman of Bramber Parish Council, and television presenter, Margaret Foster, to help raise over £20,000 towards the establishment of a school in Somalia, with Blue Circle providing the cement for the building work.

ITV's Margaret Foster, with Keith's twin sons Andrew and John, at the Yobe Project presentation ceremony

Keith's devotion to community projects was tireless. He set up an Emergency Flood Committee during the Adur Valley floods of 1987. He oversaw the replacement of the old crumbling footbridge for Beeding Bridge at a cost of £26,000. He fought to get a doctors' surgery at Beeding, thus allowing elderly residents easy access to the improved facilities. Among his many other achievements was the supervision of the building of a new school for Upper Beeding primary schoolchildren, with six new classrooms accommodating 400 children.

One of the most controversial changes in the Beeding parish boundaries took place during Keith's time as a councillor – the unpopular transfer of Kings Barnes from Beeding to Steyning. The area had belonged to Beeding for over a thousand years and was the home of the royal manor of King Alfred the Great. The change involved some thousand parishioners paying an appreciable sum in rates to Steyning in future, instead of these precious funds going to Beeding. According to the press reports at the time, there was the real fear that unwelcome development might take place in the future [2.7].

All this is about Keith, the able and devoted councillor - Keith, the public man. Having known him for over 25 years, I wanted to find out more about the private man. So those more recent conversations with such an old friend have been of the greatest pleasure and interest to me. How long we can know a person for a particular reason and in special circumstances and yet never seem to come round to asking about his life, his family, his special interests! What I discovered came as a pleasant surprise.

The Grandson

Martha White

The name Nethercoate comes from 15th century Shropshire and derives from the name for the protective garment worn under the armourer's chainmail. Keith's great-grandmother, Martha White, was a niece of the 18th century naturalist, Gilbert White, so the young lad's passion for the natural world and its secrets was in his blood.

Keith was born in Brighton in 1927, the eldest child of an old Winchester family who had also resided for some time in Bournemouth, where his uncle, John A.Nethercoate,

who was Mayor of the town, had built a substantial house, fitting his civic position, and acquired a smart Wolesely motor-car. Another uncle was organist at Winchester Cathedral.

Keith's paternal grandfather had been a pioneer military surgeon and masseur to the Maharajah of Baroda and did army service in World War I. He invented a new technique of wax massage and worked at Brighton Royal Pavilion during

Family mansion in Bournemouth, home to several Bryant branches

wartime when it was used as an emergency hospital.

Keith's mother, Louise (Lulu) Nethercoate, was an artist, and a designer of covers for *art deco* magazines. She was a founder member of the Guild of Aviation Artists, influenced in this direction by another son, David, who was chairman of the 'Popular Flying Association'. She numbered among her friends

RAF heroes Leonard Cheshire and Sir Douglas Bader. Many of her paintings can be seen at the RAF Museum at Hendon and one of her works is a centrepiece for the Red Arrows Mess. Following a stroke, she continued painting

with her left hand and produced some interesting work in this manner. She was a life-long friend (and Brighton neighbour) of the novelist, Baroness Orczy, author of *The Scarlet Pimpernel,* so it is easy to see where Keith gets his sense of adventure from. As the Baroness lived part of her time in the south of France, she wrote to Louise frequently, and I was fortunate to be shown some of this correspondence in the family archive.

Keith's mother, Louise Bryant with some of her aeronautical paintings

Keith's father was a civil engineer and followed the family occupation of builder. 'Where there was a plot of land he'd put something on it.' He was often away from home, spending much of his time travelling to construction sites.

Keith was therefore brought up by his paternal grandparents, who, as he describes them, 'regulated his upbringing'. Visitors to the house often included the eminent historian, L. F. Salzman, author of the important *Chartulary of Sele,* whom Keith always referred to as his 'tutor'. Distinguished authors and archaeologists, Dr. Curwen and his son, were also regular visitors. George Hollyman, the Brighton

Keith's father (centre) with his four sons (Keith on right)

bookseller and book-collector, in whose shop in Duke Street, Brighton, Keith could browse to his heart's content, was also a consummate guide to further study.

Keith's large collection of books on Sussex forms only a part of his wide reading, encouraged as it was by his grandfather who, in retirement, was a founder member of the Sussex Downsmen. In that capacity, he would take his eager grandson to watch 'the beating of the bounds' around the village [15.11]. This was an ancient ceremony to establish the position of the 'mere-stones' that marked the boundaries – and ginger beer was dispensed along the way! [2.9]. Keith describes his grandfather as 'the leading light of his education.' As a medical man and an amateur archaeologist and historian, he made Keith's early teens 'exciting and full of discoveries.'

With such a background, Keith, in the early 1930s, would become the youngest member of the Brighton and Hove Archaeological Society (Junior Section) and an enthusiastic collector of Neolithic implements. Many of these were discovered in later years in his own garden in Upper Beeding. The village had in former times been situated on the very edge of the Adur estuary. He was to find numerous flint borers, scrapers and blades under the soil there. Some of his collection of flint axes came from the ancient Neolithic site on Cissbury Hill across the valley [8.7].

The Schoolboy

Keith's first school was a private boarding school in Lancing, but a slump in the 1930s led to a decline in the family fortunes and he was sent to school in Brighton, in the shadows of the Preston railway viaduct, 'a gloomy place for children.' His grandfather's house was at 115 Preston Road, opposite the entrance to Preston Park, where there had once been a Roman grave and farm or villa. Artefacts abounded everywhere.

'In those days, teachers taught respect and manners as a school subject.' He recalls the many lessons enhanced by the aid of rhymes: 'In fourteen hundred and ninety-two / Columbus sailed the ocean blue' - a lead-in for the children to learning about the discovery of the West Indies. For the readers of his *Villager* articles he does not leave the thought there: he carries it through to remind us that: 'Here in Beeding it is most unlikely that anyone heard of this event for some time; the discovery of the New World or the election of a new Pope in that year would probably not have interested local people as much as the fact that the Priory of Sele was to be occupied by monks.' [5.4]

History was one of Keith's favourite subjects at school. His history master, Mr. Patching, was a veteran survivor of the First World War trenches, and was an accomplished storyteller. Soon Keith, no doubt on his many visits to Hollyman and Treacher's 'temple of the muses', or roaming around the quaint alleyways of the Brighton Lanes, began to collect old guide books of Sussex, a 19th century one for a penny, an 18th century one for tuppence, and so on.

The Teenager

It is a truism to say that the older we get the more we tend to look back to former times. Keith remarks, for example, on how the landscape has changed since his childhood. Development had closed in on the old village of Beeding and 'in the countryside many of the shaws and hedges remembered from pre-war days have been grubbed out to suit the more economical ways of farming' [3.8]. He regrets that the children of today cannot roam the fields as safely as they used to do. They are no longer allowed to collect eggs on bird-nesting expeditions (never more than one egg, even in those halcyon days). 'The wildlife of today is threatened by weed-killers and pesticides.' [5.6]

In those days, he reminds us, there was no vandalism to speak of, no bad language, and if the village children were too boisterous or naughty, there was always the local 'bobby' to lay down the law, 'who knew every scroundrel.' On Armistice Day the villagers would stand round the Union Flag as on other national occasions. The children were expected to share the reverence of their elders for the dead heroes of 'the war to end all wars' and to respect the values of their day. There was no television violence, and no computer games to distract them. He reflects on whether tomorrow's children will visit and protect the open spaces their parents fought for [5.7].

'All in all, our enjoyments were there for the taking. We made our own entertainment.' He mourns the loss of the 'romantic' measurements he learnt at school, sacrosanct British ones such as rods, poles and perches, inches and miles, ounces and pounds, which all had to give way to the demands of the European Union. School books had to be re-written for new generations of children. [11.5] He hates to see the depletion of the richness of the English language. Most of all, he mourns the loss of the little station at Bramber and the excellent train service that carried its passengers to Shoreham in ten minutes and to Horsham and Brighton within half an hour [11.2].

The Submariner

Keith as a young naval rating

With the approach of war in September 1939, Keith joined the Local Defence Volunteers, which was colloquially known as 'Look, Duck and Vanish' and later officially as 'The Home Guard'. In his time as a junior messenger (with a bicycle) he admitted to me that he learnt a vocabulary of swear-words not included in his former school curriculum!

Like most boys at the beginning of World War II, 'being young and patriotic, I looked forward to vanquishing Hitler and his regime.' Through putting up his age by one year he was able to enlist for the Royal Navy as a 'Hostilities Only' recruit (H.O.). Subsequently, he volunteered for the submarine service. His work as a submariner, mainly during the 'Cold War' 1945-50, was dealing with surrendered German U-boats, vessels driven by high-test peroxide, a highly-volatile fuel and extremely dangerous. He was exposed to two major explosions during his service. At that time he gathered up many life-long friends, though, as he sadly admits, *anno domini* is now taking its toll. 'Reunions are much smaller these days.'

At last, the war over, he came home. He remembers vividly the day when, stepping off the train at Bramber, he heard the sound of church bells ringing out across the fields, and reflects that they would have been heard only in the event of invasion by the Germans. All the same, he remarks, 'You miss things when you are deprived of them.' [3.3]

Keith with George Tranter on submarine HMS Artemis

The Naval Historian

Keith's experience with submarines led, in more recent times, to his collaboration with colleagues on three important books: *Submarine Memories*, *More Submarine Memories* and *Even More Submarine Memories*, all of which remain one of the best accounts of active service and naval action in wartime.

Keith's friendship with fellow-submariner, John Capes, led to a major investigation of great historical interest – the 'HMS Perseus' disaster of 1941. This British submarine was struck by a rogue sea-mine and, fatally crippled, sank 170ft to the bottom of the Ionian Sea, taking sixty men and officers with it. John Capes was the only survivor to tell the tale. He was rescued by local people. The world had to wait 56 years before a diver, Kostas Thoktorades, and his team began to search the depths close to the Cephalonian coast. Keith was able to give help in providing Greek author, Rena Giatropoulou, with valuable first-hand information through his knowledge of submarines and his memories of conversations with John Capes.

The Family Man

When he was 22, Keith met his future wife, Margaret, at the Brighton Ice Rink. He literally swept her off her feet! They soon paired up to do regular ice-dancing. Margaret was an artist and exhibited at the Royal Academy in London. She had her own gallery, 'The Brunswick', in Hove. She had the distinction of winning a major prize in the Festival of Britain in 1951. Keith and Margaret had seven children, including the twins, Andrew and John, followed in later years by fourteen grandchildren and 10 great-grandchildren. After a spell as site-manager of a petro-chemical company which brought North Sea oil ashore at Norfolk, Keith retired back to Beeding with Margaret. 'We wanted to rusticate', he said. 'We came here for a quiet life but it seems to have been anything but that!'

The Campaigner

In the early 1980s, all was not entirely sweetness and light in the three villages of Steyning, Beeding and Bramber. It may have been the coming of the new bypass that brought about a mood of rivalry among them. Whilst Beeding and Bramber were divided by the Adur, now they in turn were forcibly separated from their larger neighbour, Steyning. Indeed, Councillors Stuart Nutt and Miss Jess Parlour were of the view that, where public facilities were concerned, Steyning had

Keith and his wife Margaret, with Miss Dorothy Ellis, members of the Opening Committee for the bypass

won through every time. Steyning had had too much of the running on local amenities; a spanking new village hall, sports facilities and a health centre. Beeding had none of these. Why?

In Beeding parishioners, a new sense of identity began to show itself. There was perhaps some justification for their attitude, for the village had grown rapidly from 352 residents in 1951 to 4500 in 1981. There were more families and therefore more children to care for. The railway line had been ruthlessly removed by Dr. Beeching, the streets were full of aimless youth, and the local bus services had been cut down. An action group called 'Torch for Youth' was recruited, with Stuart Nutt at its head, and soon began to campaign vigorously.

Councillor Keith declared in the *Adur Herald* : 'Far too long have we been living in the shadow of Steyning.' In this, he was supported by the leader of what now might be referred to as the 'Freedom from Steyning Party', Audrey Preston-Smith. 'Independence!' came the cry. As for Bramber, 'it took too much of the limelight. We have three times as many buildings of architectural merit in our High Street as Bramber has.' The battle for recognition would be long and hard but in due course all the longed-for amenities came into being.

Another kind of rivalry, between Bramber and Beeding, began to assert itself. It came about through the wish of a few visionary parishioners that there should be a parish magazine to give an independent identity and break with the past. Keith and his colleagues set about the creation of a new study group to promote the history of the villages. The Beeding and Bramber Society ('History' was added later) began meeting in 1983. The aims were high: the collation of all aspects of that past with its attendant research programme, the noting and preservation of records with access to archives for future students to consult, and the recording of knowledge through the memories of local people.

First, all the parish records were donated by the Upper Beeding Parish Council, and the vicar of Beeding and Bramber with Botolph's, the Revd. Derek White, donated items of historical interest. It was not long before thoughts of producing a parish magazine were voiced at the group's meetings. 'History,' announced Keith,' is a treasure hunt, a detective story with exciting clues.' However, all was not well. There was about to be a storm in the village teapot!

Hardly had the announcement of the possibility of a parish magazine been voiced than strong differences of opinion began to spread. Whilst many residents welcomed the idea, tempers became frayed on one particularly sensitive issue: what was the title to be? The first suggestion may seem to us now innocent enough: *The Bramber and Beeding Villager.* But to many, it showed far too much favour to Bramber over its more populous neighbour. Up rose Miss Jess Parlour again: 'There is too much snobbery. Beeding is always put down – it makes me so angry.' Steyning, she said, wore the top hat, Bramber the bowler hat and Beeding the cloth cap!

Keith attempted to pacify the opposition by suggesting that, since Beeding had the greater population, an alternative title might be perhaps: *The Beeding and Bramber Villager.* Bramber residents claimed superiority by reason of their Norman castle and the historic medieval house, St. Mary's. In any case,

19

Beeding was really 'Upper', and alphabetically should follow Bramber. The residents of Beeding retaliated by deciding to drop the 'Upper' and so were victorious in the battle. In the end, diplomacy prevailed, the two factions agreed to disagree and the chosen title would be simply *The Villager*. Once the dispute was settled, the storm died down and no more was said on the matter.

The Sporting Man

Keith and his family often enjoyed holidays in Scotland, where they took part in the Highland Games. Keith succeeded on one occasion in winning the 'Shot Put' competition and also took part in 'throwing the hammer'. His daughter, Virginia, won the hundred yards race.

Keith was a popular helper at the Three Churches Fête, traditionally held in the garden of John and Morag McCarthy at Tinker's Court in Bramber. Once a year, he was regularly to be seen manning the 'Shot Put' competition. [15.7] The fact that he was 6 foot three inches tall and had once weighed 23 stone no doubt contributed to his prowess. In July 2001, then aged 64, he beat twenty-four other contestants with a winning 49 pound ball over a length of 22 feet.

Margaret died in 2007. She and Keith had celebrated fifty years of happy marriage and companionship at their Golden Wedding in 2001. They made many friends in the area and were always welcoming to Members and friends at the Beeding and Bramber

Keith with his twins,
Andrew and John, at the
Three Churches Fete

Local History Society meetings. It was a pleasure to meet and exchange greetings with Keith and Margaret on their customary strolls down Beeding High Street on the way to their favourite river walk.

The Local Historian

With the passing of the years, Keith began to take an interest in collecting Sussex diaries, which would reveal a more personal view of local life. He gathered together piles of old postcards, pictures, documents, deeds, leaflets, pamphlets and booklets. He joined a history study group at Sussex University. He organized a small group of Beeding local history

Keith and Margaret at
a family wedding

enthusiasts to study research methodology. The *West Sussex County Times* (11 July 1980) reported him as having collected at that time some 8000 pieces of historical evidence.

Similarly, he recreates for us in his articles his own personal 'diary' of times past. He tells us for example how, at the approach of Christmas, 'as I sit in my pew at St. Peter's before the Sunday service, I try to imagine how things would have been in the last century at this season. In these winter months, the fireplace in the north wall of the nave had a fire going, to warm the parishioners. Did those who sat nearest the fire have to stoke it during the service?' Then again, we see him in the past as he rakes the gravel path up to the church door nearly every week of the year. In the stillness of the churchyard in the spring and summer, it is good for meditation. In the autumn and winter months, the job gets harder and Margaret helps him to sweep up the leaves and load them into the barrow. [14.3]

Images of childhood fill his mind. He remembers the smell of freshly-ground coffee, the cheeses and cured hams in Mr. Lucas's village store, and regrets the modern packaging of today. He recalls the 'roundhouse' at the mill on Beeding Hill in the 1930s, in fact many things about our villages that hardly anyone remembers these days. He comments wryly that the village dustmen of today have to remove countless numbers of 'junk mail and freebies.' [8.7]

He is amused by the tale of the old woodcutter who boasted that he had owned the same axe for fifty years and didn't mention that it had had ten new shafts and five new heads in that time! [5.8] Memories of all the old crafts come into his mind, crafts now largely extinct, that he could enjoy at a time when a small boy could go and watch the local farm-workers hedging and ditching along the lanes of Edburton.

As a youngster, he spent many weekends with Edgar and Doreen Collins, friends of his maternal grandfather. Doreen gained her pilot's licence and was still flying in her nineties! She was the daughter of the well-known Bramber taxidermist, Walter Potter, creator of the museum of grotesque stuffed animals. Potter had made models for Keith's grandfather (the RAMC surgeon) for his medical lectures. Many years later, before the sale of the museum, Keith was given a saw-fish saw and a barbed wooden spear, which he later used for his talks for children [9.3].

One of Keith's great friends was Frank Gregory, the mill-wright, who made for him a model of a windmill, correct in every detail. Keith also inherited from his godfather, F. Bramwell, author of *The History of the Windmills of Brighton*, a collection of documents and photographs, a 'For Sale' notice for Beeding Windmill 'with all the details of owner and occupier at that time, the workings of the two millstones, and a fantail (to keep it into the wind), all of which remain among his prized possessions [10.12].

The Author

Keith's articles for *The Villager* comprise an assemblage of knowledge about the three Sussex villages - Beeding, Bramber and Botolphs, drawn from many sources. Each issue contained an article on a chosen aspect of our village life, sometimes exploratory, sometimes factual and informative, wide-ranging and yet comprehensive, occasionally questioning and critical, but always keeping our interest. His eager mind is constantly searching for a new idea to keep the attention of his readers. We can only admire the zeal and energy he applied on a monthly basis to the labour of research. We can enjoy that constant element of surprise, for we never know what is coming next. He explores with great charm the life and times of the villages, their inhabitants and their occupations. His occasional flights into autobiography give his writing that special personal quality, a sense of immediacy that beguiles us. Dim impressions of *Akenfield* try to break through to us, those aspects of the countryside that remain forever immutable, resisting the often brutal changes that modern life imposes on us. Keith's 'Portrait of Village Life', as I have chosen to call it, is not as directly emotional or reminiscent as *A Childhood in the Forest* or as anecdotal as *Lark Rise to Candleford,* and certainly not as consciously literary as *Under Milkwood* or as saucy as *Cider with Rosie.* Like many books of its kind, Keith's account of life in his home village of Upper Beeding arises from a deep and abiding love of his community and its people.

Enough has been written here about Keith's concern for the education of young people, the importance of the teaching of history and the value and knowledge of the past to show us the way forward into the future. He calls his articles 'Miniature Histories'.

As a matter of course, occasionally, there are among local historians, conflicting theories, but in his views Keith is forthright and to the point. There may be from time to time duplications of content, but these are only his way of emphasizing a point. His underlying motive is to draw us nearer to our history. *Domesday Book* is 'our' *Domesday Book*, Beeding is 'our' village', 'our' parish, 'the Adur river is 'our' river, and St. Peter's Church is 'our' church. He looks back to the 'good old days' of Bramber, with the Sunday trippers, the eight tea-gardens, the valley walks, the Castle pleasure activities and the scores of rowing-boats on the river. He can carry us back to our village past with all its richness of life and its infinite variety. Besides these admirable qualities, he can tell a good story. He can tell a good joke too, and with a twinkle in his eye as well.

The most attractive feature of Keith's writing is his ability to combine the factual aspects of modern life with his romantic longings for happier times, where Arcady reigned supreme. In all these things, he can be likened to Mary Russell Mitford, whose classic account of 'sketches of rural life, character and scenery', *Our Village*, was one of the best-sellers of the late 1820s. What better testimony could there be?

Peter Thorogood
St. Mary's House, Bramber
April 2011

This iconic photograph shows Keith carrying his
ceremonial spade at the opening of the new bypass,
followed by crowds of local school-children 3rd July 1981
(*by courtesy of the Evening Argus*). See page 13 and 9.7

List of articles by volume and number

Asterisks indicate articles with accompanying illustrations

Volume One

1.1	Introduction to *The Villager**
1.2	The Veteri Ponte (Part 1)*
1.3	Castletown
1.4	The Towers 1883-1983 (Part 1)*
1.5	The Towers (Part 2)*
1.6	The Schools (Part 1)*
1.7	The Schools (Part 2)*
1.8	The Schools (Part 3)
1.9	The Parish Council*

Volume Two`

2.1	St. Peter's Beeding (Part 1)*
2.2	14th October 1651*
2.3	The Roads*
2.4	The Salterns*
2.5	Beeding Bridge*
2.6	The Great Bridge of Bramber*
2.7	Kings Barnes*
2.8	The Adur River*
2.9	The Bounds
2.10	The Mills (Part 1)
2.11	The Priory of Sele*
2.12	Erringham Chalk Pit*

Volume Three

3.1	Pound House Cottage*
3.2	The Picture
3.3	St. Peter's Bells (Part 1)
3.4	The Manor of Horton
3.5	A Link with the New World*
3.6	Bramber Ghost Token
3.7	The Inns*
3.8	The Village Stores*
3.9	Beeding Police
3.10	The Post Office
3.11	The Beedings

Volume Thirteen

Volume Fourteen

Volume Fifteen

Volume Sixteen

List of Illustrations to articles

Short captions only

Volume One

Volume Two

Volume Three

3.1   Pound House Cottage, Beeding
3.1a   Penn's Cottage, Steyning
3.5   Pieces of Eight
3.5a   James I
3.7   The Castle Hotel, Bramber
3.7a   Beeding High Street, with The King's Head
3.8   Frank Lucas RFC, with his son.
3.8a   Frank Lucas delivering provisions by boat

Volume Four

4.1   St. Mary's, Bramber c1950
4.1a   Entrance hall, St. Mary's (Harry Ford)
4.2   Domesday Book (Beeding entry)
4.2a   Domesday Book: front cover
4.2b   Domesday Book (Bramber entry)
4.4   Maines Farm House. Later called 'The Old House'
4.4a   Richard Hudson and his family
4.6   West Grinstead Park
4.6a   Coal barge on the River Adur at Beeding
4.7   Bramber Station platforms
4.7a   Bramber Station
4.8   Beeding Court
4.8a   Thomas and Lucy Cross and family at Beeding Court
4.9   Drawing of the village of Botolphs
4.9a   Charcoal sketch of Botolphs

Volume Five

5.7   Old Shoreham Toll Bridge (timber) built in 1781
5.7a   Shoreham Toll Bridge, known as the 'Norfolk Bridge' 1924
5.9   William of Waynflete, Bishop of Winchester

Volume Six

6.3   Garratt's conjectural plan of Bramber Castle
6.3a   Key to Garratt's plan of Bramber Castle (see 1.2)
6.4   Magdalen College, Oxford
6.11   Templar lands as described by the Rev. Arnold
6.11a Edward II

Volume Seven

7.2   Bramber floods: delivering the bread
7.2a   Groceries arrive at Little St. Mary's
7.3   Charles I
7 3a   Oliver Cromwell
7.9   Bramber Church in 1785 by S. Hopper
7.9a   Arnold's plan of the church of St. Nicholas.

Volume Eight

8.2   Example of a Sussex shepherd's smock
8.2a   A Sussex shepherd on the Downs
8.5   An elaborately stitched ploughboy's blouse
8.5   Children at the Bramber and Beeding annual fête
8.6a   Model train in the grounds of Bramber Castle

Volume Nine

9.2   A fatal accident in the glebeland
9.3   Victorian taxidermist, Walter Potter
9.3a   Walter Potter serving in his shop.
9.5   The Revd. Dr. John Rouse Bloxam
9.5a   The tomb of Dr. Bloxam in St. Peter's churchyard
9.7   Sir Henry Gough Calthorpe, Member of Parliament for Bramber
9.7a   William Wilberforce, Member of Parliament for Bramber

Volume Ten

10.1   Alfred Musgrave, owner of St. Mary's Bramber (1899-1907)
10.1a   Miss Dorothy Ellis, owner of St. Mary's Bramber (1944-1979)
10.2   Bramber Castle. Remains of the keep
10.2a   Bramber Castle. Remains of the guard room.
10.8   Elizabeth Fry, Quaker and prison reformer
10.8a   George Fox, Quaker preacher
10.12   Beeding Mill c1891.
10.12a   Sketch of a windmill near Steyning

Volume Eleven

No illustrations for this volume

Volume Twelve

12.4   The chapel on the bridge at St. Ives, Cambridgeshire

List of Illustrations in the Picture Gallery
with related articles indicated

1. Bramber Water or Beeding River?
   Early morning mists on the River Adur [2.8, 7.2]

2. Bramber in the early 19th Century
   Old Bramber Street c1821 [4.1]
   Engraving of St. Nicholas Church [7.9]

3. Bramber refreshments
   The Bun Shop c1900 (15.9)
   The Rose Tea Gardens c1920 [15.5]

4. Searching for the Past
   Hilda Holden with a 12thC tile at St. Mary's (10.1)
   Exploring the reputed underground chapel at St. Mary's [10.1]

5. Lords of the Manor
   Sir Thomas Seymour [2.7]
   Lord Edgcumbe [1.5]

6. Honourable Members for Bramber
   Nicholas Barbon [9.7]
   Sir Richard Gough [9.7]

7. St. Mary's from 1984
   Renée Linton with Peter Thorogood c1989 [10.10]
   Peter Thorogood, his sister, Mary, and Roger Linton c1997 [10.10]

8. Beeding Celebrations
   Beeding lads with the Woolgars [3.9]
   Coronation Day at Beeding Court [4.8]

9. Bramber and Beeding Schoolchildren
   Beeding schoolchildren 1919 [1.4]
   Beeding Primary School: The new building [page 14 and 1.7]

10. Bramber Events and Recreations
    Early Tub Race on the Causeway [15.8]
    Crowds in Bramber Street [4.7, 15.5]

11. Beeding Games and Recreations
    Buns and treacle contest 1926 [14.2]
    Boating on the Adur [10.9]

12. The Bridge Between
    The working river with coal barge [5.5]
    The Adur still a navigable river in early 1900s [5.5]

13. Beeding and Bramber Local History Society [page 19]
    The Society Tent at the Stuart Fayre 1988
    Members of the Society in 2000 (Millennium photograph)

Street Maps of Bramber and Beeding

Bramber

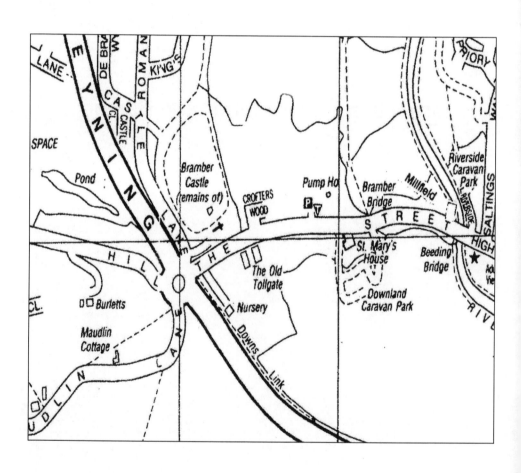

Upper Beeding

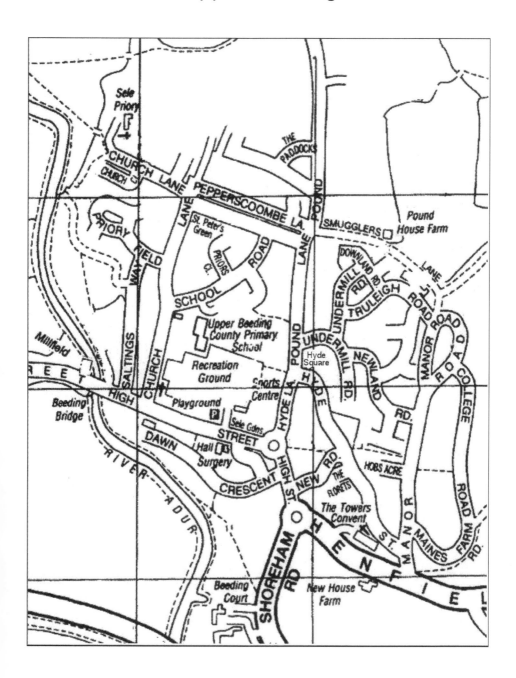

The Villager
in
Bramber & Beeding

15p

1.1 *The Villager* Volume One, Number One, April 1983

Introduction to *The Villager*

by

Keith Nethercoate-Bryant

In the hearts of many of us there is a yearning to know more about the past. History makes it clear to the observer that man is more important than what he discovers or the things he makes, even though his existence depends on them. Many of us today are in the grip of the mass media, which can make child and parent alike the passive receivers of the carefully manipulated thoughts of the advertisers, politicians, and bureaucrats. There has lately been a tendency in schools to reduce the teaching of our national history. I think this is very wrong. My long experience of life tells me that the more one knows about the past, the clearer the picture is for the future.

Man from the earliest times has recorded his lifestyle. He painted in caves, not only for decoration but to record the calendar of events in his life, dictated, as they mostly were, by the seasons of the year.

There is no dearth of source material available to the student. Vital sources of ancient history can be found in the Bible and records from Greek, Roman, Chinese, Egyptian and other ancient civilizations. In Britain, the earliest writings were inscribed by monks and scholars in *The Anglo-Saxon Chronicle.*

Our *Domesday Book*, compiled in a single year, provides a bench-mark in English medieval history. *Domesday* contains the results of the greatest survey ever undertaken in the Middle Ages – a datum and data point for the present day.

The historian has to be careful with 'folklore' based on happenings and events in the past. The mists of time do tend to bend the truth. Legends passed down through generations are bound to gain or lose something in the telling. In World War One, the story went about that a message was passed from the trenches of the front line, by word of mouth, to headquarters at the rear: 'Send reinforcements, we are going to advance,' which, when received at its destination, became: 'Send three and four-pence, we are going to a dance!'

From time to time I have written history articles for local government and historical publications as well as the local press. When the parishes of Upper Beeding, Bramber and St. Botolph's decided to publish a new magazine with a different format, to be known as *The Villager*, I was invited by the editorial committee to write a series of monthly articles on any aspect of local history around the Adur Valley that might interest the readers.

Arms of St. Peter's Church, Upper Beeding

I have attempted to present these individual miniature histories in a way that answers several questions at the same time, and in a style that I hope everyone can understand. My especial concern is for the younger members of the community, whose interest could be stirred to do further research for themselves in the future. I have tried to give an explanation of why things happened and how changes occurred, and in many cases coupled national history and events with what was happening here in the Adur Valley at the same time. There will occasionally be duplication of material used in more than one article where some reiteration is necessary.

The material I have drawn on for this series is mainly that left to us by the Revd. Dr. John Rouse Bloxam. His *Rough Notices of Beeding Parish Church and Priory* comprises a collection of ephemera, a private census of communicants, and his transcription of the Parish Registers, gathered together during his years as the incumbent, from 1862 until his death in 1891. Dr. Bloxam's book is the most important single item on the history of our parishes

Arms of St. Nicholas's Church, Bramber

In the early 1930s, the Revd. H. E. B. Arnold wrote a series for the Parish Magazine, 'The Records of Beeding Parish', based on Bloxam's material. These, together with researches in the *Sussex Archaeological Collections* and the *Victoria County History* (Sussex volume) series, have been my primary sources.

Many local residents have contributed facts and anecdotes from their memories of the past. And more important, they have asked questions. The *Domesday Book*, for example, records two churches in Beeding and, if this were so, we might ask where the second was located, for one is surely St. Peter's. And where was the mysterious 'veteri ponte', recorded in the documents of Sele Priory? Was it a bridge? Or just a causeway? Furthermore, the origin of the name 'Beeding' (or, in *Domesday*, 'Beddinges') is reputed to come from a Saxon chieftain, 'Bieda', or 'Beida' – but who was he?

It is such questions as these and a host of others like them that have inspired me most to explore the fascinating histories of our villages.

Author's Acknowledgements

'It seems no time at all that I was sitting at my typewriter composing an introduction for the history article of the first *Villager* magazine.....Friends and older residents have been most helpful with information on earlier village life, and I thank you all for your memories.'

Richard Bromfield	Jo Brooks
Jack and Jackie Campbell	George Cockman
Gill and Geoff Fox	Frank Gregory
Theo and Jessica Lloyd	Sister Mary Andrew
Pat Nightingale	Dr. Janet Pennington
Len Sanford	Stuart Stevens
Peter Thorogood	Revd. Derek White

Extract from Budgen's map of Sussex 1724

The Veteri Ponte (Part 1)

In early times the main route through our parishes was the great east-west road from Canterbury to Southampton and Winchester. This mediaeval trackway ran mainly along the crest of the downs to avoid the marshes and dangerous lowlands of the Weald (wild). Going west from the top of Beeding Hill, one river crossing ran from Castletown Lane to Kings Barns via Hyde Street and the Priory, where there seems to have been a ferry. The other descended roughly where the South Downs Way is now and crossed the river where the 25-foot contours come close together. The name 'Adur' was not used until the 17th century, before which time the river was known among other names as the 'Sore' or 'the weald ditch'.

Colonel Evans, who carried out some research here in the 1930s, was of the opinion that there was a causeway from the south of Beeding Court, near the old medieval site of 12th century Beeding, to a point near Annington, with a pontoon bridge across the main channel and either a drawbridge or swinging section to allow passage for vessels going upstream to the ancient port of St. Cuthman, near Steyning. He thought the Romans may have established it as part of a military road.

Both Hadrian Allcroft and the Revd. H. E. B. Arnold supported the bridge-crossing theory. Dr. T. P. Hudson, editor in Sussex of the *Victoria County History* agrees on the site of the crossing but points out that the word 'Ponte' or 'Pons' could mean bridge or causeway, and draws our attention to the fact that the Adur is fordable on foot at low tide at the present time.

St Peter of Old Bridge (de Veteri Ponte) is first mentioned in the *Chartulary* of Sele Priory in 1080 AD. It must be at least of Saxon origin, being described as old (veteri) before *Domesday*. Later in the 13th century the name becomes Botolphs – a saint who was known as the 'Boat Helper', and patron saint of travellers. ('St. Botolph' comes from Lincolnshire, where 'Boston' is a contraction of 'Botolphs Town'.) He is a stranger to Sussex. The name 'St. Peter' then disappears from records, so St Peter de Veteri Ponte and St. Botolphs must be one and the same.

There is no mention of Botolphs in the *Domesday* survey, but a Church is recorded in 'Haningedune' now called Annington, and, as no church or burial ground is known in the area of Annington itself, it must be St. Peter/St. Botolph. If ever there was a pontoon bridge it must have fallen into disuse when the Great Bridge of Bramber was built in the late 11th century. It has been said that when the new bypass was being constructed, a part of the old bridge was exposed.

Other local historians differ in their theories on this subject [Ed.]

For Part 2 see 10.10

1.2 Sketch of St. Botolph's Church by Margaret Nethercoate-Bryant

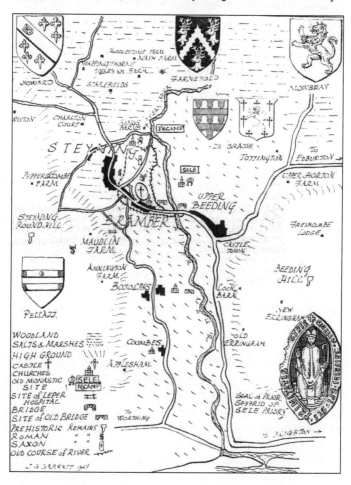

1.2a Map of the Adur valley by J.Garratt showing Botolphs (just below centre)

Castletown

The Towers, once castellated, was thought to have been the origin of the name 'Castletown', but The Towers was built after the area known as Castletown, so there must be another explanation. I was reminded of this by Miss Gravenor. She drew my attention to the wall recently exposed by tree cutting; this old flint wall with lots of interesting openings runs along Hyde Street to Manor Road turning west along the Henfield Road. It has the appearance of being fortified but is only a lightly built wall, parts of which may have surrounded the 18th century manor house near the site of the Towers, but it could have been the inspiration for the name 'Castletown'. We know that the area 'Castletown' was a farm or 'knell' which is a variant of 'knoll', a copse on high ground (see Hall's *Sussex Dialect*). There do not appear to be any dwellings, but the map is not very clear. As far as is known, the first time the name appears in print is on a map circa 1868.

In 1733, on a Beeding terrier (land ownership map) entitled 'The Land of Snelling' by J. Mason, John Backshall is listed as the copyholder of 'Knell' with titles to outlying holdings in the 'Brooks', 'Clays', and the 'Flaxlands' (east of Pound Lane). John Backshell (or Bagshall) lived at 'New House' (later called Valerie Manor), a 16th century house in the Castletown area. One of his ancestors was thought to have assisted Charles II on his flight through Bramber and Beeding after the Battle of Worcester in 1651.

In 1808 some houses were recorded in the Castletown area on land east of the Bostel Road to Beeding Hill and south of the Henfield Road. The Edwards map of circa 1820 shows what appears to be one dwelling. This is probably the existing house whose name today is Nelcote. The 1841 census records one entry under 'Nell'. The 1851 census shows four dwellings listed as 'Knell'. In the 1870s the Rev. J. R. Bloxam started his own private census of the village and records 14 entries in his index (125-139) entitled 'New houses at Nell called Castletown'. Later in the 1880s he notes that many were empty, and a wall and some doorways can still be seen. In 1983, the centenary of the Towers, the electoral role lists six residences as being in Castletown, excluding 'Nelcote' but including Castletown Chalkpit, and sixteen electors are on the roll.

Castletown Lane was once a busy coach road and was turnpiked from the middle of the 18th century. The top of Beeding Hill was an early traffic crossroads with no less than six roads meeting there. It fell into decline when the road to Shoreham (A283) was built under the Turnpike Act of 1807. This road was then called the 'New Road to Shoreham avoiding Beeding Hill' and was the top of the Turnpike Trust's agenda.

The Towers 1883-1983 (Part 1)

It would seem appropriate to mention the 'Towers' in this July article as it is the centenary of thebuilding this month and the eightieth year of the convent school. When you tell outsiders to the Adur valley that you come from Upper Beeding, the comment usually is: "Oh yes! That's where the Cement Works is," or, "Isn't there a sort of château there?"

When the Sisters of the Blessed Sacrament arrived from France In 1903, Beeding was a very different place from that of today; the Towers really had towers, the one on the south-west corner was 80 feet high and crenellated. Now, it has French-style turrets and pitched roofs.

Sadly the events in France at that time (anti-clerical laws) had led to the closing of religious houses and successful boarding schools. The communities were compelled to take refuge in England. The Superior, Sister St. Merry, accompanied by five Sisters and the chaplain Father Marcellin of the Assumptionists, arrived during the first week in October to arrange the chapel, dormitory, and refectory. On the 10th October 1903 the first five pupils, four from St. Maur and one from Montrouge, arrived from Paris escorted by two sisters.

The following description is from Sister Mary Noel, one of the five little French girls, who later became a Sister, ending her days at the Towers about ten years ago. 'It was quite dark, a winter evening, and the only lights were from two little lanterns carried by the Sisters who came to meet us at Bramber Station. There were no passers-by except a few farm workers. As we entered the drive leading to the house we fancied we saw ghosts lurking on the crenellated towers. The following day we explored our home, too grand for us, Gobelin tapestries on the walls, stag heads on the main staircase, with portraits of the Payne family below. The conservatory was full of Passion flowers and exotic and rare plants which scented the air.'

Sister Mary goes on to say that the children of royal and notable continental families were boarded at the Towers over the years, among them the Princess Charlotte of Monaco who was visited by her father Prince Louis. He was a keen fisherman and fished in the Adur when visiting his daughter. It is recorded that he often had large catches and brought them to the Convent kitchens for the sisters to fry.

1.4 The Towers became the Convent of the Blessed Sacrament after 1903.
Seen here with later tiled French-style conical turrets.

1.4a An early photograph of the first nuns and pupils. The small girl seated on the steps
in the foreground would one day assume the name Sister Mary Noel.

The Towers (Part 2)

Research into the Manor Court Book of Beeding has shown that, before 1750, the piece of land the Towers now stands on, up to the road opposite the 'Rising Sun' (formerly 'The Star') was in the ownership of a Mr. Bartlett. It was comprised of a dwelling and two acres, held of the Lord of the Manor of Beeding, Lord Edgecombe [sic*]. The land to the east, to Hyde Street and Manor Road, we believe was held by John Backshall of 'New House' (now Valerie Manor). It was described as a 'Walled Garden'; a 1733 map by J. Mason calls the area 'The Land of Snelling', which stretched from Sele Priory to Beeding Court.

We first hear of George Smith (the builder of 'The Towers') in the private census taken by Dr. Bloxam 1871-1883. Entry No.81 states him to be in residence at 'Wheelers' which was probably the former house on the site of the Towers. We know that the freehold was conveyed to George Smith from Wheeler on 5th August 1871 (Convent document). J. Wheeler must therefore be the coachman referred to in the old notes at the Convent related by earlier Sisters, as the inheritor of the rich widow's fortune, but there the story falls apart!

Nowhere is there recorded a woman as owner before Jasper Wheeler. The only coachman referred to in 'Bloxam' is Henry Marshall, who died in 1871; however further research is needed here and perhaps another report can be made in the future. The descent of the copyhold and freehold is rather complicated as there are 14 changes of copyhold owners between 1773 and 1888 and 18 changes of freehold between 1871 and 1912.

In October 1882 there is record of a mortgage from G. Smith and S. Smith to Charles Bruton and, by this time, the Towers must have been well on the way to completion. In 1897 the owner was a Mr. Walter Keymer and he leased the property to Arthur Payne at £200 per annum. As we know, the Sisters arrived in October 1903 and on the 5th May 1904 the lease was assigned to Mrs. Elizabeth Ann Wynch, who later became Sister Mary Agnes. A letter of the 1st July 1908 records the purchase of the Towers by Mrs Wynch and on the 22nd January 1918 the property was left in her will to the Sisters, and this was confirmed by her son, Major Wynch.

Some pupils remembered that during the holidays of 1911-12 the high castellated towers at the corners of the building were reduced and replaced with the now familiar, chateau type, conical, tiled towers that exist today.

*George Edgcumbe 1st Earl of Mount Edgcumbe. Naval officer and politician.
See Picture Gallery p.304

1.5 The Towers under construction c1875. The bearded gentleman,
seated with his family, is almost certainly the builder, George Smith.

1.5a The Towers: The completed building (c1883),
locally dubbed 'Smith's Folly', with its impressive castellated roofs.

The Schools (Part 1)

One of the purposes of the Benedictine order was to educate the younger sons of the barons and lower orders of the nobility, known as cadets. Not many of the Normans were literate. Under the feudal system the eldest son inherited the estate and the younger ones had to make their own way, but with a little help and learning they could become bishops and administrators. Perhaps, then, Sele Priory was the first established school in the Beeding area.

From the time the Romans left until the late 18th century, people learned of happenings only from returning soldiers, minstrels, pedlars, and visits of the clergy when inspecting their diocese. Legends passed from parent to child, and were gained or lost according to the narrator. This situation continued until the end of the 18th century with only a small percentage of the population possessing any learning.

In Beeding in the year 1530, in the will of Wyllyam Berde, there was a bequest to provide for 20 poorhouse scholars. This was possibly the first charity school in our village.

With the Industrial Revolution many reformers took up the cause of the working population. Raikes, Bell, and Lancaster, each with different motives, are remembered among the founders of our educational systems. In the early 19th century there were many small schools in our area, most of them probably Dame schools, but quite a few with a score or more pupils.

In 1833 there were two schools recorded with a total of 65 pupils, all taught at their parents' expense. The 1841 census records a school in the High Street; Richard Goddard is named as schoolmaster with ten pupils, with Charles Warner being named as a teacher, aged 15. This may have been a boarding school as the average age was 10. The 1851 census returns shows a reduced number of pupils and lists them as originating from Brighton, Portslade, Eastbourne and Middlesex.

A school existed in the early 19th century west of Beeding Bridge (once the house of Len Acton). This one appears to have been started by the Revd. Thomas Calhoun. A terrier of 1843 lists it as a workshop and school. A letter of the time says among other things that the mistress was paid £25 per annum and provided with two rent free rooms over the classroom. There was an evening school for the working boys for the six winter months. This school was known as 'Beeding Academy'. We know this from the headings of the pupils' work – some still exist and were once in the possession of Len Acton.

1.6 Len Acton's house, formerly Beeding Academy

1.6a Beeding School, founded by Dr. John Rouse Bloxam c.1872
(sketch by Margaret Nethercoate-Bryant)

The Schools (Part 2)

In a deed of 12th March 1872 entitled 'Conveyance of ground for the new school', a quarter acre of land, part of Sele Field, was conveyed from Magdalen College, Oxford, to the Revd. Dr. Bloxam. It states that the school was for the education of the poorer classes of the Parish of Upper Beeding, in the furtherance of the designs of the 'National Society for promoting the education of the poor in the principals of the Established Church.' It is signed by J. R. Bloxam, William Mills, and Peter Woods.

The first entry in the school log book, 19th March 1872, reads: 'The Revd. Dr. Bloxam came in school in the afternoon and took the first class in scripture, 64 present in school'. If we look at the two dates there is only a week between the conveyance and the opening of the school, so perhaps the land deed was conveyed after the schoolhouse was built?

The first building was designed by Charles Dalby of Steyning. This is the flint and brick part on the corner of Church Lane and School Road. The dimensions on the drawing were 'School Room 39'3" x 17'0", Class Room 16' x 12". There was a fireplace in each room and the chimneys formed the belltower with the bell hung between the two stacks – an innovation at the time.

The first teachers do not appear to be known, but we think that the first schoolmistress was Miss Ann Boler, who was recorded by Dr. Bloxam in his private census as being a lodger of Sarah Kidd living in Beeding Street in the 1870s.

A school board was formed in 1885 at which time the average attendance was 62. The number of pupils fell when the school at Small Dole opened in 1892 but, in 1912, the school was enlarged because the number of pupils had increased to well over 100. In the 1930s, with the children from Bramber and Botolphs together, the attendance was over 200. A new school building was opened in 1970. In 1983, with a new school in place, it would be fitting if the efforts of Dr. Bloxam, the founder, could be recorded in some way in the new buildings. He never married but it is evident from his writings that he loved children.

The school log makes very interesting reading. A wartime entry for 11th June 1944 reads: 'Several times today flying bombs went over the school. No air raid warnings were received at all but the children went into the corridor when danger approached.' The sound and then the silence of those V1's will always be remembered by my generation.

1.7 The pupils of Beeding School with
their teacher, Miss Mary Woolgar, 1902-3

1.7a Beeding School pupils in 1919

The Schools (Part 3)

The school at Small Dole was opened in 1892 as a Board school and later became a council school; it closed in 1952 with some 40 children on the books. In the 60 years of the school there were never more than 50 pupils on the register. The school was located to the south of the Baptist Church, and the premises were said to be leased, but from whom we do not know. The building no longer exists, but the dimensions of the class-room were given in the school log book as 16' 0" wide, 24' 0" long and 13' 0" high. The first entry in the log dated 5th March states: 'This school was opened February 20th 1892. The Revd. H. D. Mayrick came in the morning. During the week 15 children were admitted.'

The inventory of the school is an invitation to step into the past. Among the expected things are inks, blackboards and chalks, 3½ dozen slates, 3 boxes of slate pencils, alphabet cards, desks, a bell, a clock, etc. Other things that leave us wondering are: 3 bundles of white straws (what were they for? – this was long before the days of free school milk), 4 packets of thick mats, 2 packets of thin mats, one dozen tin saucers, and a ball frame (was this an abacus?). One entry brought back a flood of memories to me – just the one word: 'Bunting', bringing visions of George V's Jubilee 1935, the Coronation of George VI May 1937, 'Empire Days' on 24th May, when we all stood proudly round the Union Flag, England stood four square, 'Britannia' ruled the waves and there was pink on every page in the atlas. What have we lost? Loyalty these days seems to be to the local football team!

One of the most interesting notations in the log is the entry for 26th October 1910, which reads: "At 2.30 today we saw the 'Lebaudy' airship pass over the school; we could see two occupants at least and feel the motion of the engines and hear the whirr. It came from the south-east and travelled north-west". The entry for the 27th gives the newspaper account: it started from Moissons near Paris at 10 a.m., crossing the Channel over Rottingdean in 2 hours 12 minutes and reached Farningham in 5 hours 28 minutes.

Further research has turned up a few more facts. This airship must have been a magnificent sight in those early days of flying, being 337' 0" long with a crew of six, including Mr. Lebaudy and Major Sir Alex Bannerman. The vessel was built in France for the 'Morning Post' fund. This was the second crossing of the Channel by airship; the first had been made ten days earlier by the 'Clement -Bayard II'.

The Parish Council

Having served as the chairman of our Parish Council some years ago, it would perhaps be appropriate for me to give a brief history of our council, established under the local government act of 1884, which allowed elections to take place in rural areas where the population exceeded 300.

Ever since man has lived in a community there has been some form of tribal justice. Those great civil administrators, the Romans, first brought government from a central body, the Senate. After they left Britain in the fifth century, the roads were allowed to fall into disrepair, which tended to isolate communities. The Jutes, Angles and Saxons who followed, administered their own laws from small kingdoms. Under the Saxons, each village or area was divided into tithings (ten men). These men had to stand security for the good behaviour of the others and this was known as 'frankpledge'. Collective responsibility for securing offenders was a dominant part of English life. The Saxon 'hundred' was an area thought to support 100 families. Beeding was in the Hundred of Burbeech, which used to stretch as far as Bewbush, near Crawley. It is recorded that the Hundred Court was held in 1788 at the King's Head.

'Court Leet' and 'Court Baron' meetings were held at Beeding Court*- the main manor of Beeding. Earlier meetings were almost certainly held in the church and, although the chancel was sacred, the body of the church was used as the Parish Hall. It was often the only sheltered public meeting place with seating until after the Reformation.

Later the vestry was used and the term 'vestry' came to mean the group of people who ran the village. They appointed the 'Overseers of the Poor', established by the Poor Law Act of 1597 and the Poor Relief Act of 1601. These guardians had the power to levy a rate and to pay a dole to paupers. They could also help with medical aid and found jobs in the parish for those without work. One such task was the collection of horse and cattle droppings from the roads; farmers bid for these loads as in auction. A book was kept in which were recorded the minutes of vestry meetings, most of which were held at the King's Head, some at the Rising Sun (formerly The Star), and some in the church. The records date from 1826 to 1853, and are most interesting as they show the way the village was run at that time.

* See also 3.4. KN-B returns to this subject in 12.11

1.9 The King's Head, Upper, Beeding, where the vestry gatherings
(early parish meetings) were held.

1.9a Parish Clerk, Richard Hudson, with his wife, Harriet,
outside the garden door at St. Mary's, Bramber c.1870

St. Peter's Beeding (Part 1)

'Beida's', or 'Beada's Ing' (Saxon for 'pasture' or 'meadow'), in the *Domesday Book* is called 'Beddings' (later 'Beding'), and now, with an extra 'e', Beeding. The origin of the name of our village, which covers the area more or less south of Sele or Sela, is Saxon. Before the conquest, when there was no priory, only a church, 'Beding' was once referred to as the hamlet of Sele in a document, *The Chartulary of Sele.*

The Domesday Survey records tw churches here: 'Ibi ii eccle'.* It is possible that the first church on the site of St. Peter's was built after the Conquest, but before the Domesday survey (1086-7). The other church may have been to the east of this site. Here we are delving into *Beowulf, Widsith,* the *Anglo-Saxon Chronicle* and Bede's *Ecclesiastical History of the English People.* There is a faint chance that it was Bede's father, Baeda, whose name was used for our village. He is described as a sea rover and heathen fighter. Perhaps he was one of the people who accompanied St. Wilfred into Sussex in AD 681. (Bede was born AD 672.)

Of the church recorded in 1073 nothing remains above ground except fragments built into the walls of our present church, which can still be seen. Looking at and around the south churchyard wall, it is not clear whether the present church was originally the Priory Church, as it may have been built after the original Priory.** It abutted the north side; the north wall of the Church had no doors or windows. A new building was consecrated on the 24th February 1308 and rededicated to St. Peter and St. Paul.

Two additional altars are recorded: the one to the south dedicated to the Blessed Virgin Mary; the other to St. John was to the north of the existing Chancel. Some of the remains were discovered during a 'dig' in 1966, so it follows that the column of stonework in the NW corner of the Chancel could have been part of that old chapel. The existing Chancel is mainly 16th century. It incorporates materials thought to be from the old Priory Church at the time of the dissolution and the arcaded window and door in the south wall are reliably dated as being circa 1300 (*Victoria County History*). In 1852 an extensive alteration took place; the medieval south aisle was removed between 1627 and 1801 and replaced with the one that exists today.

For Part 2 see 5.8 and for Part 3 see 6.2

* Page 28a column (i) of the original record

** This could be in the original south aisle known to exist in 1627 on a map by J. Gotham but had disappeared by 1801 [KN-B]

2.1 St. Peter's Church, Beeding

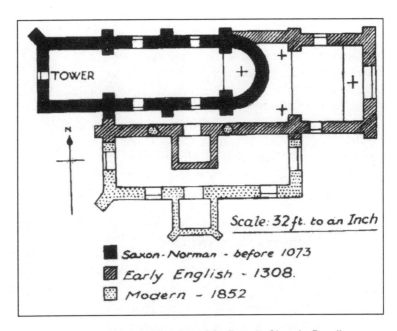

TOWER

N

Scale: 32 ft. to an Inch

■ Saxon-Norman - before 1073
▨ Early English - 1308.
▨ Modern - 1852

2.1a Revd. W. Arnold's plan of St. Peter's Church, Beeding,
showing periods of construction
(see 7.9a for plan of St. Nicholas Church)

14th October 1651

In 1830, during the dismantling of a house at Racton, near Chichester, which was the home of the Gounter family, a document was found in the secret compartment of an old bureau. The document, now in the British Museum (add; Mss; 9008), is a missing link in the tale of the escape of the future Charles II. Col. Gounter was given the task of guiding the young King's party through Sussex after his defeat at the battle of Worcester in 1651. This document makes a nonsense of the tales told of the places the King stayed at on his last night in England. Charles was in a similar position to his grand-nephew, Bonnie Prince Charlie, who, almost a hundred years later, was defeated at Drummossie Moor on 16th April 1746, the final chapter in the Stuart cause.

Gounter's narrative (made shortly after the event) is perhaps the most accurate of all the accounts that relate to our area. He was a Sussex man and often travelled to Brighton, then known as Brighthelmston, to visit relations there. The King's account, recorded in code by Samuel Pepys, was written down nearly thirty years after the escape. We take up the story at Hambledon, where they stayed at the house of Gounter's sister, Ursula (Mrs Symons). The party left at day-break on Tuesday the 14th October and made their way eastwards along the line of the Downs. At Arundel they were nearly captured when they ran into a hunting party led by the Governor, Capt. Morley, but by dismounting and descending a steep hill they avoided a confrontation.

At Houghton, they stopped at an alehouse for bread and beer: "From thence they came to Bramber, where they found the streets full of soldiers on both sides of the houses, who unknown to the Colonel came thither the night before to guard Bramber bridge and at this time had come into the town for refreshments". The party proceeded to Beeding, encountering yet more soldiers, but were unrecognised.

The Colonel had arranged a stop for refreshments at Mr Bagshall's house (Backshell), while he surveyed the rest of the route. This house was always thought to be New House farmhouse (now Valerie Manor), but we have discovered that the 'Priory' and Horton farmhouse were both in the possession of the Backshells. It was the opinion of Dr Bloxam that the way they went was along 'Gypsy Lane' (which was formerly the high road to Henfield and now Smugglers Lane). If they stopped anywhere at all it was at Horton, going on from there to Edburton, over the Downs to Southwick and on to Brighthelmston, where the King spent his last night in England at the George Inn in West Street. He remained in exile in France for the next nine years.

2.2 Charles II
(St. Mary's Archive)

2.2a Valerie Manor, formerly New House, one of a number of houses owned by
John Backshall

The Roads

"The Foul Ways of Sussex People" – so wrote the Revd. H. E. B. Arnold. This was not intended as any reflection on the habits or morals of Sussex folk; it was a quaint reference to the roads of our county which a century and beyond were the worst in the whole of England.

The fine highways of the Romans gradually fell into disrepair when they left these isles in the 5th century. No more proper roads were built for 1000 years and those that did exist from that time were only way-leave, i.e. the right of passage over private property. These were little better than paths. A statute of 1555 charged that the maintaining of roads be laid on the parish. Later in the 18th and 19th centuries the Turnpike Acts were passed. Turnpike trusts were set up and roads were built and paid for by tolls which laid the costs, rightfully, on those who used them.

'The New Road to Shoreham Avoiding Beeding Hill' was the name of the trust that built the road which was later to become the A283. This specific act was passed in 1807 and endured until 1885. One toll booth was at Bramber, near the Tollgate Restaurant, and the other between The Rising Sun and Beeding Court. The latter is now re-erected at the [Weald and Downland] open-air museum at Singleton. The occupants of Beeding Court were exempt from tolls. Before this time the road to Shoreham went up Castletown bostel road to Beeding Hill and down through Erringham.

Most travel in earlier times took the routes along the top of the Downs and the high ground where possible; other tracks like the one to Edburton and Poynings were called 'Hollow-ways' and were almost impassable in the winter months. The road to Henfield was Smugglers Lane, but in very bad conditions the Maines Farm road across Windmill Hill was used as an alternative route.

The east-west road along the top of the Downs ran from Southampton to Canterbury and, before the Great Bridge of Bramber was built in the late 12th century, it crossed the parish at two points. The most direct one was that which follows the now South Downs Way from the site of Old Beeding village, crossing the Adur at the Veteri Ponte to Botolphs. The other descended the bostel road to Castletown down Hyde Street and round in a natural curve to the Church and Priory crossing to Kings Barnes via a ford probably near the White Bridge, formerly New Bridge. The top of Beeding Hill was an early spaghetti junction, as six roads met there and still do, but are now only used by hiker and horse-rider.

2.3 Bramber toll house and toll gate,
demolished following a road accident

2.3a Beeding toll house, re-erected at the Weald
and Downland Museum, Singleton

The Salterns

In the days before freezers and cold stores, there was only one way to preserve meat for any length of time and that was by putting it into brine or salt. Before the 20th century, farmers were not able to keep enough feed to see all their stock through the winter, so towards the end of the year they butchered their surplus stock and salted them down. Up to the end of the 19th century the staple diet of the Royal Navy was salt beef, pork and dried vegetables. Instances of meat being in the cask for over twenty years have been known.

Old medieval salt workings, some just a few feet across, others 200ft long, are found in estuaries like the Adur valley. There are many ways that salt can be extracted in tidal areas and it is reasonably certain that in this English climate the evaporation had to be assisted by artificial means.

Salt making was quite a flourishing industry in earlier times; here in the Adur Valley many references to salt workings and salt payments are to be found in the documents of Sele and other manors.

The remains of our salterns over the past century are being reduced by ploughing. Not many are left now, but if you want to see one, look north-west from the top of the Priory steps, or stand in the car park in Bramber and look north. In earlier times there were many on each side of the Adur.

Documents show that salt was exported from Sussex fairly regularly up to the 14th century and then declined; plague and wars may have helped towards this decline. In the years 1323 - 1329 the recorded shipments of salt from Sussex were 58; in the years 1395 - 1399 only three are listed.

Salt is mentioned in the Bible and was a valued condiment. The word 'salary' was from the money allowed to Roman soldiers to buy salt. Now that it is manufactured and mined in huge quantities it has lost the importance it once had.

For more on one of KN-B's favourite subject see 12.3, 12.8, and 13.1.

cf. E. W. Holden & T. P. Hudson. *Sussex Archaeological Collections* Vol. 119.

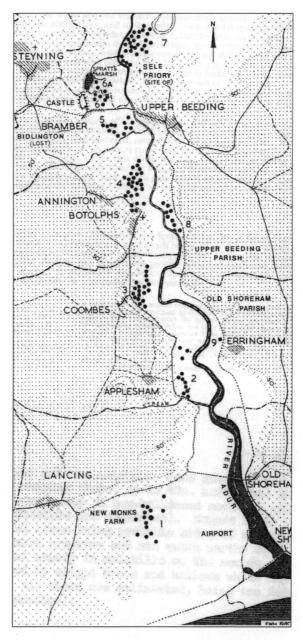

2.4 Plan of salterns in the Adur Valley
(by kind permission of the Sussex Archaeological Society)

Beeding Bridge

I wonder how many people who cross Beeding Bridge, as I do many times a week, pause and give a thought to its age, the builders, or indeed why it was built in the first place. There were two river crossings in our parish before the Conquest, one at the Priory – Kings Barnes and another at a place near St. Botolph's.

At the time of the building of the castle at Bramber, a causeway and two bridges were built. The great stone bridge of Bramber, 170 feet long with a chapel on the central pier, crossed the two minor navigations of the river near St. Mary's. A wooden bridge crossed the main course of the Adur where Beeding bridge does now. References to this first timber bridge mention it as the lesser bridge of Bramber, 1260 A.D. A watermill existed on the north-west side (Millfield) which was probably some of the first reclaimed land; salt pits adjacent are also mentioned.

A timber bridge similar in construction to the Old Shoreham toll bridge but shorter is shown on a map by John Gotham in 1627. By this time the causeway had been built on, and now forms the High Street, Beeding and The Street, Bramber.

Our brick and stone bridge was built in 1785 in consequence of an Act of Parliament passed in 1765 which enabled a turnpike road to be built, the builders being empowered to use materials from the ruins of Knepp Castle. Many old buildings went this way and no doubt much of Bramber Castle is now under our feet. The cost of the bridge is not mentioned, but Magdalen College, Oxford, paid the bill as owners of Sele Priory; the Vicar paid one fifth as the upkeep of the bridge was his responsibility. A letter dated 9th April 1785 from the College to the Vicar, Dr. Nicholas, said that owing to several points, not least the poor condition of the then present bridge, it would be best for the College and their tenant to lay out money for the erection of a more substantial bridge.

The bridge was widened on its north side in 1845, the iron footbridge was added in 1926 to keep the pedestrians away from the increasing motor traffic, and how many of you remember the clay barges and the little tugboat that lowered its funnel when passing under Beeding Bridge?

2.5 River Adur, looking south

2.5a River Adur, looking north with the Bridge Hotel on the right

The Great Bridge of Bramber

As we have seen in earlier articles there were, in our parish, two main crossings of the River Adur before the Conquest. Much has been said about the great stone bridge, 170 feet long with the chapel of St. Mary on the central pier. This was built in the late 11th century and probably with other events caused the decline of the old port of St. Cuthman located further north.

Wharves from this period have been discovered east of St. Mary's. These are recorded as being used by the Knights Templars when they left for the Crusades. There has been speculation that the original bridge was of Roman origin but this is unlikely if one remembers the other two crossing points of the Adur. Thurston Hopkins, in his book *Sussex Rendezvous,* calls our attention to the blocks of Sussex marble used in the rebuilding of Horton Hall.* These, he says, are of the same fretted appearance as those blocks cut by the Roman artificers to build Stane Street and quite different from the blocks of Isle of White stone, which are recorded as being used circa 1480 to repair the bridge. The blocks of marble, he says, were cut at Pulborough as were those used in the construction of Stane Street. Five of the stone piers of the great bridge were discovered in 1839 two feet below the surface. These were excavated and sold to Sir Charles Burrell who used them for rebuilding the foundations at Horton Farm [now known as Horton Hall] where they can be seen..

Some of you may remember that around 1957 a trench was dug along the entire length of Bramber street for new sewers. During excavations numerous wooden piles from the causeway were exposed, as well as further traces of the bridge. These wooden piles which were mainly upright, were 4 to 5 feet long and covered a distance of 200 feet. There was no rubble infilling which suggests that there was a timber roadway across.

Traces of a 30-foot causeway of limestone rubble from Bembridge were found east of St. Mary's. It was 5 foot deep connecting directly with a 7 foot section of masonry (Greystone Wealden marble) which may be part of a pier of the bridge. The bridge and chapel are recorded as being in existence in 1538 but were gone by the 17th century. Much of the material was used in the building of the Turnpike roads and if you look around at old buildings you will no doubt see some visible traces there.

*Some fragments of Sussex marble (winklestone – fossil shells) were incorporated in the garden wall at St. Mary's during the 19th century restorations. A piece of cornerstone from the bridge and some pieces of the pilings can be seen at St. Mary's House [Ed.].

2.6 Garratt's conjectural sketch of the Great Bridge of Bramber

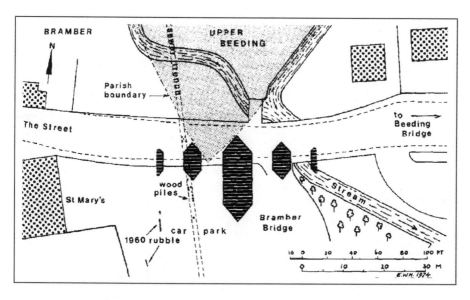

2.6a Eric Holden's excavations of the Great Bridge of Bramber
(by kind permission of the Sussex Archaeological Society)

Kings Barnes

The Royal Manor of 'Kings Barnes' was a farm and royal residence of the Saxon kings. It was part of the Saxon kingdom that was known as Wessex; its capital was Winchester. The Manor included parts of Bramber and Steyning and reached to Wiston and Ashurst. King Ethelwulf died and was buried in the Manor of Kings Barnes, He was later re-interred at Winchester by his son, King Alfred the Great, who was also buried there in 901 AD. What is believed to be Ethelwulf's marker stone is in the porch of Steyning Church.

King Alfred is known mainly for his struggle to regain his kingdom from the Northmen and his great victory at Edington. He is also known to ex-sailors like myself as the founder of the Royal Navy. He must have spent periods of time in his manor house here and when he died he left Beeding in his will to his nephew Aethelm. King Edward the Confessor is named as being in possession prior to the conquest and this is recorded in the Domesday survey.

Kings Barnes occupied a strategic position; it was in direct contact by river and sea with Winchester and it was a major point in the crossing of the Adur. As we saw in earlier *Villager* articles, it was one of the two crossings of the river; travellers crossed at Botolphs, or descended the bostel at Castletown and forded at the Priory of Sele, where a ferry was also recorded. At high tide the waters of the estuary reached from the Priory to the port of St. Cuthman, at Steyning.

The name 'Kings Barnes' is first mentioned in the Pipe Rolls in 1210. It was probably always known as a Royal Residence and was in the possession of Thomas, Lord Seymour, in 1547. In circa 1600, it belonged to Sir Edward Caryll; in the 18th century it was in the ownership of the Clitherow family. At least five kings are connected with the Manor, including Alfred's brothers and his father, Ethelred, whose relics were removed to Winchester Cathedral.

After a period of over a thousand years of belonging to Beeding, that quiet little area of Kings Barnes will shortly be transferred to the Parish of Steyning. Perhaps few will be aware of the change, the rates may be higher, pensioners will no longer receive their bus tokens, but life will not be much different. Historians will note the event and that will be that.

2.7   Alfred the Great
(St. Mary's archive)

2.7a St. Andrew and St. Cuthman's Church, Steyning

The Adur River

When we mention the Adur these days many will think of the annual 'Bath Tub' race, or the river banks as a nice place to walk the dog. As a child I have memories of bathing near Beeding bridge; older folk will remember the years before the war when that most convenient railway line from Brighton to Horsham brought visitors from all the surrounding district to Bramber station for the pleasure of a day out on the river. Scores of boats were for hire in those days on both sides of Beeding bridge and many tea rooms flourished in the two villages.

In earlier times the river was of much greater importance to the whole of the Adur Valley than it is today. From Roman times till the coming of the railways almost all heavy materials, stone, timber, lime and all the products of the iron industry in this part of Sussex, went by water. The pack horse was the only other means of transport through the dense marshy Weald in medieval Sussex.

'Adur' is a fairly recent name. Michael Drayton, in his work *Polyolbion** (1622), was the first to mention the Adur; he may have thought that the estuary was the site, as many did, of the old Roman 'Portus Adurni'. Sore, Score, Weald Ditch, Bramber Water and Beeding River – all these names and others have at various times been applied to our river.

John Camden wrote, in his *Magna Britannia,* that ships with full sail could reach as far as Bramber in the 17th century. The Vicar of Beeding owned the fishing rights on the river from Old Shoreham to Bedney corner, north of the Priory of Sele. As far as we know he still does, although others claim it! The fishing must have been quite good, as a complaint to the Revd. Dr. Bloxam in 1882 by residents shows. A letter still in existence, asks him to put a stop to fishermen from Shoreham using fine net to trawl the river, as they were taking 80 to 100 lbs of fine fish at each sweep.

On a map by John Gotham of 1627 we find many ox-bows [lakes] shown on the river. Most of these were straightened out in the years after the Navigation Act was passed by Parliament in 1807. The Baybridge Canal Co. made the river navigable for vessels up to 70 foot long with a 4 foot draught, as far as West Grinstead, where the wharves can still be seen. Salt making was another valuable product of the river

* *Poly-olbion* – from the Greek, 'having many blessings' [Ed.]

For more on salt-making see 2.4, 13.1

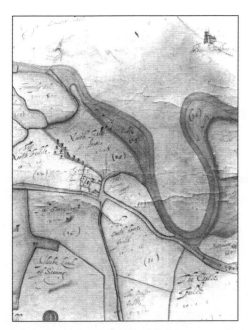

2.8 John Gotham's 1627 map of the River Adur showing ox-bows

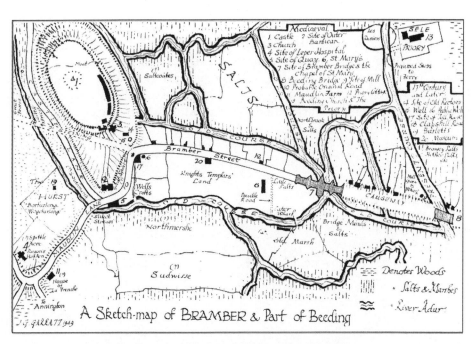

2.8a Plan by J. G. Garratt of Bramber waterways,
purporting to show the land of the Knights Templar

The Bounds

When I was a lad back in the early thirties my grandfather, a founder member of the Society of Sussex Downsmen, and one who had a great sense of occasion, took me to witness a 'Beating of the Bounds'* ceremony in East Sussex. This is an experience that all children should have at least once in their lives. It was something that I will never forget; it was a dusty walk, but at several points large earthenware jars were produced and home-made ginger beer dispensed to all and sundry.

What was the object of all this? Well, you could ask any child in Beeding or Bramber today where the boundary of their parish was and it is very doubtful if they could answer with any accuracy – if at all! But a child of the last century knew exactly where the limits of the parish that he lived in were, as they had been pointed out to him or her during the walk.

The ancient custom of 'Beating the Bounds' dates back to the 9th century; it took place at Rogationtide and was traditionally led by the Vicar and Churchwardens. All the children and most of the population took part; it was a happy day out and a holiday for all except the 'Meresman', who was appointed by the parish each year to establish the position of the mere or bound stones, the roads, bridges and watercourses.

We have a record of the boundaries of our villages as they were in 1871. At that time the Ordnance Survey department was engaged in a survey of Beeding and Bramber; the findings of this survey are contained in the 'Meresmans Report Books'. These were compiled by William Mills, Meresman for Beeding, who was the tenant of Pond Farm, which in that time was the area of the Memorial Playing Fields and land south of Pond Farm House. With Charles Woolgar acting for the late Bridger Woolgar, Meresman for Bramber, the man appointed to take charge of the survey by the Ordnance Survey Department was John Stirton, a corporal in the Royal Engineers. (A corporal was a very responsible position in those days – he was classed as a surveyor). They perambulated the boundaries of the two parishes for several days in June 1871; the results make very interesting reading.

* KN-B returns to the subject in 15.11/12

The Mills (Part 1)

Some older folk may remember seeing the remains of the roundhouse of Beeding mill; I saw it in the 1930s. There was quite a lot left then but modern farming methods have reduced it to a scatter of broken brick and slate. The site is easily identified; one only has to walk up 'Maines Farm' road to the crest of Windmill Hill and you can define the track off to the north-east that led to the mill, barn and, probably, living quarters. Later millers lived at Castletown.

This mill was built around the turn of the 17th century. It was a post mill with four sweeps and a fantail to keep it into the wind. It was badly damaged in a gale in 1888. A mill is recorded as being on this spot from at least the year 1384 (600 years).

The Lord of the Manor owned the mill in early times, when mills were very important to all. Everyone gave service to the Lord. After the harvest, when the milling was completed for the Demesne farm, the Yeoman and peasant had their grain ground and paid a commission, usually a part of their flour or grist, as coin was not used by the lower classes until the 17th century, except for monastic tokens.

No windmills were recorded in England before 1191 A.D. From Roman times till then, the watermill supplied all the power. Mills were the energy sources of yesteryear; they not only ground cereals but drove furnace bellows and trip-hammers of the iron industry, and powered sawmills in the last centuries. Windpumps reclaimed estuary land and many other tasks. We are again tapping the sources of wind and water. Tidemills are producing electricity as are experimental wind generators. Free energy with no pollution! – what a thought for the future? A watermill stood on the north-west side of Beeding bridge (Millfield), replaced later with a windmill. The site of a windmill base can be seen near the top of Beeding hill, a cross in the grass where the post rested.

There was a watermill owned by the Priory of Sele in the 13th century. This was traditionally thought to be at the foot of the Priory steps where much dressed stone can be found. This location was known as Monks Walk, which is now the name of a road in another part of the village. A survey from the bell tower of St. Peters has shown what archaeologists think is the millpond.

For Part 2 see 10.12

The Priory of Sele

The house known today as the Priory was built on the site, a little to the north-west of the original monastic structure. This was erected in the years 1788-1790 by the then Vicar, the Revd. Thomas Hutchinson D.D.

The earlier premises had been pulled down and rebuilt without the full permission of the owners, Magdalen College, Oxford. This is perhaps reflected by their contribution of £150, to the £800 that it cost Dr. Hutchinson for the new building. Several of the incumbents had spent big money. As the records show, the Revd. James Ventris much improved the 'convent garden'. To quote Dr. Arnold: 'Both the front and rear of the house were laid out in exquisite taste'. He spent £700 improving the premises. The extension on the south side was a new kitchen added about 1832. The college granted him £100 for this and for deepening the well. This is then how we see the house now, a nice secluded Georgian property.

The first Priory was built sometime before 1096. It was founded by William de Braose as the Benedictine cell of the Abbey of St. Florent near Saumur. The cloisters of this early building were joined to the North wall of the nave of St. Peter's Church, then dedicated to St. Paul as well. That is why there were no windows in the North wall until the rebuilding of the church in 1852.

In the 1480s, after nearly four hundred years, and in a state of decay, the Priory closed and was acquired by Magdalen College. At this time, the Carmelite Friars at Shoreham were gradually being pushed farther and farther into the town by the increasingly heavy tides on the Adur. The sea began to invade their premises until, in 1493, they were allowed to occupy Sele Priory. The rent for house, Chapel and four acres was 10 shillings (50p) per annum. They rebuilt the Priory from ground level – only the cellars of the first building remain. An excavation in 1966 showed that the rebuilt cloisters were eight feet wide and were paved with plain yellow, green and purple glazed tiles, bordered by bricks glazed in pale blue. We know that the stained glass windows were removed to Buncton Church and were re-erected in the exterior chancel walls. There is evidence that rebuilding took place in Tudor times and again in the 18th century when the Revd. Thomas Newlin refurbished the property to the tune of £200 in 1724/5.

See also *Windows into the Past* 6.4

2.11 Fragments of arches from Sele Priory at Buncton Church
(by courtesy of Anne Ketteman)

2.11a Sele Priory (c1790) as it is today. The cellars and remains of the
original wine store still exist. It is sometimes referred to as Beeding Priory.

Erringham Chalk Pit

Have you, as I have lately, had occasion to be stopped by the temporary traffic lights on the A283 at Dacre Gardens? Perhaps you have reflected on the cement works there and how it evolved. Why is it where it is? The Adur is one reason, as up to the 19th century most heavy goods were transported by water. The Sussex Weald was without proper roads and very marshy. It is speculation but it was probably the Romans who organised the kilns for limeburning in this area and the site has probably been in use since then. The two other chalkpits, one at Golding Barn, previously a tip, and the other at Castletown, were limited by access – neither was adjacent to the Adur.

Limeburning was vital to agriculture and was also needed for mortar, with horsehair for plastering, and for limewash which was about the only cheap weatherproofing material used on the exterior of small buildings. A kind of cement was used 6000 years ago in the pyramids by the Egyptians. Here in 1796 a man named Parker produced a 'Roman cement'. Smeaton who built the first Eddystone lighthouse had discovered that clay mixed with limestone made excellent hydraulic cement, but it was left to a bricklayer, Joseph Aspdin, to patent 'Portland' cement – a name used because it set like Portland stone.

Local records show that the pit on the site of Beeding Cement Works was in use from the early 18th century, but had probably been worked from a much earlier period. In 1895 the firm of H. R. Lewis took over the works that had been established by the Beeding Cement Company* about 1882 and were themselves taken over a year or so later by the Sussex Portland Cement Company. By 1912 it was in the hands of the British Portland Cement Manufacturers Ltd. Production increased and clay that had previously been brought in from outside of the area was now (from about 1900) extracted from Horton claypit near Small Dole and brought down the river by barges After the war, in the late 1940s, the clay was sent by a pipeline which passes west of Pound Lane across the playing fields and along the side of the village hall and on down the river.

The terrace of houses known as Dacre Gardens was erected in the first decade of the 20th century. In the early 1950s the works were transferred to the east side of the A283 which had been built under the Turnpike act of 1807. Many of the old chimneys disappeared.

*In December 1984, Blue Circle were manufacturing 7000 tonnes of cement a week [annually some 3,000,000 tonnes] and employed about 250 local workers [Ed.]

KN-B returns to this subject in 11.2

2.12 View of Dacre Gardens and Beeding Cement Works with the Mission Hall just visible in the foreground

2.12a Interior of Beeding Cement Works, showing the rotary kilns

Pound House Cottage

I wonder how much is missed by residents of the village as they go about their daily business? How many of us stop to look around us? Life moves at such a pace these days that few of us pause to survey our environment or to wonder what happened at such and such a spot long before any of us was born. The only way forward is by building on information from the past as we can only improve on something that we know about. History, therefore, is vital to us and for the generations that follow.

Where did 'Pound House' get its name from? One usually associates the name with the local 'pound' as being near to or part of it. This was the place which in earlier times was where stray animals were kept when found roaming loose or on grazing ground not owned or leased by the owner. Sometimes, too, the owner would exceed the number he was allowed to pasture on common land. A fee was payable for the release of each animal detained. In Beeding in the 1840s the Village Pound was situated just off the High Street, as shown on the Tithe map. Perhaps the pound was originally at the bottom of Gypsy Lane (the name changed to Smugglers Lane sometime after 1650 for reasons that need no explanation).

Pound Cottage was once two dwellings and is now a listed building with a thatched roof   A mainly flint construction with brick quoins two storeys high, the cottage was built sometime before 1700. It has a well in the front garden that is about 20 feet deep, lined with brick and rendered. It is still usable, but whether the water is pure with all the pesticides in use today is questionable.

The house stood alone in earlier times, on the high road to Small Dole and Henfield that crossed the river by the church. It is said that by the house was a gate made of poles called Peppersgate and this may have been a tollgate of some sort.

Dr. Arnold quotes an interesting fact, dated 26th April 1655:

"The same first day George Fox had a meeting at Ninian Brocketts house at Beeding".

The piece goes on to say that the Quakers living in Sele were accustomed to meeting at Peppersgate, and were seldom fewer than 220, yet the population at this time was probably less than this. It is possible that open air meetings took place for the whole Adur Valley here, until the sect obtained the use of Penn house in Steyning in 1678.

3.1 Pound House Cottage

3.1a Penn's Cottage, Steyning
(sketch by Harry Ford)

The Picture

I have no doubt that many of you have read *Highways and Byways in Sussex* written by E.V. Lucas in 1903. There is a little bit relating to Beeding which always makes me chuckle. It is the story of the 'picture'. I quote: "It was not long ago that a masterpiece was discovered at Beeding, in one of those unlikely places in which with ironical humour fine pictures so often hide themselves. It hung in a little general shop kept by an elderly widow. After passing unnoticed for many years, it was silently identified by a dealer who happened to be buying some biscuits. He made a casual remark about it, learned that any value that might be set upon it was sentimental rather than monetary, and returned home. He laid the matter before some friends, with the result that they visited Beeding in a party a few days later, in order to bear away the prize.

Outside the shop they held a council of war. One was for bidding at the outset a small but sufficient sum for the picture. Another for affecting to want something else and leading to the picture, and so forth. In the discussion of tactics they raised their voices too high, so a visitor of the widow, sitting in the room over the shop, heard something of the matter.

Suspecting danger but wholly unconscious of its nature, she hurried downstairs and warned her friend of a predatory gang outside who were not to be supplied with anything they asked for. The widow obeyed. They asked for tea and she refused. They asked for biscuits, she set her hand firmly on the tin lid. They mentioned the picture, she was a rock. Baffled they withdrew. The widow, now on the right scent, took the next train to Brighton to consult an expert. The picture, thought to be the work of either Romney or Lawrence, was found to be a portrait of the actress, Mrs. Jordan." A little tale that probably was true.

If we consult Dr. Arnold's unpublished history papers on Beeding, he says that the Revd. Dr. Bloxam taught young ladies at the Priory, and on the walls of his study hung many sketches and drawings by his uncle. At certain times he would ask his pupils to select a drawing which he would then present to them. Many of these drawings probably still exist in our area as quite a number were distributed. There are three references to these gifts, and one person (who does not wish to be named) still has one. Dr. John Rouse Bloxam, Vicar 1862-91 was the youngest son of Dr. Richard Rouse Bloxam and his mother was Anne, the sister of Sir Thomas Lawrence, President of the Royal Academy.

St. Peter's Bells (Part 1)

You miss things when you are deprived of them. Church bells ringing out over the Sussex countryside bring back vivid memories to me. I stepped off the train one Sunday morning in 1946 having just been demobbed from the Royal Navy, to be welcomed by a peal (not just for me!). Church bells were silent over the war years, with invasion by the Germans being the only occasion when they would have sounded.

What treasure we have in our church of St. Peter! Probably the oldest things still working in our neighbourhood are the two medieval bells in the tower, which are recorded as being cast in Southampton between the years 1307-1340. It is evident that these large bells, weighing 7cwt. and 8 cwt., would have been transported by sea and river from Southampton.

The heavier bell is dedicated to the honour of St. Katherine and the lighter to St. Margaret. A new church building was consecrated on the 26th February 1308. It does seem likely that the bells would have been in place then and rung out across the estuary to tell the world.

A little over three hundred years later another larger bell was added. This 9cwt. bell was cast by Thomas Giles of Chichester in 1613, but could have been made at Lewes as he also had a works there. This large bell was removed in 1892 and melted down to make four new bells, with a total weight of a little under 19cwt.

I contacted the makers, the Whitechapel Bell Foundry, and they sent me a copy of their daybook for 27th March 1892. There is no indication as to where the other half ton of bell metal came from. It is claimed that it was donated by Clement Budd (Churchwarden 1887-1908) whose name is on one of three cast onto the bells, and was perhaps made up of fittings salvaged from barges sunk on the Adur.

Two more bells were added in 1898 to make a peal of eight, and they are still in place. Let's hope they are never silent again.

KN-B's original title was *The Bells of St. Peter's*

See also 12.7 for Part Two

The Manor of Horton

The 'Manor' was a unit of administration in ancient times and there are today people who are still entitled to call themselves 'Lord of the Manor'. The Manor was held by a Lord appointed by the King or through a nobleman to the Lord of the Rape (in Sussex). The person so appointed was empowered to hold a Court Baron or Court Leet.*

Usually once a year at one of these courts a statement was read from the 'Customal'. This was a document which recorded the duties and services owed by the free and unfree tenants and the rights and obligations of the Lord to those tenants. Annual appointments were made, those of the burgesses, haywards, way-wardens and the pinder (who looked after the village pound). Payments could be made to avoid this service. The courts recorded the ownership of land and regulated village life. The freeholders were usually the ruling bodies. The copyholders, by custom, held land from the Lord by a written copy of their entry in the court rolls – hence 'copyhold', which endured until 1926.

The area of the Manor was usually in the form of a strip of land as was Horton. This included good agricultural land pasture, woodland and sometimes a chalk pit which provided lime for the land and for building. Horton stretched from the borders of Henfield to the sea. There is record of a perambulation of the bounds in the manor rolls on September 4th and 5th 1771:

"Also at this court the Homage present that they, together with John Gates of Beeding alias Sele in the county of Sussex, yeoman, and John Kidd of the same place, carpenter, have on the day before and on the day of the holding of this court perambulated and gone over the bounds of the said Manor and in particular have found that the said Manor extends itself on the beach of the sea-shore in the parish of Southwick from a place called Fishersgate to a place called Kingston East gate and from the south of the river there to low water mark." (Presumably this included the new harbour area).

The first recorded Lord of the Manor was William de Bonevile who lived in the last half of the 13th century. He left no male heir and the manor passed to Sir Philip Maubank of Dorset who married Bonevile's daughter Emma. Several generations later the manor passed to John Horsey by marriage, so we have the manor of Horton, Horton Maybank, and Horton Horsey, over the years.

* See 1.9

A Link with the New World

A year or two before the last war a small leather bag was discovered during minor repairs and redecorating to the old toll cottage that used to stand south of The Rising Sun. It contained a few old coins, among which was a silver crown-sized coin dated 1734. That along with the other minor pieces in the bag was acquired by my grandfather, a medical man, who was also an archaeologist and keen numismatist. How the bag was left there or why it was hidden remains a mystery. The fact that it was concealed could perhaps indicate a 'fiddle' by the tollkeeper who was only paid 9/- per week by the person who held the right to levy tolls from the turnpike trust. The trust was titled 'New road to avoid Beeding Hill' and was wound up in 1885. The coin in question was a Spanish milled dollar or 'Piece of Eight' minted in Mexico. This was probably the most popular coin and certainly the most romantic piece of currency ever. The phrase 'Piece of 8' usually excites the imagination of children and without doubt quite a few adults as well. Who has not read R. L. Stevenson's *Treasure Island* and day-dreamed of finding buried treasure on some Caribbean island on the old Spanish Main?

These large silver pieces were accepted here and in most countries in the 18th and 19th centuries. They were issued countermarked by the Royal Mint and also restruck and circulated as the Bank of England dollar in the early 1800s. The silver was of a very high standard. The mintmaster was responsible for the fineness of the metal. The penalty for debasement was loss of a limb or death and this gave assurance to traders. The Spanish/American 8 reals (pronounced re-als) was the origin of the U.S. dollar of today, (Dollar evolved from Thaler or Daaler, European crowns).

When small change was short the coin was cut into ½, ¼ and 1/8s in pie-shaped segments called 'bits'; that is why the U.S. ¼ dollar is to this day known as 'two bits'. In colonial America they were known as 'Dos Mundos' as they depicted the two hemispheres (the old and new worlds) between two pillars (the pillars of Hercules, entrance to the Mediterranean). Settlers and merchants in the New World, when writing home or about their wealth, would write the '8' between two pillars (thus: |8|) to indicate the dollar unit and one can easily imagine a hastily written |8| as the $, which is, of course, the U.S. dollar sign of today.

KN-B takes this subject further in 20.3 *Numismatics*

3.5 Pieces of Eight

3.6 King James I.
He introduced small change into the currency
(*St. Mary's Archive*)

85

Bramber Ghost Token

In the late 1930s there appeared in the window of a Bramber shop an advertisement by a collector who wished to purchase a 17th century Bramber halfpenny token. This trade token was first noticed in the list of Sussex tokens in 1888 by J. Lowe-Warren and was described thus: 'obverse-Robert Higginson-his half peny...reverse-In Brambare-1666-RHA.' It later appeared in Boynes' *17th century Tokens* (1891 edition) – the standard work on the subject at the time. The advertisement remained for a long period and offered a very high price for the coin, but without result as the token did not exist! This came to light on the discovery of a token in the collection of A.H. Baldwin (a dealer and coin expert). His coin was in fine condition and read: '....obverse-Robert Higginson-his half peny...reverse-in Elsmeare (Shropshire) 1666-RHA'. It can be clearly read so the legend of the Bramber token may have been founded on a very worn specimen of this.

At this stage you may well ask 'what were tokens?' If, like the character in the film, you owned a £1,000,000 note and nothing smaller, your purchasing power was somewhat restricted. This, too, was the predicament that people were in in the 17th century and at other times in this country when there was a shortage of legal currency. Trade suffered badly when this occurred as the man who had a shilling piece could not buy an article costing a half penny if the seller did not have 11 pennies in change.

The official coinage of England from Saxon times was of silver, the penny being cut into half or quarters for halfpennies and farthings (four-things). In Elizabethan times the silver ½d was the lowest denomination but, weighing only 4 grains and about half the size of the now defunct ½ pence, was not very popular. James I (1603-25) recognised the need for small change and commissioned Lord Harrington to strike copper farthings. These were only 3 grains and were suppressed by Parliament in 1644. During the civil war little coinage was struck and no official copper was issued during the commonwealth period. From about 1648 traders took action and produced their own token coinage which was accepted almost everywhere in the country and many inn-keepers and trade guilds are recorded on these pieces.

The Inns

Inns and alehouses from early times were situated where they would attract most business, usually the main street of the town or village. Almost all communications, news of foreign wars, happenings in the capital, even local intelligence was passed through the inn. With the mail coach era and the building of the turnpike roads, many small premises were rebuilt or enlarged to take advantage of the increased trade. They were often staging posts for changing the coach-horses and for the use of the passengers; frequent stops were necessary as coach travel was mostly very uncomfortable.

Although several inns have been recorded in Beeding, the one mentioned as an unlicensed alehouse in 1647 was probably the present King's Head. On a coaching map of circa 1780 in my possession, the only inn shown is the King's Head. It was certainly thriving in 1788, as the meetings of the Hundred Court were held there from that date and on into the early 1800s. Later on most of the vestry meetings were held there.

The King's Head was, without doubt, named after Charles II, and probably from the the time of the Restoration in 1660. Charles II escaped from the battle of Worcester 1651. Cromwell's men occupied these villages on and off during the English Civil War, so it is unlikely that Charles's head would have appeared until after Cromwell's death. It is interesting to note that the sign changed at the beginning of this century when Edward VII's portrait replaced his ancestor, but not for long, as a photograph taken after the First World War shows Charles II back in favour.

In the national census of 1841 the inn was in the occupation of Henry Marshall and his wife, Rebecca. They are recorded again in the 1851 census and described as 'victuallers', with two lodgers and a female servant. The premises are in the conservation area of Upper Beeding and are listed buildings recorded thus:

'18th century or before, altered and refaced, two storeys, six windows, stuccoed, hipped tiled roof, some casement windows, some sash with glazing bars intact, modern public-house front on ground floor'.

The barn is recorded as being 19th century and was once part of Pond Farm. I suspect the earlier King's Head building was once the medieval farmhouse.

3.7 The Castle Hotel, Bramber,
immortalised by Hilaire Belloc in *The Four Men*

3.7a Beeding High Street, 1905, with The King's Head on the right

The Village Stores

Along with the inn, the local store was the hub of weekday village life in the days before the last world war. It sometimes had the dual role as Post Office/Grocery store and was often an iron-mongers as well. There exists a late 19th century photograph showing Mr. Goddard outside his shop in Beeding High Street (later the Lucas Stores); the forecourt is crowded with spades and forks, buckets and brooms, and so on.

My recollections, as a lad, of the inside of the store, was an atmosphere pervaded with the pungent aromas of freshly ground coffee, cheese, cured hams, and newly baked bread – smells that are not enjoyed today with modern packaging and marketing methods. Service was the watchword then; customers were served by the proprietor from behind the counter. Butter was weighed and put into shape by wooden pats with designs cut to give an attractive look to the rich yellow colour. There were a couple of bentwood chairs for the elderly and/or valued customer. The floor had fresh sawdust daily.

Our High Street store was in the occupation of the Lucas family from 1913. A sale catalogue of 1914 describes the premises as the Beeding Grocery and Provision Stores. It states that it is let to Mr. Obadiah Lucas on seven years' lease from Christmas Day 1913 'at 30 pounds per annum' and that he pays the land tax of £1.2s.11d. Among the things described in the list is a flint and brick built shed used as an acetylene gas plant. This was to provide gas light to the shop and was probably installed before 1888 when town gas came to Beeding, (electric light did not reach the village until 1921).

Obadiah Lucas came from Fulking village where he owned the bakery and shop. His son, Frank, was born there. The family had other branches in the area. Frank took over the Beeding stores in 1923 after service in the Royal Flying Corps, and ran it for over thirty years, then his son Douglas became the proprietor.

Frank is a village stalwart with a record of public service second to none, (I discovered in conversation with Frank that we had both attended the same school, but not at the same time I hasten to add!). He was a churchwarden and organist at St. Peter's for more than thirty years. He served on the Parish Council for the same amount of time and has also served on the old Rural Council. In 1950, he was presented with an illuminated Scroll to mark twenty-five years of service, fifteen as chairman. He had much to do with the acquisition of the playing field as a memorial to the dead of both world wars.

3.8 Frank Lucas RFC, with his son. He kept his Grocery and Provision Store going for forty years

3.8a Frank Lucas delivering provisions by boat to his flood-marooned customers

Beeding Police

Until the early 1800s there was no regular police force. Order was kept by 'The Military'– a much hated practice that resulted in affrays such as the terrible 'Peterloo Massacre'. In 1829, a regular Police force was established in London by Robert Peel; 3000 'Bobbies' or 'Peelers' replaced the old 'Bow Street Runners' which were few in number. This force was controlled by the Home Office and was unarmed except for wooden truncheons. The new system drove the criminal out of the big towns and into the countryside, so other towns began to employ the same methods until, in 1856, every county and borough was obliged to maintain a police force.

Researching the old parish records, I came across two entries in the 'Vestry minutes'. On 1st April 1831 it was resolved that a pair of handcuffs be bought for the use of the Parish. At a later Vestry meeting in the King's Head on the 30th November 1837, a proposal was put by the Parish Chairman, Richard Goddard:

'It was agreed upon that a man should be appointed to act as a Police to watch the Parish of Upper Beeding, in respect of property of every description. There shall also be appointed three Inspectors for the district; Mr. Joseph Morris of Beeding Court shall be one, Mr. William Mills the second and Mr. Henry Patching of Toddington Farm [Tottington] the other. The said Policeman shall every day call on one of the Inspectors to know his destination for his nightly watching and an assessment shall be made according to the act of Parliament to defray the said expence'.

The first mentioned as a policeman was John Carter on the 13th February 1839, but it is unclear as to whether he was the first one appointed. It was probably no coincidence that the Beeding inspectors were farmers. They were the most robbed by way of their livestock. It must be remembered that penalties were very harsh. Stealing an animal was a capital offence and if caught in the act it was an advantage for the thief to try and murder his captor rather than face the death penalty. The old saying was - "You might as well be hanged for a sheep as a lamb".

In Saxon times order was kept by a system known as 'Frank-Pledge'. This formed men into groups of ten known as tithings. These men were responsible for the actions of each other, should one commit an offence it was up to the others to secure his attendance at the court of the Lord of the Manor for punishment. Perhaps a revival of this ancient order would do much to help the community with the present cutbacks which make the village bobby an endangered species.

KN-B has more to say on this subject in 14.12

The Post Office

Charles I founded the Royal Mail. Communications were very poor until the 18th century, with no national delivery network before 1720 when Ralph Allen of Bath was granted the monopoly of all deliveries outside London.

John Palmer, best remembered for his mail coaches, was awarded a contract by the Post Office in 1784. It was this success that led to the mail-coach era, which existed until the coming of the railways in the 19th century. The stagecoach, as its name implies, changed horses at certain stages of the journey, carrying passengers and mail and was exempt from tolls. On approaching the toll gates, the toll-keeper held open the gate to avoid delay. All coaches gave way to the Royal Mail.

Before the Regency period, the London-Brighton mail passed through Beeding, coming via Guildford, Arundel and Petworth. Around 1807, before the A283 was built, the route was up Castletown Bostel and down through Erringham by way of Beeding Hill. The *Sussex Weekly Advertiser* for 11th December 1775 records a mail robbery at Erringham, in which the Shoreham and Brighthelmston letters and three shillings were stolen. This offence often carried the death penalty and, on execution, the culprit was hung in chains to rot at the scene of the crime. I cannot find any record of this felon being caught.

The King's Head is marked on an early coaching map, but whether it was a post collecting-point or stage is unclear. Holly Cottage was the post office at the time of the 'penny post' in 1840. The Reverend Doctor Bloxam refers to it in documents. There have been at least four different sites for Beeding post office over the years. In the Sussex Kelly's for 1915, the Postmaster, Arthur Vinall, dispensed many money orders and telegrams from the 'Telephonic Express Delivery Office'. Locally, letters were delivered at 7am, 11am and 6.45pm.

Some years ago, the postmistress at Beeding let me see her deeds. In 1914, the property known as No. 1 Adur Villas was a private dwelling occupied by Frederick Elms. The annual rent was £19. Happy days!

The Beedings

In *The Christian* [the former 'Parish Magazine'] for 1982, I wrote an article on the apparently illogical use of the prefixes 'Upper' and 'Lower' for our parishes. Many people since then have asked me the same question, so perhaps it is time for a replay with additions. The name 'Sussex' is a contraction of 'Suth-Sexia' which indicates that it is the land of the 'South Saxon' (cf. Wessex - West Saxon, Essex - East Saxon). Before the Romans, it was the land of the 'Regni'', the tribe that occupied Sussex and parts of Surrey. 'Regnum' (Chichester) was an important place, and there is abundant evidence that our county was occupied from the earliest times. Neolithic, Bronze and Iron Age settlements surround us, so the land had been inhabited for thousands of years before the *Anglo Saxon Chronicle* recorded the coming of Bieda and his father, Port, in the year 501 AD. 'Bieda' is recognised by many historians as the source of the name Beeding (also Beddingham). 'Ing' (or 'ingas') is an early form of meadow or pasture or community, so one can easily see how five centuries later 'Bieda's ing' or 'Beida's ingas', came to be written 'Beddinges' in the Domesday survey. The Victorians wrote 'Beding'; and we added an 'e' in this century, so the name has been used in one form or another for 1500 years.

The county was divided in the Norman period, north to south, into 'rapes' – an Icelandic term (the Normans not being French but 'Men from the North', or 'North-Men'). Each 'Rape' had a river, castle, port and forest. Ours was St. Leonards Forest, part of the parish of Beeding near Horsham. Sussex was divided in another way by the Downs; north was Wealden Sussex and at one time was dense forest. South of the Downs was 'Maritime Sussex'. This was the most important part, having ports, fisheries, fertile land and links with the continent. It was, therefore, the upper division of Sussex, so when in 1838 that part of the parish near Horsham (the area of St. Leonard's forest), was detached for ecclesiastical purposes, it being in the lesser or lower division, became Lower Beeding. On the other hand, we in the south were Beeding in the upper division of Sussex, and so became known as Upper Beeding.

Bewbush near Crawley was also a detached part of our Parish called 'Bewbush Tithing' and remained so for some time after the detachment of Lower Beeding. However, Ordinance Survey maps of the last century show one Lower Beeding and two Upper Beedings, which must have been very confusing for travellers from outside the area.

A Link with the Past

King Wenceslas, who lived from 1361 to 1419, was King of Bohemia as Wenceslas IV. He may or may not have been related to the King in the carol, but one thing we do know for sure is that he had a sister who married King Richard II of England (the only surviving son of the 'Black Prince'), who was born in 1367 and reigned from 1377 to 1399.

The young King Richard appeared to be stubborn, delicate and effeminate, but he had great courage, which he displayed at Smithfield (then Smoothfield) on 15 June 1381, confronting the leaders of the 'Peasants Revolt'. Accompanied by his advisers (those who had not been executed by the rebels), he met Wat Tyler and leaders of the rising. It must be remembered that the previous day the rebels had occupied the Tower and parts of London, and had killed Sir Robert Hales, the Grand Master of the Knights of the Hospital of St. John.

After receiving demands and insults from the rebel leaders, the Lord Mayor of London, Sir Robert Walworth, killed Wat Tyler and the rebellion failed. 'The Rising' was the last straw in a chain of events which began in the early 1300s. Famine in 1315 and the years that followed reduced the population almost as much as did the 'Black Death' of 1348 (the cause is now thought to be anthrax by historians and not bubonic plague, since the symptoms and results are similar). Plagues continued to occur regularly until the 17th century.

With the King on that day was a former Lord Mayor and M.P. Nicholas Brembre, who was later knighted for his services on that occasion. Sir Nicholas, according to the Reverend H.E.B. Arnold, was a descendant of Philip de Brembre.

The name 'Brembre' appears on many of the documents recorded in the *Chartulary of Sele Priory* and it is obvious that they were great landowners in our area. About 1387, Sir Nicholas was involved in a plot and, accused of treason (it was said later, falsely), denied the right to defend himself in single combat as a Knight, and was hanged. These were days in which, if you did not get rid of your enemies they would soon get rid of you.

St. Mary's, Bramber (Part 1)

Richard I, born in the year 1157, was the eldest surviving son of Henry II. 'Richard the Lionheart' won personal glory as the greatest of Knight Errants and his exploits are known to all. Post- war historians have shown that he was not 'whiter than white', but no one has tried to take from him his military reputation as a fearless leader. He reigned from 1189 to1199 but did not spend very much time in his native country. His wife, Berengaria of Navarre, never set foot in England.

One aspect of the Crusades was to open up the Middle East to Europe for trade and commerce. Among those engaged in the holy wars were the 'Templars', a religious and military order of Knights founded in 1118. They were quite active in Sussex and had preceptories in Shipley and in Sedlescombe (near to the Devil's Dyke).

At Bramber, they occupied a house on the present site of St. Mary's. The site of ancient wharves were discovered nearby in the 1970s by Mr. E. Holden F.S.A. and excavated by him. The radiocarbon date from the timber piles is given as being between 1010 and 1170 AD. Mr. Holden suggests that the quay was built after the conquest as an unloading place for the materials to build the castle.

A document at the Clerkenwell headquarters of the Knights Hospitallers (successors to the Templars in 1312) records the gift by a Norman lady (died c.1125), which reads:

"CONFIRMATION of the GIFT of 5 acres of Aanor de Braose by William her son To all men of the Castlery of Brembre, as well clerks as laymen, and to all sons of the Holy Church . . . KNOW YE that I have confirmed the gift that my mother Aanor gave for the souls of our ancestors, and for the redemption of our sinning selves. . . to the Knights of Solomons Temple; to wit 5 acres of her dower at the port of Brembre."

St. Mary's stands at the centre of this area of land and is of great antiquity, but the present edifice was probably re-structured and added to during the Tudor rebuilding period in England. The timber framework is dated around the middle of the 15th century and an article by W.Godfrey puts the date for this as the time of the repair by Bishop Waynflete of the great stone bridge in 1477.*

*Sussex Archaeological Collections lxxxvi.

For Part 2 see 10.1. For more on St. Mary's see 5.9 *The Causeway*.

See also note at 10.1 for modern-day nomenclature.

4.1 St. Mary's House, Bramber, during the time of Miss Dorothy Ellis

4.1a Drawing of the Entrance Hall at St. Mary's House, Bramber,
by Harry Ford, one of a series of interiors, 1988

900 Years On

1986 was the anniversary of the great survey of England known to all as the *Domesday Book*. 'Domesday' is thought to be derived from 'Domus die', the place where the books were deposited in Winchester Cathedral. The first account of King William sending his men out into the Shires was recorded in the *Anglo Saxon Chronicle* in 1085, and tells us how much the annual dues were from the holdings of his Bishops and Earls. The Chronicler says that "so very thoroughly did he have the enquiry carried out that not one Hyde or Virgate of land, not even one ox or cow nor one pig escaped his survey." This is an exaggeration; the book does not include Northumberland, Cumberland, Durham, a large part of Westmoreland, part of Lancashire, and also omits in some instances landless men and those owing military service to the crown.

The returns of this census were in the following order:- (1) The ownership of the estate or manor, always beginning with that owned by the King; (2) the name of the 'hundred' (unit of administration, supposed holdings of 100 families, replaced by District Councils in the 19th century); and (3) the tenant and description of the property.

It also gave values of property before the Conquest and was a basis for future disputes to be settled. A total of 275,000 persons were mentioned in the text and, assuming each was the head of a family, the population of England would have been around 2,000,000, allowing for the counties that were not enumerated in the survey.

The entry for Beeding starts thus: "The Land of WILLIAM de BRAIOSE - in BURBECE [Burbeach] Hundred - William de Braiose holds BEDDINGES - King Edward [the Confessor] held it then vouched for 32 hides*. It has not paid geld. Of these Hides, William de Warren has 10 Hides in his rape [Lewes] and William de Braiose holds the others. There is land for 28 ploughs. In a demense [the Lord of the Manor's farm or 'domesne'] are 4 ploughs, and 62 Villeins [unfree tenants owing service to the Lord] and 48 Bordars [villein cottagers] with 24 ploughs. There are two churches and 6 acres of meadowland; wood for 70 hogs, and 20 hogs for rent, and 2 sextaries of honey."

Of the 285 Manors of Sussex William de Braose held 38; Upper and Lower Beeding being one manor then.

*A Hide or Hyde was supposed to be the area of land able to support one family and dependents, with one plough. It varies from 60 to 180 acres.

4.2 Domesday Book (Sussex entry) from a facsimile copy in the Library at St. Mary's, Bramber. Beeding measured 32 hides, had land for 29 ploughs, had 72 pigs, 62 villagers and two churches.

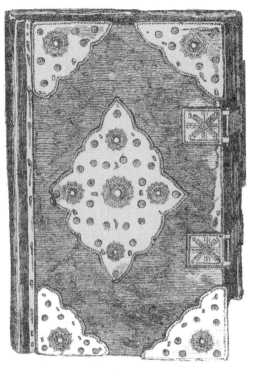

4.2a Front cover of the Domesday Book (facsimile 1767)

Ipse Witti ten' WISINGETONE. Guerd tenujt. T.R.E. Tese defd.p.L.je. hid. Modo ñ dao geldu. In una exhid. sedeq, castetu BREBRE. Tra.e. xxc. iiii. car. In dñio sunt. V. car. 7 c. xx. uitti 7 xx v. bord cu. xxx iiii. car. Ibi. v. saline de c x. ambris salis. auc. je-sot 7 ii. den. 7 iiii. ac' pa. De pasnag' silue: lxc. porc. Ibi. vi. serui.

4.2b Domesday Book (Sussex entry). Bramber Castle had 59 hides,
land for 34 ploughs, 120 villagers, five salt-houses,
and 110 ambers of salt at a valuie of 9s 2d, 60 pigs and six slaves.

Medieval Mysteries

One question that pops up frequently among historians is that of the deserted medieval village. Over 2000 sites are known and probably as many undiscovered, all of various shapes and sizes. Examples are: the nucleated village built around a crossroads or a church; a settlement around a green or open space, or a village built on either side of a highway.

How does one recognise the site of a long gone village? A church standing alone is one indication; footpaths leading to a central point for no apparent reason, another; raised earth platforms where there are no modern buildings; and squares, oblongs or shallow depressions where buildings once rested. Why were they deserted?

There are many theories: land exhaustion, engrossment and enclosure from Saxon times by landlords (which deprived the peasant of the rights of common field and pasture), the severe famine of the early 1300s, the 'Black Death' of 1348, which reduced the population of England from seven million to two and a half million and recurred regularly until 1666 before finally dying out around the 18th century.

There are several vanished villages in our neighbourhood. These once existed because of the river crossings, fords in early times, bridges later. The medieval settlement of Sele existed along the route from Beeding bostel through Castletown and along Hyde Street in a curve to the Priory Church. There were Saxon houses along this line; one was discovered not long ago during the building of Maines Farm Road.

Other remains probably exist at Kings Barnes on the other side of the estuary. South of the Manor house of Beeding Court is the now extinct village of Beeding (Bieda's ingas – See 3.11) probably attached to the farm. Excavations show pottery up to the 1300s, but not later. Could this be a village destroyed by the Black Death? Across the Adur is the Church of St. Botolphs. Before the Conquest, this was once a thriving village.

Allotments

A French bishop once said: "There are only two kinds of men, those free and those un-free". The difference in medieval England was not as great as it would appear. Medieval English society and peasantry had, to the observer of today, a most complicated arrangement. The manorial system was in use before Saxon times and endured, in name only, till early this century. Residents of a manor were subject to the rules and obligations that were the custom of that manor. The 'Lord of the Manor' was supreme, owing allegiance to the monarch, or in our case in the Rape of Bramber, to the sovereign through the lord of the Rape, de Braose.

A variety of seemingly strange customs applied in the manor, one being 'foldsoke', which obliged tenants to fold their animals, mainly sheep, at night in the 'demesne' (Lord's Farm). This provided the lord's land with much needed manure, the pens being shifted regularly. Tenants owed free service to the demesne, their commitment laid out in the 'customal' read out at annual manorial meetings. The obligations of each tenant were listed: some supplied firewood, some labour for ploughing, weeding and stone clearing and other duties, but nearly all were bound to be present at harvest time.

Free and un-free men held land by copyhold (copy of entry in Manor Court book or roll). Both had access to common land for grazing and for firewood, their only source of heat for cooking. Common land owned by the lord or others was available to most for grazing when not under crops, the number of animals allowed being regulated by the 'customal'. The un-free man was bound by the Manor Courts whereas a free man had access to the national jurisdiction for his grievance.

Improved farming methods led to 'enclosure', which took place from early times by common consent and, from the 17th century on, by Acts of Parliament. This was a transition from the old open field system. Walls, fences and hedges were erected to make private to the owners the once common land. This made for a better use of land but became very difficult for the subsistence farmer especially if he had animals and little land of his own.

These Enclosure Acts provided compensation for some whose rights had been extinguished, by making them allotments of land sufficient for themselves. Later in 1892, in order to avoid a burden on the local rates under the 'Poor Laws', further allotments were provided by the Vicar, the Revd. H. D. Meyrick. By 1913 the management of these allotments had passed to the Parish Council. They were sited in what was Sele Field and were moved to a new position. Originally a part of Pond Farm, they are now the Memorial Playing Field.

4.4 Mains Farm House, built in early Tudor times.
Later called 'The Old House'

4.4a Farmer Richard Hudson resting on his hoe, with his family in the orchard at St. Mary's c1860. Mrs Harriet Hudson seems to be doing all the work!

The Flaxlands

The cottager sitting at her spinning wheel is a scene popular with many artists noted for their rural pictures, but so often they fail to capture the harsh reality that lay behind these pleasing scenes. From early times up to the industrial revolution most villagers clothed themselves mainly by their own efforts at the spinning wheel and hand loom. It is not known precisely when we stopped wearing the skins of animals. The Greeks and Romans wore woven cloth, as did the Egyptians, 4,000 or so years ago while here in Britain we were in the Neolithic period.

Weaving in our area started most probably in the Bronze Age from 2000 to 500 B.C. and was well established in the Iron Age, testified by the many loom weights and spindlewhorls found around here. Wool was the material that was woven then. From late Saxon times woven goods were a main export of England and were so until the end of the 19th century. As long ago as 1300 we were exporting 35,000 sacks of wool annually, but before this time we had imported much finished cloth. The 14th century saw the start of our export textile industry and even the Black Death of 1348 did not initially make any reduction in the export of wool and cloth to Europe and the Baltic states. The growth of our exports ran parallel with the development of the 'Hanseatic League' (entrepreneurial German states in the 14th and 15th centuries).

During a slump in the reign of Charles II, acts of parliament passed in 1667 and 1678 declared that no corpse of any person shall be buried in a shroud that is not pure wool (repealed 1814); in Dr. Bloxam's book of Beeding Parish notes there is a printed certificate for use of the incumbent, an affidavit to prove compliance with the acts.

A commodity important to us here in Beeding was flax (linum usitatissimum). Not only did it provide the seed for making oil (linseed) but the fibres could be processed by soaking and shredding to make the linen cloth used by farmworkers. The pale flaxen-coloured unbleached material made the smock with the tuckered yoke which seemed to be worn by all field workers up to the end of the 19th century. Estuaries and fenlands made the best places for the growing of flax and on a local map of 1733 there is an area of land in Beeding called the 'Flaxlands' south of the brooks occupying what is now Newbrook Farm and Cattle Copse with Pound House field. This must have been a magnificent sight before harvest as the flowers are blue and the ten or so acre site must have been visible from the surrounding hills.

The Baybridge Canal

Our river has been a source of employment for local folk from medieval times. Salt making, fishing and transport have all played a part in Beeding life. The Industrial Revolution played little part in our village, but countrywide it was a tremendous alteration to the predominantly agricultural way of life that man had followed since he first learned to grow crops. Canals had been in use in Italy since the 12th century but nothing much had been done in England to improve water transport until the late 17th century. The Duke of Bridgwater and his engineer, James Brindley, are probably the best known canal builders, but it was the network of canals in the West Midlands connecting the Black Country, the South Staffs coalfields and Birmingham and its regions that made the most impact. Before that, coal and raw materials had to be carried overland at great cost. With the canals, the transport of these commodities was cut by half.

Before 1800, the Adur was without any improvement, apart from embanking which had been carried out from medieval times. In 1807 the Commissioners of Sewers for the Rape of Bramber (under whose jurisdiction was the river) applied for an act of Parliament by which they could rate all lands above Beeding Bridge likely to benefit. Within three years they had made the river navigable as far as Bines Bridge on the western arm and Mock Bridge on the eastern arm of the Adur.

The River Adur has always been tidal and never a canal in the proper sense, but a new stretch of the river was cut along the half mile, under Sele Priory at Bedney, to connect the neck of an ox-bow that reached Kings Barnes in a great loop. This appears on a map by John Gotham, was surveyed in 1627 and can still be seen on a modern map as a series of drainage ditches.

In 1825, the Baybridge Canal Company obtained further powers to extend the western arm of the river to West Grinstead at a cost of £6,000. Locks were built at Lock Farm, Partridge Green and above West Grinstead Church and can still be seen. Craft up to 70 feet long with a 4-foot draught could use the waterway to take up coal, lime and slate from Cornish quarries (look at the number of slate roofs along the river). They often returned with grain and Horsham stone from the Weald. The coming of the railways killed the canal trade and the Baybridge Course was abandoned from about 1875. St. Peter's Beeding was known by the barge population as 'River Beeding Church' and was considered to be the home parish of generations of river people. The Parish Registers testify to these baptisms and burials.

4.6 West Grinstead Park

The River at Beeding

4.6a Clay barge being towed back to Small Dole from the Cement Works at Erringham

The Railways (Part 1)

Records tell us that railways have been in use in the gold and silver mines of Central Europe since the Middle Ages. These were very primitive affairs, the rails being squared timbers and the wagons small wooden hoppers pulled by man or horse. In 17th century England, in the early years of the Industrial Revolution, horse-drawn wooden railways proved their worth to the collieries of the North Midlands. Overland journeys to the emerging canal system with coal and raw materials were increased fivefold by the trackways. As production of iron increased, iron plateways were laid. These were flat interlocking pieces of cast iron with a flange on the inside edge which enabled ordinary carts to be run on these tracks, sometimes for a toll.

With the invention of the steam engine thought was given to its application to self-propelling vehicles. Steam road carriages were running many years before the locomotive on rails. In 1767, the first iron rails were laid for horse-drawn wagons at Coalbrookdale. Richard Trevithick, a mining engineer [who had already built a steam road carriage] designed the first locomotive for a railway, which he demonstrated in 1804. It was not really powerful enough to sustain motion for long and was too heavy for the cast iron track. Others engaged in this problem, Blenkinsop, Hedley, Hackworth and, perhaps the best known, George Stephenson, were not able to progress far until the invention by John Birkinshaw of a method of rolling, wedge-shaped, wrought-iron rails in 1820, a tremendous improvement on the earlier, more brittle cast iron permanent way. The Stockton and Darlington is credited with being the first steam railway [1825], but this was really a hybrid as horses were still being used to pull the trains much of the time. The Liverpool and Manchester Railway [1830] was the first substantial railway to rely completely on steam power.

Here in the Adur valley the railways came late, as did many other rural lines. The Brighton to Shoreham was opened on 12th May 1840, Shoreham to Partridge Green 1st July 1861 and continued to Horsham on 16th September of that same year. The London-Brighton and South Coast Railway emerged from a number of other companies and became the Southern Railway in 1923. Bramber was a much used station for Sunday school outings and excursions; one attraction was the castle, another the hire of boats on the Adur at Beeding Bridge and almost all visited 'Potter's' Museum of taxidermy. With hindsight it was a rather morbid place, but the 'Death of Cock Robin' and other displays delighted generations of children. Oh! Dr. Beeching! What have you done?

For Part 2 see 7.6

KN-B returns to this subject in 15.9

4.7 Bramber Station

4.7a Coming into Bramber

Beeding Court

Following the archaeological dig at the site of the burial ground at Botolphs, I thought it may be a good idea to find an explanation for the existence of two medieval villages.

The manor house at Beeding Court stands on the same gravel bank as does the church of St. Peter. These were well drained sites on high ground close to the river. The settlement at Beeding Court was only approachable on foot from the east, as water surrounded it on the other three sides. In earlier times, it was also important as the centre of a farming community and as one of the crossing points of the Adur valley. The great east-west road through southern England from Canterbury to Southampton crossed the river here. St. Botolph's was known before the Conquest as St. Peter de Veteri Ponte (St. Peter of the old bridge). In the documents of Sele the bridge or causeway is referred to as 'old' in the llth century. The remains of a medieval village exist in a field south-west of the bypass roundabout. Past excavations have revealed pottery and other artefacts dating up to the 14th century. Is it possible that this early 'Beding' village failed on the decline of the old bridge? Or perhaps when the Great Bridge of Bramber was built after the Conquest? Or even as a result of the Black Death of 1348?

A manor house has been recorded here from 1326, but the present building is probably from the late 16th century and incorporates earlier parts. A dovecot was recorded on the site in 1398. This was a most important and useful appendage as it provided eggs for the pantry, and meat in times of need for the household. Many former occupants were absentee landlords mainly because they had country seats in other places. Previous owners included William de Broase and the Earls of Arundel, one of whom, Thomas Howard, sold it in 1641 to Piers Edgcumbe. Later his successor, Lord Edgcumbe, sold the estate to Harry Bridger of New Shoreham.

I am indebted to Mrs. Diana Durden for information on one of the best known owner/occupiers to reside at Beeding Court [See Select Bibliography]. He was Thomas Daniel Cross, a Somerset farmer, who, with his family, farm animals and implements, uprooted himself and his family, lock, stock and barrel, and boarded a train at Crewkerne, arriving at Steyning six hours later with his 'Noah's Ark', much to the amazement of the locals who witnessed the event. His two eldest sons, Tom and Oliver, each drove a team of horses by road, loaded with more goods, through Bramber Street to Beeding. Mr. and Mrs. T.D. Cross are acknowledged as the founders of the Baptist movement in Upper Beeding. In more recent years, William and Phyllis Fretwell owned the property.

4.8 Beeding Court, later the home of Phyllis Fretwell,
benefactor to the poor of Beeding
(*by courtesy of the Cross family and Diana Durden*)

4.8a Thomas and Lucy Cross and family at Beeding Court

Botolphs

After being involved in the 'dig' at the new burial ground at Botolphs, I thought a report would be in order. This archaeological excavation has emerged as one of the most important discoveries in Sussex for many years. It was undertaken by the Institute of Archaeology and was led by Mark Gardiner, one of their field officers.

This survey has shown human occupation from the Middle Stone Age up to medieval times. Stone implements from the Mesolithic and Neolithic era were discovered. Evidence shows that there was Anglo-Saxon occupation from the time the Romans left these shores, circa 450 AD. to 650 AD. Post-holes found indicate the existence of an Anglo-Saxon hall.

Other disturbances in the soil confirm that there were 'sunken featured' buildings attached to this settlement. Further evidence indicates that the builders of the settlement pillaged a (so far unknown) Roman temple or villa site. Fragments of tile and bronze artefacts found, have been sent to the British Museum for proper identification and preservation..

There appears to be an occupation gap of some two hundred years and then the site was again inhabited from circa 850 A.D. until the Conquest. That is not to say that the people had left the area, as it has been proved that dwellings such as these have been re-located within the village or parish boundaries over the centuries, so other areas of occupation may be close by, and as yet undiscovered; (there are traces to the west of the Botolphs road).

Domesday listed fifteen 'villani' (serfs), and thirty-four 'bordars' (cottagers) in Annington and Botolphs, which indicates that at that time the area was well populated. Parts of the Sele Priory estates are recorded as being in this area, which was formerly the property of the Kings of Wessex.

It may be significant that the medieval occupation of this site in 13th and 14th centuries is similar to the deserted village on the opposite side of the Adur. There is not much doubt that there was an important river crossing at this point. Whether it was by causeway/ford or bridge is a matter for conjecture. The river can be forded on foot at low water now, but in earlier times the water levels were higher. There are references in the 16th century to 'causeway stiles' lying to the east of Annington Street.

St. Botolphs Church

4.9 Drawing of the village of Botolphs by J.G. Garratt

4.9a Charcoal sketch of the village of Botolphs by Monica Leighton Hicks

111

Riots at Beeding

From 1795 to 1832 Sussex suffered disturbances and riots among its agricultural workers and, too, unrest in the militia stationed around the county. 7000 soldiers were camped in Sussex during the Napoleonic wars. The militia were poorly paid and fed and, while awaiting the call to action, were used to quell civil disorders. There are instances of them refusing to fire on rioters, many having probably been plucked from farms to serve in the army. This was a time when new machinery was being used by farmers who turned to casual labour instead of employing full time workers, which put many on parish relief. Another problem was created by the Parliamentary 'Acts of Enclosure'. In the first thirty years of the 19th century, three and a half million acres of common land had been enclosed. Although enclosure was relatively small in Sussex, it put many off the land that had been traditionally used by the community and had made many self-sufficient.

Before 1832, when the last of the labourers revolted, agricultural workers, while still protesting, demanded that prices should come down in times of bad harvest. It was not until after the 'Labourers Revolt' that they asked for wages to rise. The price of bread doubled in the early 19th century. A four- pound quartern loaf was over a shilling, this being 10% of a weekly wage.

The plight of the poor was such that they often gathered in large numbers at market places. Their method of protest was to impale pieces of meat or bread on long poles, occasionally lowering them, indicating to the traders and market authorities that the price of these commodities must come down. This happened in Brighton market place, by the 'Druids Head'. This idea of 'fair prices' was shared by many churchmen and magistrates, and was known and described as the 'Moral Economy'.

During this disturbed period in Sussex bands of hungry unemployed roamed the countryside, burning ricks and barns belonging to the 'Guardians of the Poor' (often farmers). Such a band of these unfortunates came to Beeding around 1830. They surrounded the Priory which was in the occupation of Mr. James Ventris, the Vicar at that time. I quote part of a letter from Edward Ventris to Dr. Bloxam 20th March 1865:

"The love of peace was so predominant in him that he would never consent to return to Beeding lest there should be another outbreak. Mrs. Ventris gave me a history of these disturbances, the most vivid recollection of which my mind now is, that the mob entered the Vicarage armed with bludgeons which they struck forcibly upon the floor demanding 'bread or blood'."

Field Names (Part 1)

The English language is one of the world's richest in terms of the number of words available to the writer. This is no doubt due to the fact that so many different cultures have inhabited this island of ours. When the Romans departed in the fifth century many tribes settled here, each bringing their own traditional patterns of land tenure, administration and tribal customs practiced in their continental homelands. The Jutes occupied what is now Kent, known earlier as the Jutish Forest; the Angles and Frisians settled mainly on the East coast, adopting names of Scandinavian origin like Axholm, Ine, King of Wessex, first mentioned 'Sud-sexia' (Sussex, the land of the South-Saxons) in AD 678. Many of these continental tribes had served as mercenaries in the Roman armies and were not strangers to Britain, but the poor indigenous peasant carried on working for whoever the land owners were. The soil always had to be tended in this agrarian society or starvation would surely follow.

The Saxons tended to name their settlements with a combination of local place features and more importantly, as in Beeding, with the name of a worthy. The origin of field names holds the secret of their meaning, while this may often prove to be the key to some archaeological question which has not yet been solved.

Sometimes, as in Beeding, fields took the name of the owner. A piece of land to the east of Bramber Castle was known as 'Butchers Field', recorded in 1627 by John Cotam*. Many years later it was called 'Spratts Marsh'; Colonel Evans gives it as 'Prutts Marsh' in the 1930s. It was a detached part of Steyning Parish until 1933; Dr Arnold refers to it in a small plan of the area (AD 1102) in his unpublished history and says that it was designated as the new port area to replace St. Cuthman's port when the Adur receded in the late 11th century, but he does not give his source.

Other field names gave the use they were put to, as in the 'Flaxlands', the 'Clays' and the 'Brook-lands', denoting the type of terrain.

Lands belonging to the clergy as part of their benefice are in the main called 'Glebe-lands'. King Ethelwulf, father of Alfred the Great, once a resident of 'Kings Barnes', legalised tithes around AD 855, giving to the church one tenth of his kingdom.

So, it may come as no surprise that land between St. Peter at Sele and Kings Barnes should be called 'des deniers' or 'le deniers'; denier was a small coin, a fabric weight, or a tenth (tithe). This land was known in recent times as 'Diggoners'. What's in a name?

* i.e Gotham. See 11.1 for Part 2

Owling

'Owling' was the name given to smuggling, and those who took part were called 'owlers'. No one can be sure when this clandestine business started but it must have been from a time when duty had to be paid on goods leaving and entering the country. 'Owling' seems to be an appropriate name as most activity probably took place at night by the light of lanterns. It was in early times an export trade in wool. There was a great demand for English wool from weavers on the continent in the medieval period and a duty was put on it at the time of Henry III. Edward III attempted to prohibit the export of wool and to ban imports of foreign cloth, and Charles II later passed an Act forbidding any corpse to be buried in anything but a woollen shroud.

Import smuggling was not very active until the time of William and Mary, but at the end of the 17th century, wars with France made it a lucrative profession. Silk, lace, spirits and all manner of luxury goods were brought into the country in loads that sometimes involved up to thirty or forty packhorses. The routes and systems previously used by the wool owlers were ready-made for this.

Sussex and Kent were the prominent smuggling counties due to their proximity to France. Information in times of war was exchanged and it is recorded that newspapers and correspondence were sent from Bexhill direct to Bonaparte during the Napoleonic Wars. Rivers were one of the main routes inland for illicit goods. It is recorded that in our own area the Sussex Pad inn, adjacent to Old Shoreham toll bridge, was the entrepôt of the smuggling trade here; the original building was burned down in 1905.

There is an amusing tale in Revd. J. Warner's *Sea-board and the Downs* [Vol.1]. of the old Parish Clerk called Miles. The Revd. T. G. Calhoun, Vicar of Beeding, did not live in the Parish. Due to failing eyesight he resided in Goring, his former parish, and the churchwardens had to report to him there from time to time. Miles was supposed to meet with him after a dinner party with his pony but he failed to turn up and the poor Vicar had to walk home. Miles had in his earlier days been a free-trader (smuggler) as had many of the 'well to do'. He had spotted a cask of spirits half-buried in the sand (casks were buried like this sometimes to be concealed until transport was available). The next morning the contents were found at the Vicarage; Miles appeared disguised in a Geneva cloak and, as the Revd. J. Warner related, "there was the smell of the Hollander [spirits] about him, it was got rid of in caudel [spiced gruel] to the perfect satisfaction of the old ladies of the village".

Taxes (Part 1)

Ever since there was some form of tribal law and administration there has been a need for taxation to pay for those who oversee, to finance the defence of the community and to wage war on other communities. Tax gatherers are mentioned in the Bible, especially the oppression of the Romans and their system; very efficient, but based on a society with a lower tier of slaves and un-free colonies. So it was with our country. We paid taxes first to the Romans and after their departure in the 5th century to the marauding Scandinavian warriors, the Vikings, who extracted payments from us for immunity from attack by them. Alfred the Great, till his death at the end of the 9th century, did much to reduce the payments by his opposition to the Danes. *The Domesday Book* records how much each Hundred and each Rape paid in 'Danegeld'. We were in the Hundred of Burbeach and did not pay geld. Exemption here may have been due to the poverty of the area. There was a prayer of this time reflecting the serious nature of the Viking threat: 'From the Fury of the Northmen, Good Lord Deliver Us'.

The descendents of those very same Northmen, the Normans, who settled in the area now known as Normandy, came here in 1066 to administer the laws and extract taxes from the native Briton. As we have seen, King Ethelwulf legalised the lay taxes to the church, the 'tithe' (one tenth) being introduced around 855 A.D. Thereafter, the church made its own tax arrangements with the sovereign.

The non-clerical body of the country was subject to what is now known as the 'lay-subsidy' and some of these subsidy rolls are still in existence. Much information can be gleaned by local historians as the earlier returns, such as those in 1296 and 1327, named the individual taxpayer. There were many different ways of establishing how tax was levied. Some examples are: poll tax, land tax, and the most used: tax on moveables (the content of a house and barn except for tools of a trade) and all harvested crops. Standing corn however was not counted, but calculations were usually made after harvest.

In 1296 Beeding paid £6.6s.– a very large sum for that time – but this included Lower Beeding which was the forest of St. Leonard and Bewbush near Crawley. In these times there were no established surnames, so names like Richard de Bedyng indicated that he was of our village, while William att Sele meant that he was there, but may not have been of our village originally. One name seems to have come through to the present day from those early tax rolls – that of Greenyer (an occupation). This name is mentioned in the Tudor rolls of 1523-24, and, in the present electoral roll and phone book, appears as Grinyer.

The Poor Law*

The aftermath of the Black Death of 1348 left the population of England greatly reduced. Labour was in short supply and wages rose as landholders vied with each other to acquire the necessary workforce to till and harvest their crops. Prior to the plague a surplus of labour meant that the manor had tight control on the movement of people. In 1351 an Act, now known as the 'Statute of Labourers', was passed, reinforcing an Ordinance of 1349, fixing a maximum wage rate for workers corresponding with that twenty years earlier. This forced men to accept any work offered in their manor or parish.

The Peasants Revolt of 1381 was due in part to the poor treatment of the working population, which was aggravated by the 'Poll taxes' of the 1370s culminating in a levy of three groats (1s.) on every person aged fifteen to sixty – a large sum in those days. Jack Cade's revolt of 1450 was one of many civil disorders in medieval times. The writings of John Wycliffe and his followers, the Lollards (the first non-conformists), helped to stir things up. Yorkist and Lancastrian plots added fuel to the flames of unrest in these times. Fears of revolt were ever present in the minds of the nobility and landowners. The polarisation of rich and poor was very much greater than it is today and many laws and statutes were passed to suppress the lower tiers of society.

Laws of 1388 and 1494 enabled parish officers to return vagrants to their own parishes. Those capable of work could be whipped, have their ears cut off or be hanged. Other laws put the responsibility of the poor and infirm on the parish and enabled 'overseers' to levy a rate on the working population. Help was restricted to parishioners and non-locals found in the area had to have a certificate issued by their own parish indicating that they would foot any bills or liabilities.

An entry in Dr. Bloxam's book records the carrying out of one of these punishments (all parishes kept a register of vagabonds). It says: 'Thomasin Dunford, a sturdy vagrant (the wife of William Dunford), Rachell Stone her daughter and Mary, Eleanor and William Dunford, were May 26th in ye 31st year of King Charles ye 2nd [1679] openly whipped in this parish according to law, and sent to Mayfield Parish where she saith she was born and three of her children.' The Elizabethan Act says that 'they shall be stripped naked from the middle upward and be openly whipped until his or her body be bloody and sent from parish to parish to where they were born'.

*KN-B's original title was *The Poor (Poor Law)*

See 18.1 for types of charitable help for the poor

Industrial Beeding

The words 'Industrial Revolution' usually conjure up a vision of coal- mine winding-wheels, tall Midland chimneys belching smog, and the 'dark satanic mills' of Victorian times. This is how many of us view this period of great change in late 17th century Britain. Canal networks and railways of the 19th century made communications and the rapid transport of heavy and high volume goods easier and cheaper. Time was standardised throughout the country in the early 1850s, but prior to this the coach proprietors working the turnpike roads carried expensive chronometers set to gain or lose a certain amount of time, depending on the direction of travel. Local time in Plymouth differed by sixteen minutes from the local time in London, to give one example.

An agricultural revolution took place at this same time. Innovations of the industrial revolution spread to the landowners and farmers and machinery began to be used on the land (not without opposition). Many people left the rural areas to seek their fortunes in the cities, with machines making up the shortfall in labour required to feed the rising town populations. This, then, is a brief view of early industrial Britain.

An earlier revolution took place in the weald of south-eastern England. Many manufacturing areas were developed for textiles, tanning, brickmaking, bell-founding, glass and iron, with the latter being the best known Sussex medieval industry. The area between the north and south Downs was the 'Black Country' of Sussex and Kent. Huge forests provided charcoal, ironstone was easily dug, and abundant water powered the trip-hammers and bellows of the blast furnaces. St. Leonard's Forest with Bewbush was a part of our parish until 1838 [see 3.11]. It was an area where iron was produced in great quantities and it is recorded that, in 1254, the sheriff of Sussex had to supply Henry III with 30,000 horseshoes and 60,000 nails. Cannon and shot were made from the late 15th century and Sussex is credited with casting the first one-piece gun barrel (1543).

The names of 49 miners working for Edward Carryll in St, Leonards forest are recorded c.1587 and it is mentioned that Sussex had 50,000 iron workers at this time (but no proof exists to support this).

The reduction of the forests led to Elizabethan laws restricting the use of timber. With the discovery of large deposits of coal in the Midlands, our industry declined. Little remained at the end of the 18th century and Sussex returned to a full agricultural life. The hammer ponds remain, but little else to remind us of past glory when Sussex supplied guns to beat the Armada.

The Monks of Sele* (Part 1)

When I was a schoolboy many lessons were enhanced by rhymes and that I have remembered them speaks for the success of that system. Recalling a history lesson in my early years, the couplet "In fourteen hundred and ninety-two, Columbus sailed the ocean blue," was a reference to the discovery of the West Indies and subsequently America. Here in Beeding it is most unlikely that anyone heard of this event for some time; the discovery of the New World or the election of a new pope in that year would probably not interest local people as much as the fact that the Priory of Sele was to be re-occupied by monks.

The Benedictine occupation of Sele began in 1073. These monks probably re-built the Church of St. Peter, which is recorded as being the subject of an order for repair in 1283. It was decided at that time that the tower and nave be repaired by the village at a cost of 40/- and the monks would be responsible for the chancel. On 24th February 1308, the Church was re-dedicated to SS. Peter and Paul. Parts of earlier building could still be seen in the churchyard walls in the years before 1480.

The Carmelites were founded at Mount Carmel in Palestine in the 12th century. Their Shoreham house was in a direct line to the south of the Buckingham Road – perhaps somewhere near the modern footbridge. At that time, the Adur discharged to the east of new Shoreham. Owing to changes in the coastline, the Carmelite house was under threat by the encroachment of the sea; the monks were forced to move inland and took over the ailing Priory of Sele. Their distinctive white habits would have been easy to notice around the village.

The annual rent was ten shillings (50p in today's values) for the site at Sele; this included four acres of land and the chapel (probably the chapel of St. John built in 1308 and adjoining the north wall of the chancel). The existing buildings were in such a delapidated condition that the Carmelites re-built them from ground level and re-roofed the cloisters in green glazed tiles, circa 1493. The Order remained for forty years and, at the dissolution of the monasteries, Henry VIII sent the Bishop of Dover to Sele, who found it empty, with the doors wide open – in the words of the Revd. H. E. B.Arnold: 'they had done a bunk!.

KN-B's original title was *The Monks.* See 12.1 for Part 2

River Beeding Church

The River Adur has been used as a highway into the Sussex Weald from the earliest times. Heavy and high volume goods were taken upriver as far as Mock Bridge near Shermanbury and to West Grinstead past Bines Bridge, and from there to Reigate and Horsham overland. Coal, chalk, lime and Cornish slate went up, along with other commodities, and down came hay, grain and other agricultural produce to the several seaside resorts developing from the early 19th century. From this time depots were set up along the line of the river and wharves were established at Erringham, Beeding Bridge, Horton and beyond. This was made possible by an Act of Parliament of 1807 with the creation of the Baybridge Canal Co.

Barge families were likened to water gypsies, never settling anywhere for long. Like the snail, they lived in their shell (the narrow boat), very cramped, but comfortable enough for the times they lived in. The Revd. H.E.B. Arnold, in his unpublished history of Beeding, refers to the thick north-country accents of the bargees, but many of the families on the river were local stock whose names appeared in the Parish registers from Elizabethan times. Dr. Bloxam's transcriptions list names that are even today found in the local telephone directory: Blann, Boniface, Nye and many others. However, the occupation 'bargeman' does not occur before the 19th century.

What we do not know for sure is whether they were regular worshippers at St. Peter's Beeding. Given their mobile lifestyle it is not likely, but their designation of our church, 'River Beeding Church' was testimony to their faith. The registers record their baptisms, marriages and burials in the churchyard, from around 1813 to the 1870s.

The 'London, Brighton and South Coast Railway' branch line from Shoreham to Horsham was opened in the 1860s and from then the barge traffic dwindled until, in the early part of this century, only the clay barges from Horton to the cement works were paying dues, a sad end to a colourful occupation and lifestyle that had risen in the 17th century and set in the 20th.

Reflections

Having lived locally as a boy, it is very noticeable how the landscape has changed since the Second World War. Development has enclosed the old village of Beeding and in the countryside many of the shaws and hedges remembered from pre-war days have been grubbed out to suit the more economic ways of farming. No one in my day uttered the cry 'there's no facilities'; few worried about things for children to do as they could roam the environs in safety. Birds-nesting was one of the many pursuits. Some children had collections of eggs that would be the envy of smart modern museums, but now no longer are we allowed to collect eggs because it 'endangers the species'. Few children though, would take more than one egg from a nest and then only if there were several. I wonder how much damage we did compared with the concrete of the developers, or the weed-killers and pesticides of the modern farmer, which are rapidly reducing the areas where wildlife can still flourish.

There were, of course, seasonal games - one could go to the blacksmith (where the Beeding Garage is now) and for a few pennies purchase a thin iron hoop. Skipping was enjoyed mainly by the girls; boys played 'pitch and toss' with halfpennies and farthings. 'Fag cards' featured in a game of skill, and in the autumn, following the conker season there were marbles or glass alleys played along the street gutters (in comparative safety) and there cannot be anyone born before the war who does not remember 'whips and tops' (cost about ld.). The whips were more prized if they had a leather thong instead of string, which tended to fray at the end. The Saturday penny had to be earned, but what a lot it would buy – 'Spanish root', 'tiger nuts', and other strange delights, or 'Sharps' toffee fragmented by a special hammer from large trays. One could walk for miles and not see a discarded 'coke' can or crisp packet. The worst that could happen was to step in a 'cow-pat' in Hyde Lane when the cattle from Hyde Farm were driven down to graze in the field where Dawn Close and Dawn Crescent are now. 'Oh happy days!'

Armistice Day, Empire Day, (when we all stood around the union flag) and other occasions gave our generation some sense of civic and national pride. No vandalism then – young minds were fully occupied, and then there was the village P.C. who knew every young scoundrel. We were not subjected to hours of TV violence and foul language, as is the modern child. Our enjoyments were there for the taking and we made our own entertainment. But what of the future? Will today's schoolchildren in years to come have to visit the inner cities' parks and gardens, to view with reverence, the last remaining green open spaces in England?

Bridges across the Adur

Back beyond memories and the known facts of history, which we call time immemorial, there have been crossings of the Adur. In earlier times there was only one way across on foot and that was by the old 'Veteri Ponte' at Botolphs. We know this because St. Botolphs was known before the Conquest as St. Peter de Veteri Ponte (St. Peter of the old bridge). Other ways across were by ferry of some sort. This old bridge or causeway fell into disrepair around the time the bridge at Bramber was erected just after 1066. By 1250 the 'Great Bridge of Bramber' had been rebuilt in stone – 170 feet long with a chapel on its central pier. It endured after being rebuilt circa 1477, until sometime in the 17th century, by which time the river had receded.

Beeding Bridge, which has always spanned the main course of the river, was of timber up to 1785 when it was rebuilt by Magdalen College, the owner from 1459. Bricks were used then, and again, when it was widened on the north side in 1845. The footbridge was added in 1926. The timber bridge known as the 'Old Shoreham Toll Bridge' and was built in 1781 because the ferry had become increasingly dangerous. This ferry was owned by the priory of Hardham. In 1387 the revenue was said to be £20 per annum. The Duke of Norfolk built the bridge, which was rebuilt by the Railway Co. in 1916 to the same dimensions as the original. Another bridge of the trestle type was built to the south of the toll bridge around 1845. This carried the London, Brighton & South Coast Railway to Worthing and beyond, and was replaced by the present one at the end of the 19th century. The first 'Norfolk Bridge' was opened on May Day 1833. It was a suspension bridge designed by Tierney Clarke, the architect of Hammersmith and Marlow Bridges. There was some influence from Captain Samuel Brown, the builder of the Brighton 'Chain Pier' (1822/3). One of the toll gates from this first bridge can be seen at the entrance to Sele Priory. The cantilever bridge which replaced the first one was built in 1924, and owing to the growing congestion, tolls were finally abolished in 1927. This structure was replaced, using earlier supporting piers to give a new wider concrete deck.

In our parish alone, four bridges now span the Adur – the South Downs Way Bridge, the bypass bridge, Beeding Bridge, and the old foot-bridge to Kings Barnes, built originally in 1724 but replaced in 1905 and known locally as the 'White Bridge'. During recorded history there have been, or still exist twenty-two bridges across the Adur, south of Henfield.

KN-B returns to the theme of bridges in 19.10

5.7 Old Shoreham Toll Bridge (timber) built in 1781
(*Photograph by courtesy of Alan Durden*)

5.7a Shoreham Toll Bridge, known as the 'Norfolk Bridge'
built in 1924, the tolls being finally abolished in 1927

St. Peter's Beeding (Part 2)

I have always been amused by the tale of the old woodcutter who boasted that he had owned the same axe for 60 odd years. The fact that it had had ten new shafts and five new heads in that time did not persuade him that it was not the same axe. Our church has stood for over a thousand years and is the same church, with the fabric altering over the years. Domesday records two churches. At that time when the Adur was unembanked and higher, the buildings must have appeared as beacons from the west bank, situated as they were on the gravel mound that provides the highest point along the river - a magnificent sight. To the question: 'Why is the church there?' the obvious answer must be that once it was the centre of the village of Sele (Beeding was to the south). Churches very seldom stand alone and this was the case with St.Peter's. The remains of many medieval buildings exist around the area of this raised gravel bank. Sele was an important traffic node and river crossing of the Adur. The great Canterbury-Winchester road descended from the downs at Beeding Hill by Castletown bostel, curving in a semi-circle along Hyde Street to the church and priory, where a ford is known to have existed from the 11th century (the site of White Bridge*).

The oldest things still working in the Adur Valley are surely the two medieval bells in the tower, dedicated to St. Katherine and St. Margaret, (probably in 1308 when the church was rebuilt). The lower part of the tower dates from at least 1283**. Earlier historians were unaware of a map that exists in the Duke of Norfolk's Library, dated 1627, by John Gotham which shows clearly that there was an earlier south aisle to the church, probably built and dedicated to the Blessed Virgin Mary in 1308. This had disappeared by 1801 as shown in a drawing in the Sharpe Collection (Brighton Reference Library). The Revd. Dr. Arnold produced a chronological diagram of the plan of the church which is still in the present guide. This shows only the modern south aisle (1852) and does not record the earlier one. He says that if we wish to see St.Peter's as it was in the 11th or 12th centuries, we should go to Manningford Bruce in Wiltshire and look at the church of St.Peter there; the original design being from the church of St. Mellon in Rouen which goes back to A.D.250 (Roman times). Bruce was the Scottish version of the name Braose, and it was our William de Braose who was responsible for the building of our church. During excavations for underpinning the chancel a few years ago, a piece of Roman tile was found.

For Part I see 2.1 (with Arnold's plan) and for Part 3 see 6.2

*For 'White Bridge' see 10.10 and 11.11

** *Chartulary of Sele Priory XV*

The Causeway

The area between St. Peter's in Beeding and Bramber Castle was, at high tide, a wide expanse of water. When the ebb came it reverted to a saltmarsh and was almost impossible to pass on foot. It was dotted with raised mounds called salterns. Here the manufacture of salt occurred in the milder weather and as there was no Beeding or Bramber street and no bridges, access was upon wattle hurdles laid flat.

The building of the causeway probably started around the 11th century as a single bridge was recorded in 1086 and again in 1103. This was most likely over the narrower deeper channel at Beeding Bridge. Two bridges are recorded for the first time in 1230. The Great Bridge of Bramber, 170 feet long, with four arches, and a chapel on the central pier, was almost certainly completed before the beginning of the 14th century as repairs to the chapel are recorded in 1304. It was this new way across the Adur (then called Bramber Water) that probably assisted the demise of the village of Old Beeding (south of Beeding Court) and Botolphs. In the Hundred Rolls, in the 51st year of the reign of Henry III (1266/7), there is reference to Simon Barnes, who was Constable of Bramber. Complaints were made that he had cut through the causeway to gain access to the castle for boats bringing stone, sand and chalk from Bramber Bridge.

There are remains of a wharf in the grounds to the east of St. Mary's (excavated by Eric Holden in 1974) probably dating to the 11th century. This predates the castle and was most likely erected to land building materials for it. St. Mary's today is part of the structure that is recorded as being repaired or rebuilt in 1477 by William Waynflete, Bishop of Winchester, when the great bridge was also repaired. The contracts are still in existence, referring to John Cowper, stone-mason of Winchester. The legend that the house was a leper hospital is unlikely; this was on higher ground south-west of the castle. There was an earlier house on the site before St. Mary's and was probably the dwelling of the bridge wardens, appointed by de Braose. Sited near the wharf, it was a good vantage point for seeing that no one escaped paying the tolls required for crossing the bridges, and maybe also for collecting excise dues on imported goods such as wine that may have missed collection at Shoreham. It may also have served as the residence of the priest who was appointed to look after the chapel on the bridge. St. Mary's was referred to as the 'chapel house' as late as the 16th century.

To the north of, and behind the Old Priory and St. Mary's Lodge, there is a site of similar proportions to St. Mary's today (discovered by Eric Holden but as yet unexcavated). This seems an unusual site and poses the question 'Was there a twin to St. Mary's that was burnt down at this time?' Maybe it was just a moated area to contain cattle? Perhaps one day we will find out.

5.9 William of Waynflete, Bishop of Winchester, restorer of the
Great Bridge of Bramber and adjacent 'Chapel House',
now known as St. Mary's
(St. Mary's archive)

When Bramber Burned

With the 400th anniversary of the coming of Spanish Armada, one's thoughts have turned to the subject of fires – the fire ships of Drake, Hawkins and Frobisher and the fire beacons along the coast. Of the 129 Spanish ships only sixty-three ever returned to their home ports. A combination of fire and gales led to their defeat. Queen Elizabeth I struck a medal to commemorate the event; the Latin inscription read: 'God blew, and they were scattered'.

Three hundred years earlier the wind may not have been so helpful to Bramber. It is recorded in the *Chartulary of Sele Priory* that in the time preceding July in the year 1286 there was a great fire which destroyed the village. The chartulary does not refer to the cause of the fire but to the re-allocation of property afterwards.

Bramber at that time was probably more populated then than in 1832 when about two score houses were recorded. The mainly wooden houses with thatched roofs, once alight, were impossible to extinguish, as was found later in 1666 when the capital burned. Until quite recently Bramber was full of thatched houses; chimneys were not generally known until Tudor times and then they were very tall to take the sparks clear of thatch. Many houses around us still have tall chimneys although now the thatch is replaced with tile or slate.

Bramber in 1286 was the service area for the castle, and the population was perhaps many times more in the castle area than today. The way the destruction of the village is recorded leads one to interpret it as being a deliberate act of arson that went with the sacking of places by raiders. Whether it was that, or as a punishment for wrongdoing by the inhabitants (as sometimes happened when people offended the feudal Lord) is now almost impossible to solve. Could it have been for revenge that the village was fired? At this time there was a very unpopular de Braose and an equally unpopular steward, Andrew de Lechepole, at the castle.

There are, recorded on the Rolls, many incidents of oppression by this steward. On one occasion when the castle was lacking in wood for fires and cooking, he seized some cart loads of wood from peasants, who were on their way to market at Shoreham. They were abused and not compensated for their timber. Was this their protest?

*The original title of this piece was called *The Great Fire*, but I have borrowed the above title from the identical deleted article (18.9/10). [Ed.]

Remember! Remember!

On the annual anniversary of the 'Gunpowder Plot' it would seem appropriate to look back to the foundation of the 'Beeding and Bramber Bonfire Boys' (a society from 1956). Celebrating the fifth of November does not appear to have taken place before the beginning of the 18th century. Riot and protest seem to have been the main theme; groups assembled to express their displeasure of political and religious figures. The 19th century was a time of revenge for real or imagined grievances. Very often the houses of the 'Guardians of the Poor' and those in local ruling positions were attacked and their fences burned for bonfires. Rockets were sent through upper windows, sometimes with dire results. In this century the bonfire societies took on a different role – that of raising money to help those less well off. Guy Fawkes replaced the Pope and out-of-favour clergymen on top of the fire.

Earlier bonfire supporters here appear to be grouped around Steyning but, since the last war, Beeding seems to have taken on this role and the first bonfire dinner for the elderly was given. Helpers called at every house in the villages of Beeding and Bramber to make sure no pensioner was left out. Meetings of the society took place in the home of Mr & Mrs Norris in Priory Field (built 1946). Wally Norris who was a committee member then, had the minute books for 1955-59 and also the original Bonfire Society banner. In the early years the set pieces for the firework display were assembled in Wally's front room! The whole display of fireworks, lasting half an hour or more, cost in the 1950s around £25. Money was raised by various means – monthly dances were held in the village hall. One entry in the minutes refers to the nuisance of 'Teddy Boys' and resolved to ban them from dances in the future!

Bonfire processions took place through the main streets, usually starting from Bramber railway station and ending on the Memorial playing field and Sele Field (now School Road). Magnificent costumes were worn – Zulu, Redskin, Pirate – and many innovative ideas for wearing apparel were displayed. There was always a Bonfire Queen and many well-known local names appear in the minutes as Queens or attendants over the years. Torches for the procession were stored in baths of paraffin which were locked in an old air-raid shelter which older residents will remember was on the bank in Hyde Street near the police house. Many other Bonfire Societies took part here, and in return Beeding and Bramber visited other towns. Upwards of 300 costumed participants taking part was not unusual. Sadly the parade no longer takes place, but the annual 'old folks' dinner survives.

Woodland and Hedge

As the Christmas Season approaches one is usually drawn to the fireside and the traditional Yule log burnt on Christmas Eve. There was no alternative to the fire for cooking until 1888 when gas was laid to the villages here. Electricity did not arrive until 1921. Older residents will remember the cast iron kitchen range. Old postcards show smoke issuing from chimneys at all times, even in summer with the trees in full leaf. It had to be this way otherwise there would simply be no hot water or cooking.

New methods of cooking have made things much easier and cleaner, but before coal was easily available, wood was the only fuel here. The woodlands were harvested just as any other crop. In earlier times St. Leonards Forest (a part of Beeding Parish) was a veritable cornucopia with wood and charcoal for the iron industry and the blacksmith's forge, bark for the tanner, timber for building. Pollarded trees produced leafy grazing for the forest animals (an ox could survive in winter on tree and hedge clippings unlike horses which needed oats and grass or hay). The art of coppicing was a fascinating subject. The woodsmen wielded their hachets, fashioning, with swift strokes, fencing posts, bean poles, and hazel laths for the hurdle maker. Many of these old crafts are now almost extinct. I remember as a small boy watching the local farmworkers hedging and ditching along the lanes towards Edburton. When they had finished a hedge it was an almost impenetrable barrier through which only the smallest creature could pass.

Before the Conquest, much of Sussex was the forest of Andredswald [See 10.11]. The Anglo-Saxon farmers had cleared and ploughed large parts of the woodlands. Sussex was more than half forest at the Domesday survey (1086). A number of hedges started in the Anglo-Saxon period still survive in our locality to this day. There is a formula worked out by historians and horticulturalists that is used for determining the age of hedges. For every different species of shrub within approximately 100 yards allow 100 years of age. If there are ten different sorts of shrub the hedge will be older than the Norman period. This criterion is not a perfect guide, but in the absence of any other yardstick it must suffice.

Since 1945, more than 140,000 miles of hedgerow have vanished under the concrete of the developers or grubbed out by the farmer to enlarge fields for bigger machinery to operate in order to feed an expanding population. There comes a time when enough is enough...surely unwanted grain mountains point to a solution; return some land to woods to cut down those imports of foreign timber, and grow more flax and similar commodities that we currently have to import at vast cost.

Unusual Occupations

In 1538 instructions were sent to every parish by Thomas Cromwell for them to purchase a 'sure-coffer'. The incumbent was to have a key, and a duplicate was to be held by the churchwarden. This mandate directed every minister to enter in a book every marriage, christening and burial at which he officiated. The entries were made after the service on a Sunday and witnessed by the churchwarden. This book was to be kept in the newly acquired coffer. It is these records that the local historian will almost certainly consult first when he begins to study a parish, because they give a list of inhabitants, and in some cases their occupations. So, to the student of early modern history (1500-1750), these records are as valuable as the *Domesday Book* is to the medievalist.

There are many taxes that can be referred to which reflect people's life-styles. Perhaps the best known is the 'Hearth Tax' (1662-89) replaced by the 'Window Tax' (1696 abolished 1851). A national census was taken in 1801 and has continued to the present day at ten-yearly intervals. Statistics are obtained for immediate use, but the details are only made fully available to the public after a hundred years. From 1841 the names of residents and their occupations were recorded by a local literate person. In Beeding, a schoolmaster Richard Goddard was among the Victorian enumerators.

The most recorded occupation is the 'ag lab' (agricultural labourer) which reflects the local land use. One essential trade was the shoemaker or 'cordwainer' (cordwain was a Spanish leather used for shoes). The designation of 'cobbler' was for the repairer of footwear. 'Huckster' is another name for pedlar, street seller of ale, mainly carried out by women, but Hugh and Thomas in Beeding street were named in the 1841 census as hucksters. 'Higgler' is probably derived from 'huckster' or vice-versa. The higgler was probably the forerunner of the 'barrow boy'. Chapman is also another name for a pedlar, while 'Clapman' is the town crier. Other occupations may be second or voluntary jobs, William Mills was a farmer residing at Pond Farm. He was also the 'meresman', who looked after the parish boundaries, marked by the 'merestones'. A 'hayward' supervised the common fields, saw that the fences and hedges were in good repair and took any stray cattle, pigs or sheep to the 'pinder' who managed the village pound and charged those who allowed their animals to wander. The Pound was near The King's Head. A 'parker' was one who looked after game on enclosed land and was responsible for these areas. Many of these second occupations were unpaid, but excused the holder from paying the Poor Rate.

St Peter's Beeding (Part 3)

The very first printed book was produced in China around 868 AD. Printed books came into being in Europe around the middle of the 1400s. The first dated printing from moveable type was a papal document from Mainz in Germany. In England some six hundred years later William Caxton set up his printing press at Westminster in 1476. He was the first recorded printer and publisher in this country. He had wide-ranging abilities and obtained his expertise in the art of printing in Cologne in the early 1470s. Among his best known early published books are Chaucer's *Canterbury Tales,* which gave a vivid picture of life in the 14th century, and Aesop's *Fables* from the 6th century BC.

On the 12th September 1412, Stephen de Sens, or Stephen Sennis as it is sometimes written, took an inventory of all the moveable articles belonging to the Priory of Sele. This existing document covers several vellum pages and lists the contents of Sele, the church and the chapel on the bridge at Bramber. As each place or room is under its respective heading, we are able to know exactly what was in the church that was not screwed down or cemented in. At this time there was a medieval south aisle and a chapel to St. John attached to the north side of the chancel. Many objects, some perhaps unfamiliar today, are recorded: '3 silver chalices, a tin holy water pot, a wooden box, 4 candlestick; a copper thurible (a censer), 3 old copes and one tunic, 4 cruets, 6 towels (3 at the altar of the Blessed Virgin Mary), 8 old decayed amices (cap, hood, or linen squares), a copper water basin, 2 corporals (altar cloths), 2 wax torches for Mass, 2 osculatories (small wood statues), 2 old albs (white vestments reaching to the feet), 2 old chasubles' [sleeveless vestments of the celebrant with colour regulated by the feast of the day]. Only one new thing is mentioned and that is a vestment bought from Master Felewyt by the Prior.

A total of 15 books are recorded as being in the church, quite a large number when you consider that at this time they would have been produced by the hands of several monks and scholars. Two Missals are on the inventory...illuminated books containing the service of Mass; a book of Martyrology containing the Rule of St. Benedict, another illuminated volume, and a book recording the Legends of the Saints. There are 2 books Antiphon (verses of Psalms intoned or sung alternately by two people or two choirs).

Sadly, only part of a bible is listed and not one complete. These books, if still in existence (maybe in Magdalen College, Oxford?), would at present-day prices be worth in excess of half a million pounds depending on their condition!

For Part One see 2.1 and for Part Two see 5.8

Bramber Castle 1643

It has been said by many people that Bramber Castle was reduced to its present dilapidated state at the time of the English Civil War. In fact, it was, they say: 'one of the places Cromwell knocked abart abit'; but this may not *be* so. We know that the strategy of the Royalist army in 1643 was to advance on London from the southwest. This route took the king's followers through Sussex and they had to secure the river crossings at the Arun and the Adur, guarded respectively by Arundel and Bramber castles. Bramber was a strategic place because at that time of year (December) the countryside around and above Bramber was almost impassable and certainly unsuitable for large guns and the army baggage trains.

It is recorded that earthworks were set up to defend the bridge at Bramber and that is where most of the fighting took place. In command was captain James Temple (later promoted colonel), defending Bramber for the king. It appears from existing narratives that Temple withdrew to the castle after having some nine men killed repulsing an attack on the bridge on the 12th day of December 1643. It is also recorded that the castle was later taken by the 'cannon' of Sir William Waller. We will never know what really happened, but modern evidence is in the many cannon balls found in the area around the castle. The custodian, whose title is the 'Key Keeper of Bramber Castle', had a collection of shot of many different sizes picked up in the neighbourhood. Gordon Alcoran passed some cannon balls to me that he unearthed in his garden. This points to there having been a gun position, as shot which has been discharged is seldom found in tight groups. Whether it was a royalist or parliamentary cannon is still open to discussion. The foregoing may point to the belief that the castle got into its present state during the civil war. This, though, is most probably not so as there is in existence a contemporary picture by Hollar showing the castle in a ruined state early in the 17th century, before the fighting took place.

One theory is that Sir John Fagge of Wiston damaged the castle with gunpowder in 1642 to prevent it being used as a defensive position by the royalists as it is said by Cheynell that Temple was defending a neglected castle. It is much more likely that the castle, then owned by the Duke of Norfolk, was allowed to fall into disrepair because his main residence was at another castle in Arundel.

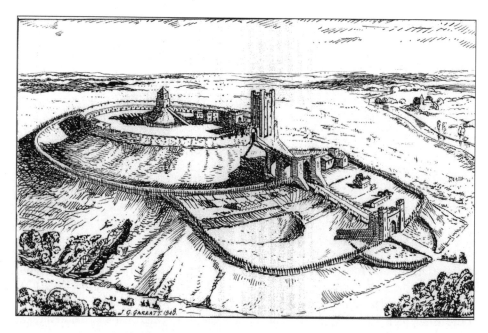

6.3 Conjectural drawing of Bramber Castle by J. Garratt

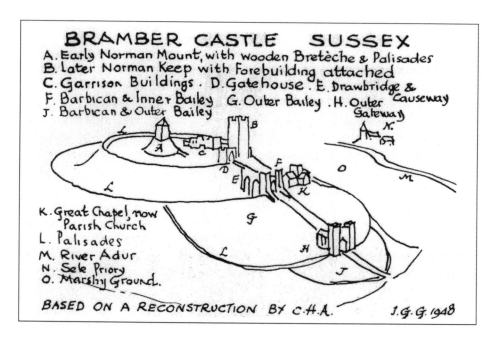

BRAMBER CASTLE SUSSEX
A. Early Norman Mount, with wooden Bretèche & Palisades
B. Later Norman Keep with Forebuilding attached
C. Garrison Buildings. D. Gatehouse. E. Drawbridge &
F. Barbican & Inner Bailey G. Outer Bailey . H. Outer Causeway
J. Barbican & Outer Bailey   Gateway

K. Great Chapel, now
   Parish Church
L. Palisades
M. River Adur
N. Sele Priory
O. Marshy Ground.

BASED ON A RECONSTRUCTION BY C.H.A.   J.G.G. 1948

Windows into the Past

Our national history is reasonably well recorded and knowledge of happenings in earlier times is constantly being revised as more material is uncovered which gives us a more accurate picture of past events. It is usually down to local historians to bring to light the things that are not of such national importance, but when many local researchers produce findings that differ from region to region assumptions made as to national behaviour based on one area have to be rethought.

In this series of articles, I have written several times of Sele Priory. This information is based on archive material at Magdalen College, results of excavations in 1966, observations by the Revd. Dr. Bloxam and Revd. Dr. Arnold, and my own local knowledge. Further material is from research by Edward Turner and which I use here. As we have seen [2.11], the first priory was built sometime before 1096 and occupied by the Benedictine Order as a small monastic establishment with never more that a dozen monks in residence. In the 1480's it was derelict and in the ownership of Magdalen College. The College leased the ruined buildings to the order of Carmelite Friars, whose house at that time was being inundated by the encroachment of the sea at Shoreham. They paid 10/- (50p) per annum and rebuilt the Priory from ground level; only the cellars of the first building remain. The cloisters were to the north of the church, they were eight feet wide and paved with plain yellow, green and purple glazed tiles, bordered by bricks in pale blue (some of these tiles were unearthed from the chancel when the church was underpinned a few years ago).

One can only guess what the original building of the 11th century was like from excavations and fragments that still exist, but we do have an eye witness account of the structure prior to the last rebuilding. Sometimes a voice filters down from the past that has been recorded by a well known and trusted accurate historian, and one such man was the Revd. Edward Turner. He recorded the observations of a close relative who lived to be 100 years and 8 months old. This person was very familiar with the buildings in the times before 1790 and this 'peep into the past' records them thus: "The vicarage-house was then part of the ancient priory, and the dining room the refectory of the monks. The house was, at that time, connected with the church by a cloister and there were fragments of old walls of flint and stone and ruined arches, standing in and about what is now the kitchen garden lying between the house and Church (north of chancel). These began to be removed in 1785 and their total demolition was effected upon the erection of the present house". The description continues with the details of the beautiful chapel of St. John attached to the north of the chancel.

See also 2.11

6.4 Magdalen College, Oxford, founded by William of Waynflete, Bishop
of Winchester, who owned lands in Beeding and Bramber

The Meresman

Travellers, landowners, and military men have a need for maps. Pilgrims usually follow a well beaten track, but others need to seek the best route to their destinations or follow the extent of their operations. The stewards and bailiffs of the landowners needed to know how much land the lord owned, who occupied it, and how much rent was paid. Similar information was required by the ecclesiastical authorities in 1836, when their tithes were commuted into annual money rents instead of the former tenth part of the produce that had existed since the time of King Ethelwulf, and so the tithe map was added to our store of records of the past.

Gerhardus Mercator (1512-1594), the Flemish geographer, is probably the best known cartographer. He was a pioneer of navigational maps and charts. He worked out the way in which meridians and parallels of latitude cross each other at right angles, which enable compass bearings to be drawn as straight lines. Christopher Saxton (b1542), John Speed (b1552), with Norden, Morden and John Ogilby are among the best known cartographers to produce English county and road maps. The most famous series of maps is that issued by the Ordnance Survey; founded in 1791 as the Trigonometrical Survey, they established the 'one inch to one mile' national scale (earlier maps used local measurements which differed from county to county – the mile varied from 1830 to 4300 yds).

A few maps of our parish exist as estate maps. One of the earliest (1627) by John Gotham, shows ox-bows in the Adur. These were removed by the Navigation Act of 1807, which provided for barge traffic. Beeding Bridge is of timber and it also shows a south aisle to Beeding Church, a fact that is not recorded in the current church guide. Perhaps the most beautiful and informative is the 19th century map of the Rape of Bramber, surveyed in 1824. Engraved by Davies and published by Edmund Cartwright in 1830, it shows the geography of the area with every house, park, woodland, pond, and watermill. Sadly only ninety copies ever reached subscribers to the original edition as there was a fire in the storeroom, no one knows how many of those ninety remain today and apart from my own copy I know of only two others.

On 9th June 1871 the 'Meresman' for Beeding, William Mills, the tenant of Pond Farm, set out with Charlie Woolgar for Bramber, and a corporal/surveyor from the Royal Engineers to plot the joint boundaries for the new Ordnance Survey series, begun in 1840. The meresmen's report books drawn and written that day are still in existence and make very interesting reading.

Edburton – Siamese Twin?

The little village of Edburton stands on the upper Greensand bench at the scarp foot of the South Downs; it occupies a position astride the ancient 'hollow-way' that connects Upper Beeding with Pyecombe. At one time it was an ecclesiastical parish but was divided by the boundary of the Rapes of Bramber and of Lewes. The manor house of Edburton Manor was Aburton farmhouse, built in the early 17th century on the site of an earlier house. The parish of Edburton is mentioned in the *Domesday* survey (1086).

In 1889 East and West Sussex became two separate administrative counties and, when in 1894 civil parish councils were formed, part of Edburton came within the boundaries of Fulking civil parish. In 1933 over a thousand acres were added to Upper Beeding civil parish, establishing a boundary line that ran north-south a little to the west of Edburton School, known sometimes as 'Boundary House'. The earliest deed of the school is recorded as being 1874; it was then closed in 1930 and the pupils divided between East and West Sussex, with some going to Small Dole and Henfield, and others to Poynings and Hurstpierpoint.

For the early history we are indebted to F. A. Howe of Henfield who produced a *Chronicle of Edburton and Fulking* (1958). Nathanial Blaker was born in 1835 and came to Edburton the following year. He records his impressions of the Rector, the Revd. J. G. F. Tufnell: 'In a very short time he had gained the confidence of everyone, and every local matter was referred to him. One of his first acts was to procure the extension of the penny post to the parish. I perfectly recollect the first time a postman appeared in the parish, in the shape of a pale youth, dressed in a white frock smock, who came from Beeding'. (A stranger on those roads was so rare as to attract attention then). Previous to this, letters for anyone in the parish were left at a neighbouring turnpike gate, and were forwarded by any chance conveyance or pedestrian who would take charge of them, sometimes arriving a week late. Letters from the parish were sent in the same uncertain manner. Even after the postman's daily visit was instituted, all letters had to be ready for him to take back, so that no answer could be sent to a letter on the same day it was received. 'Penny Blacks' were issued in 1840 but it is thought they were not sold locally until after 1843, so a penny had to be ready for the postman for each letter. The foregoing must say something about the honesty and co-operation of villagers and their trust in each other.

The Tools of our Ancestors

Mankind is distinguished from all other living things by having the power to reason as well as the ability to make and use tools, and it has been this way for over two million years. Stone, especially flint, has been widely used for various implements since the Palaeolithic (Old Stone Age) period, and, later on, in the Neolithic (New Stone Age) period, which ended c.1800 BC. In biblical chronology this would be the time of the patriarchs Isaac and Jacob. Many very finely-made instruments were fabricated. Stone had other important uses too; Stonehenge was built and rebuilt over the period 2100 to 1600 BC, and a high degree of intelligence would have been required to work out the mathematical calculations for that edifice/ 'observatory'. Flint was still being used in this century by tribesmen for their flintlock muskets, and until the end of the 1800s by aborigines in Australia. Up to the Second World War some people in the Highlands and Islands still made use of the 'tinder' box with flint and steel. Over the last few decades I have assembled a collection of Neolithic flint implements that have been found locally. My own garden, which in earlier times would have been on the higher ground at the edge of the estuary, has been most fruitful. Without digging, more than a dozen scrapers, borers and blades have been picked up. Truleigh Hill is another place where flint tools have been found. Some have come to light between Summersdean and Bushy Bottom around the Celtic lynchets – ridges formed by ploughing – whilst Thundersbarrow at the south-east end of the parish has also yielded one or two small items. Almost all of my stone axes were fabricated in the Cissbury area which is the site of a number of flint mines.

As a lad I was present when some of the mines were excavated in the thirties. Flint mining declined with the onset of the Bronze Age (1800-500 BC) which was followed by the early Iron Age (circa 500 BC). These flint tools, which were very necessary for his survival, were also a form of currency to early man. It is the general consensus that people from areas which did not have a readily available supply of stone themselves, bartered for the roughly fashioned implements with the people that mined and 'knapped' them. Having obtained the rough tools from the 'nappers', man would then give them a better shape and a polish with some whetstone of very hard material. These polished axes and blades would be among the very highly prized possessions and be buried with him when he died.

In the hearts of many of us there is a yearning to know more about our past; it is true to say that without knowing the past one has no yardstick for the future.

The Blacksmith (Part 1)

At the age of 13 years 8 months, my father apprenticed me to an engineering firm in Brighton. The first few weeks were occupied with endless sweeping up, making tea and running errands. In the second month, Mr.Gill the manager packed me off to William Dawkins, the owner of the forge in Marshalls Row, near the old open market in Brighton, to learn (in three months) all about the blacksmith's trade. The events and scenes of those early days of my life became vividly fixed in my memory. Start at 6 a.m., light the forge, work the bellows, strike for the smith, straighten old horseshoe nails, sweep up, work till 4.30 p.m. Apprentices in those days had to make their own tools of the trade from scratch, tongs, pincers, set squares and rules for measuring hot RSGT cold iron. Years later, after the war, as an engineer in charge of sites, my early skills proved to be of the utmost importance. The power of practical knowledge gives one good leverage when dealing with others.

Half a century ago, the village blacksmith was a person who could be described as a 'jack of all trades'. Life in rural parts would have come to a standstill without him. Horses were shod in the smithy and the oxen in the fields. He repaired agricultural machinery and made hinges and latches for a variety of doors and gates. Sickles and shears were fashioned from the rough lumps of iron, tempered and given a keen cutting edge, as were axes, knives, and many of the carpenters' and joiners' saws, chisels, spoke-shaves and plane irons. The smith was almost indispensible, especially in a place like Beeding, where in earlier times boat-building was carried out, and cleats, rudder pintals and iron straps were needed. Before the Industrial Revolution the local blacksmith made most of the nails required in his district.

Beeding Forge stood opposite The Rising Sun, where Beeding Garage is now. My records show that it is likely that Harry Tribe of Hyde Street was the smith. Others are recorded as living in the village at different times but Harry Tribe was working for around fifty years until his retirement mentioned in the 1861 census returns. With his wife Martha, he is buried in the churchyard at St. Peter's, Beeding. Their grave is on the left, shaded by a large yew alongside the path near the lamp post. Martha died in 1868, and Harry in 1873.

As with many forges at the turn of the century, the coming of the horseless carriage forced many blacksmiths to turn to vehicle repairs along with dispensing oil and motor spirit. Perhaps some of you will remember Mr Upton.

See also 6.10 *Beeding Garage*

The Hyde

Hyde Square, Hyde Lane, Hyde Street. These places probably took their name from Hyde Farm which was located in earlier times in the area of the Hyde Farm Estate that now covers much of the eastern part of Beeding Village. So why, where or what, was a 'hyde'? The name has endured for practically 2000 years with just slight differences. The 'hyde' or 'hide' of the Middle Ages was a land measure. It was the area of land that could be ploughed in a year using one plough. This was generally believed to have supported one family unit and was also known as a 'husbandland'.

The hide was a part of the 'hundred', which was of Saxon origin, but the Normans continued the use after the Conquest. We live in the Norman hundred of Burbeach. The hundred was thought to have been made up of a hundred hides or family units and was the subdivision of a 'Rape', another Norman land division. There were originally five Rapes in Domesday Sussex which were increased to six later. Each Rape had a castle, a river, a port and a forest (ours is St. Leonard's Forest).

The area of a hide varied considerably. Much depended on the quality of the soil, but generally it was between sixty and one hundred and eighty acres. The hide was sub-divided into quarters and these were known as 'Virgates' or 'Yardlands'. 'Wista' is a Sussex term for a Virgate. A quarter of a Virgate was known as a Farthingdale and below a Farthingdale was the now English standard land measure - the acre. In agricultural terms this was as much land as could by ploughed by a yoke of oxen in a day and was standardised by Edward I as forty rods long by four rods wide. The English Furlong was one furrow long and is now one eighth of a mile. In ancient law, a Saxon 'Ceorl' had to possess 'fully five hides of his own land, a chapel, a kitchen, a book and a bell', before he could become a Thane. In mediaeval times anything up to fifty hides would be under the support of a Knight and his family.

Going metric may make things much easier for the scholar of today, but I mourn the passing of the 'inch' (three grains of wheat end to end), the 'foot' (supposed to be the size of the foot of Henry VIII), the 'yard' (the measure of nose to outstretched finger tip of the average man). 'Pole', 'perch', and 'chain' have almost disappeared now and so has the 'league' (three miles), a well loved measurement of the writers of 'Once upon a time' books.

Beeding Garage

Leonardo da Vinci had plans for a kind of automobile in the 15th century. It is recorded in Vatican archives that the Emperor of China, Ch'ien Lung (1736-1795), witnessed the movement of a self-propelled cart invented by a Jesuit priest. These carts were almost certainly powered by steam. Frenchman Etienne Lenoir is the man credited with building the first passenger-carrying, internal combustion engined (I.C.E.) vehicle. His motor car had a successful journey from Paris to Joinville-le-Pont in 1862. He used gas under pressure, electrically ignited. The first roadworthy vehicle with an I.C.E. using a liquid fuel, (petroleum spirit) ignited by electricity, was made by German-born Austrian, Seigfried Marcus in 1865. His three-wheeled cart carried no passengers, but in 1874 he had a motor car running on the roads around Vienna. He was a Jew, so evidence of his innovative ideas was destroyed by the Nazis in 1938. Gottlieb Daimler and Karl Benz are generally credited with the production of I.C.E. automobiles as we know them today.

We saw [in 6.8] that the service station developed from the blacksmith and wheelwright businesses, and inns like the King's Head sold petroleum spirit to passing motorists. Beeding Garage was one of the earlier Sussex service stations selling petrol, oil and tyres. Spare parts were not usually available 'off the shelf' in the first decades of this century – these had to be fashioned by the local mechanics with their blacksmith background. A major extension to the buildings was made in the early 1980s with the development of the quality car sales on display and the workshops tucked away at the back. It was in the time of Obed Henry Upton's occupation that the blacksmith's forge became a garage (around the time of the First World War). The workshop opened on to the High Street, and motor spirit was dispensed to customers' cars by hand-operated pumps. Mr. Upton's son, Harry, told me that he had been involved in building the first proper garage, now a part of the present buildings, with the bronze lamps atop the facade. They generated their own electricity then, since electricity did not come to Beeding until 1921, when the Steyning Electric Light Co. was authorised to supply the area. While excavating for the petrol tanks installation, mammoth tusks and the remains of prehistoric animals were discovered. Before the extension was made to the garage, a bungalow stood to the north. This was a timber-framed building purchased from Brighton barracks and Harry still has some of the bills covering materials required to re-erect the structure. Mr. Upton sold to a Mr. Radford who then sold it to the present owners.

This piece is a sequel to 6.8 and repeated as 20.2 under a new title
The Blacksmith (Part 2)

The Knights of the Temple

The 'Knights of the Temple' derived the name of their Order from the convent and church of the Temple on Mount Moriah at Jerusalem. The Order was founded in the year 1119 (1180 in England), Hugh de Payens heading the list of eight soldier knights. Their original purpose was the maintenance of safe passage for pilgrims going to and from Jerusalem, along the roads of Palestine. They grew in numbers and in 1128 A.D. they received the sanction of the Church. A set of rules was instituted by St. Bernard himself – a triple vow of poverty, chastity, and obedience. The Order was divided into three classes. At the highest level were the soldier knights of the nobility who regulated their affairs through a middle level of clerks and chaplains. The lower tiers were occupied by craftsmen, farmers and free men. The knights were attired in the well-known white mantle with a red cross (recognised by schoolchildren as Crusaders), the other serving brethren wore a black surcoat with a red cross. They rendered service to Christianity showing great bravery and devotion in eight of the Crusades and became very wealthy and powerful too, being able to finance kings and princes. Sadly for them this influence led to their downfall. Pope Clement V saw them as a rival influence and abolished the Order in 1312.

The Templars were very active in the Adur Valley during the hundred and twenty-eight years of their existence here. They had settlements at Shoreham, Sompting. Shipley and Seddlescombe, and owned at least five acres and a wharf where the present St. Mary's now stands [See.4.1]. It has been said (E.W.Collins), although unsupported by evidence, that Richard I, the 'Lionheart', left England for the third Crusade (around 1180) from Bramber Castle, and would have used the jetty at the site of St. Mary's to board his vessel.

Edward II pre-empted the Pope as, without warning, on the night of the 10th January 1308, he had his sheriffs seize the English Templar estates and imprisoned all the occupants without trial. It is recorded that in 1320 St.Mary's was so impoverished that it was excused all taxation. After being plundered by the King, the Templar lands and what remained of their possessions were transferred to the Knights of St. John, the Knights Hospitallers or Knights of Malta. For the observant there are clues to the Hospitallers in St. Nicholas' Bramber, where a carved Maltese cross in the stonework can be seen.

St. Peter's was re-dedicated on 24th February 1308 by Bishop Enaghdun (acting as a suffragan). Rev. Dr. H. E. B. Arnold was of the opinion that the cost of rebuilding was funded by a gift from Emma, widow of Sir Philip Maybank of Horton, and loans from the Templars at Bramber.

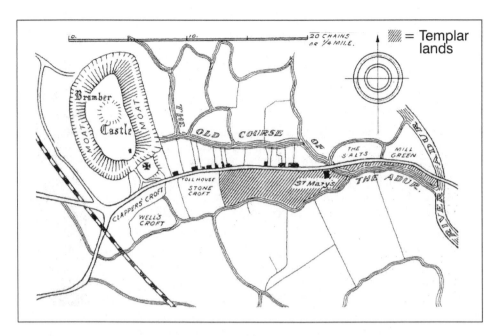

6.11 Templar lands in Bramber by Revd. Arnold

6.11a King Edward II.
He seized the English Templar estates in 1308

The Apothecary

Today if we feel a bit off colour we wait in the surgery in comfortable surroundings and are seen by a doctor who has the latest gadgets to assist in his diagnosis. If necessary, he will give you a prescription that the chemist will make up for you using the up-to-date products of the pharmaceutical companies. What was it like in earlier times? In the Middle Ages there was much endemic disease and in 1348/9 we learn what an epidemic really was when half the population of Europe perished in the Black Death. New thinking floats the idea that it was not 'bubonic plague' as was thought, but anthrax. This disease of man and beast recurred at four year intervals and this is how the Black Death progressed until the 18th century. The records, civil and monastic, are very good in this sphere.

In the medieval period there was a leper hospital recorded to the west of Bramber. It is doubtful if any cures were effected as it existed merely to keep the lepers away from the populated villages and was more of a hospice than anything else. Up to the early 19th century if one had toothache or any intense pain, there was little anyone could do to help. Alcohol or drugs of the time could not entirely relieve suffering, but great strides were made in Victorian times, chloroform discovered by Liebig and used by Simpson, and antiseptic surgery by Lister relieved much suffering. The local apothecary was the general practioner of the times before the 20th century. Not many villages had an M.D.[local doctor]. The apothecary was originally a person who kept a drugstore and until 1617 was classified along with the grocer. He was the only hope of relief from illness for most of the villagers. I should like to relate an amusing tale from the Ransome (K. Underwood) unpublished family history. It is a true story.

'An old labourer who worked on Newlands Farm complained of constipation and was sent to the Apothercary/doctor at Ditchling, which could be reached by a footpath which still runs along the back of the Downs today. The Doctor appeared to know the old boy and his habits, and invited him to take a glass of beer while he waited for his medicine. The old labourer was not slow in accepting the beer but did not know the doctor had laced it with a generous dose of 'Jallop'. After receiving his bottle of medicine, he proceeded home across the fields but it was not long before he was compelled to hide behind a hedge to obey a very urgent call of nature. Later he was observed approaching the farm with the bottle of medicine tied to the end of a very long stick and held at arm's length. Asked to explain this, he replied that "it was mighty powerfel medicine and 'worked' you through the Bottle"'!

The Growth of Beeding

The emergence of a new local plan for our area has worried many residents who fear an overcrowded environment with a poor infrastructure. As we have seen in earlier articles, Beida was the founder of the village around 501 A.D. The original Beeding is most likely to have been the medieval site to the south of Beeding Court. Sele was around the church, a well-populated place in the Middle Ages; both names are now synonymous of our area. The existence of Beeding-Sele was without doubt the fact that here were two places to cross the river – a ford at Sele and a bridge and causeway to the south; a field called 'Bridgeways' is recorded as late as 1842 south-east of Beeding Court. Botolphs was called 'Old Bridge' up to the 13th century. Steyning was the nearest market town and Bramber hardly existed until the Conquest when the castle was built.

St. Peter's is probably the oldest building (1308) with part of the tower dating from before 1283 A.D. The Saxon linear village stretched from Castletown along the line of Hyde Street, in a curve, to the church and priory. Remains of Saxon dwellings have been located along this line. If one pays attention to the schedule of 'Listed Buildings', it records 'Candytuft' in the High Street as being the oldest building used as a dwelling, although Beeding Court has parts that date back to the 13th century. There are still a few Elizabethan houses to be found in Hyde Street. Several also exist in the High Street including 'Beam Ends', the chemist (formerly Lucas Stores), Manor Cottage and the Dilly. There was nothing in the High Street before the 12th century when a causeway was formed (the sea was receding at this time). There are many 17th and 18th century buildings but they have been altered and enlarged over the years.

The 19th century saw the start of the expansion of Beeding village. This is primarily due to the fact that land was cheap here, and also available. During this century the school was built (1871), as were the Towers (1883), Cliff House (1890s) and many good Victorian buildings. The beginning of the 20th century saw houses being built near the school in Church Lane; Dacre Gardens was developed by the Cement Works company* and tenanted by the employees (1910); Sele Gardens, Beeding Garage (1920s) and Shoreham Road (1930s) followed. After the Second World War, Priory Field was developed as an enclosed square with a green open space. Dawn Crescent and Dawn Close were started in the 1950s and in the 1960s, a gap was made in the High Street to form Saltings Way and the spread of the Hyde Farm estate. The 1970s brought the march into the 'brooklands' with the Driftway development. What next, I wonder?

*Blue Circle

The Floods

Many local postcards and photographs of the late 19th and early 20th century show the inhabitants of our villages enjoying themselves skating on the ice of frozen flooded fields adjacent to the river. The main streets of Beeding and Bramber provided venues for bath tub races, provisions were delivered to the upper storeys of affected houses and water came up to the hubs of horse-drawn vehicles. Flooding was a regular feature of village life until the raising of the banks in the 1950s put an end to this natural threat for the time being. The villagers who suffered the misery of soggy carpets and damp furnishings on a regular basis must have been overjoyed to see the banks raised above the tidal surges which take place every season.

From the 11th century the sea began to recede, leaving St. Cuthman's Port (at Steyning) high and dry, but at high water the sea was several feet deep between the steps of Sele Priory and the ditches of Bramber Castle. In the 12th century, two bridges were built and connected by a causeway spanning the two (or possibly three) main courses of the Adur, then known as the Soare or Weald Ditch. Land was reclaimed and the causeway was built upon. The main bridge near St.Mary's at Bramber was 170 feet long and may have been built across the confluence of two courses; it now exists as footings of the piers under the present roadway. Beeding Bridge, originally a timber-built structure, was re-built in brick in 1785 by the owners – the Vicar, and Magdalen College Oxford.

The early 1980s saw flooding return to the area of the bridge. The banks north-east of Beeding Bridge had to be increased in height by 15 inches to replace sand-bags put there earlier to prevent water inundating 'Riverside' at high tide. Why should this be, you may wonder? The answer is simple. Our only bridge is like the plughole in a bath, or a pinch in an hour glass. All storm water north of us from as far as Horsham and Crawley, Haywards Heath and Burgess Hill drains through this 'choke point'. Flooding risk is most dangerous at a time when there are tidal surges coming upriver and millions of gallons of rainwater are trying to get through this narrow defile. The volume of flow is increasing as development to the north is putting more and more surface water through the bridge. The water authorities have designated the water meadows each side of the Adur as holding areas or soakaways. Many residents have been worried about the Saltings area being built upon. One inch of rain there produces some 700 tons of surface water that will be pumped into the river at its highest.

7.2 Bramber floods: Frank Lewis with Harry Adams
delivering bread to Mr. Bacon

7.2a Groceries arrive at Little St. Mary's.
Note the tall chimney built to take away sparks from the
former thatched roof.

A Bramber Regicide

In the year that Queen Elizabeth I died (1603), the Reverend Stephen Goffe was appointed Rector of Bramber-cum-Botolphs by Magdalen College. He was also said to have been the Rector of the Parish of Stanmer, although there is no evidence to support this, except a brass in the church to the memory of his wife Deborah who died in 1626. Goffe, a Puritan, fell foul of Bishop Lancelot Andrewes, who deprived him of his benefice in 1607. His three sons came to be better known. The eldest, Stephen, took Holy Orders. In 1636 he is recorded as being chaplain to Charles I, and the diarist John Evelyn reports Goffe as being chaplain to Colonel Goring's regiment in 1641. In 1647 Stephen assisted Charles in his flight from Hampton Court and, although arrested, somehow managed to rejoin the King at Carisbrook Castle. Later he was chaplain to Henrietta Maria (Queen Mother) and tutor to Charles II's natural son, who was to become the Duke of Monmouth. Stephen died on Christmas Day 1681. The second son, John, inherited the ecclesiastical views of his father and he also took Holy Orders. His stated views in 1645 led him to be imprisoned for several years, but with his younger brother's help he was released and given a rectory at Norton. At the Restoration, John Goffe was restored to his former vicarage at Hackington near Canterbury.

William, the youngest son, was a different 'kettle of fish'; being adverse to academic learning, he was apprenticed to a London salter. At some time he became a soldier for the 'Blessed Cause'. He joined the Presbyterians and was made a colonel in the Parliamentary army. He sat as one of the judges at the trial of Charles I and his seal and signature are the 14th on the Death Warrant of the King.

Cromwell made William a 'Major-General' over Hampshire, Sussex and Berkshire and it was said that he would have been successor to the Protector. The Civil War created many family divisions – brother fighting brother – but William did help his brother John by getting his release from prison in 1652. At the Restoration (1660), William, as one of the 'regicides', had to flee the country. He, with his father-in-law, Lieutenant-General Whalley, escaped to Boston, Massachusetts, where Governor John Endicott welcomed them with open arms.* The following year, two King's Men arrived to arrest them and they had to hide in a cave near Newhaven, Massachusetts. In 1675 Goffe put his military talents to good use by assisting his American protectors when the settlement at Hadley was attacked by Indians. It was Goffe's leadership that saved it from destruction. His last letter to his family was dated 2nd April 1679, so it is presumed that he died about this time.

*A descendent of the Goffe-Whalley family, Major M. D'arcy was a visitor to our villages. He was on holiday from Australia and was impressed with our records. [KN-B]

7.3 King Charles I. Stephen Goffe assisted Charles in
his flight from Hampton Court.

7.3a Oliver Cromwell.
He appointed William Goffe as Major-General of Sussex.

Jack Cade – a local man?

Mediaeval times produced a way of life that included fear of war and civil disturbance as things to be expected rather than unusual happenings. Sussex men, along with those of Surrey, Kent and Essex were in the forefront of many of the risings of this period. In the aftermath of the 'Black Death'(1348) came the 'Statute of Labourers' (1351) which attempted to peg wage rates for the depleted workforce and to restrict the movements of labourers within their own area. Landowners desperate to get their land tended, were unable to offer more than the going rate. Unrest festered. The poll-tax of the 1370s was increased threefold and with the events at Fobbing (Essex) the 'Peasants Revolt' of 1381 broke out. [3.12].

Nearly seventy years later, the risings of 1450 was the first revolt to produce a coherent manifesto of aims and objectives of those involved, mainly because many taking part were small landowners, artisans and freemen who had a little more learning than the peasants in 1381. A weak king (Henry VI) had allowed many of our overseas lands to be retaken during the 'Hundred Years War' to the dismay of the population. There was much extortion and confiscation of holdings of lesser yeomen, illegally by those in authority. Lord Saye and Sele was indicted by the rebels and beheaded; Robert Est was also hated. The trigger for this uprising was the killing of the Duke of Suffolk at Dover on his way to exile for his part in the loss of our French possessions. The rebels wanted political reform in London and 'good government' for Sussex and Kent. Perhaps one should be reminded that this was the eve of civil war, later termed the 'Wars of the Roses'.

There is evidence that Jack Cade lived locally. It is known that he resided in the Sussex household of Sir Thomas Dacre. Early in the revolt, a commission was appointed to arrest Cade, but Robert Poynings, an esquire from Twineham and Poynings who headed this body, defected to Cade and later became his swordbearer. Cade led the rebels to London and invaded the city. Among the opposition was another local man, Matthew Gough of Bramber, who was killed with many more, defending – London Bridge. The King's forces repelled the rebel host, persuing them south. Cade was wounded by the sheriff of Kent, Alexander Iden, at Heathfield, Sussex and died of his wounds. His body was hanged, drawn and quartered in London.

Jack Cade (if that was his real name) adopted the name of Mortimer and proffered the notion that he was a cousin of the Duke of York. It was said that Cade was of Irish origin, and since the thirteenth century the Mortimers, forebears of the Duke of York, were substantial landowners in Ireland. A Yorkist plot? Who knows? Among those pardoned after the rising was John Frenssh [?], who lived near Bramber Castle.

Prisoners at the Priory

During the last two world wars, prisoners captured in battle were `guarded in special P.O.W. camps and only repatriated during the conflict if they were no longer capable of fighting, through some disability such as wounds or illness. In earlier times things were very different. During the wars with France in mediaeval days, prisoners were only taken if they were worthy of ransom (Richard I, captured on his way back from the Crusades, was worth 70,000 marks). The Hundred Years War with France (1335-1453) produced many valuable prisoners of high status.

As we have seen in previous articles, Sele Priory was built around the first decade after the Conquest and given by William de Braose to the Benedictine order at St. Florent in Saumur. The ground plan of the first priory was much larger than the present configuration, and cloistered. During the Hundred Years War (to 1378), the Papacy was in Avignon and in the control of the French monarchy. Many of the population saw the Pope as the friend of the King of France and, therefore, an enemy of the English. Money was not allowed to be sent to St. Florent during much of this time. At one time the King ordered Sele Priory, as an alien establishment, to remove itself from the coast. William de Valence (son of King John's widow by the Earl of Marche) interceded and the monks remained, but had to pay a penalty of half the income (£25 13s 4d) to the king and to billet hostages awaiting ransom.

Prisoners of war were, in the main, of the nobility and, as such in that age of chivalry, were allowed a certain amount of freedom to walk locally and to share the hospitality of Sele. They had to give their parole that they would not attempt to escape during the period their ransoms were being raised, it being a great dishonour to their families and nation if they broke their bond.

Prisoners billeted at Sele lived reasonably well. It is recorded that Robert Curling, the gateporter, received daily one wheaten loaf, one black loaf of household bread, a gallon of convent ale and meat or fish as served to the monks.

The Railways (Part 2)

The 1830s and 1840s brought a tremendous amount of innovative railway projects to England. Hundreds of railway companies were floated on the Stock Market and numerous Acts of Parliament were enacted. For those with a little under the mattress, shares were the 'in' thing as engineers, designers, and architects competed for a place in the history books. The London to Brighton line had opened in 1841. The London and Brighton Railway Co. had beaten off the attempt by Mr. Vallance to create an AtmosphericRailway' to Brighton from the Metropolis, first proposed in 1826.

An advertisement appeared in the *Pictorial Times* 11th October 1845 headed: 'The Dorking, Brighton and Arundel Atmospheric Railway'. It read 'This company has been formed for the purpose of giving to the populous and wealthy district between Dorking, Shoreham, Brighton and Arundel the advantage of a direct railway communication with the Metropolis and the coast, from which at present it is excluded. It is proposed that the line shall be constructed on the Atmospheric principle, by which a cheap, speedy, safe and frequent means of transit will be secured to the country through which it passes. It may be observed that if any doubt has hitherto existed as to the efficiency of this principle, that doubt has been most satisfactorily removed by the recent trials on the Croydon Railway, the results of which have exceeded the most sanguine anticipations, and proved that railways constructed on the atmospheric principle must eventually supersede all others.'

The atmospheric system propelled carriages and wagons by means of a vacuum tube situated below and between the rails. The train was coupled to a piston which was drawn along the tube by means of an exhauster engine station every three miles, creating a vacuum in front of the piston. This method did away with heavy locomotives and eliminated the chance of field fires.

The route proposed crossing the Adur from west to east at the Priory, passing thence through Beeding. Why was this safe silent railway not built? Among other difficulties, the leather seals on the vacuum tubes were eaten by rats!

For Part 1 see 4.7

Well! Well!

My grandfather once told me of a discovery made by his Society at Beeding Court, which was then in the occupation of the Cross family. Interest centred upon a well with passages leading off like the spokes of a wheel, but at different levels. This was a puzzle at the time and they were somewhat mystified as to its purpose. Was it an old galleried mine now used as a well? Did it serve a more clandestine role, openly a well but a store for smuggled goods at other times? [4.12) The use of these shafts became apparent some weeks later, when at No.3 Denmark Villas, Brighton, a similar well was drawn to their attention. An expert was consulted and he pronounced that they were, or had been, a century or so earlier, 'ice wells'. These were used by local gentry to store domestic supplies of ice until the summer.

Victorian London had many ice wells. Some had been used since mediaeval times. The largest was owned by Messrs. Leftwick in Little Albany Street. This was a huge commercial enterprise and held some 1500 tons of ice. Smaller ice merchants owned wells, and it is reported in newspapers of the time that London alone consumed more than 4000 tons of ice in the summer months. The ice was vital to the fish and confectionery trades, long before the general use of ice-making machines.

The gathering of ice provided work for many labourers in the months when there was little field work to be done. Owners of large bodies of water, such as canal proprietors leased the use of their water and several 'crops' of ice could be had. It was a different story in mild winters; then ice was imported from Norway and the Baltic. Victorian winters must have been more severe than the present cold seasons as it was common to have ice more than a foot thick. It is recorded that forty men and twelve horses could cut and stow 400 tons of ice daily where the areas of water permitted. Probably the best re-cycling exercise of all time!

Ecclesiastical Treasures

Before the 11th century there was very little gold or silver plate in ecclesiastical use in the British Isles. By the 16th century its use was much more widespread. This is reflected in records of the time. In 1536 Henry VIII's jewel-keeper received some nine tons of gold and silver plate from the suppressed monasteries and houses.

In mediaeval times, churches and monasteries were only allowed to dispose of their treasures in emergencies such as famine or for ransom payments. An object of interest in our parish is, perhaps wrongly, described as a 'porringer', a fairly recent name for a child's porridge bowl. The porringer is based on the shape of an earlier chalice. Arculf, a French bishop, who travelled in the Holy Land in the late 7th century, described two such cups. They were kept in a cave at Golgotha. One was said to have been used by Our Lord. Both cups were of silver, both had two handles, their capacity was equal to one sextarius, probably just exceeding half a pint.

The vessel from St. Botolphs matches the description of the earlier chalices and is the same shape as some depicted in a mosaic of the 6th century which shows a 'tulip' design. Our chalice/porringer has acanthus leaves in the body with laurel leaves around the rim. It is dated 1683 and the maker's mark is S.D. There are also the initials T.M. with C over, making a pyramid shape. These may refer to the donor, possibly a Thomas Middleton, with his wife's initial for Catherine above, as is often depicted on private tradesmen's tokens of the 17th century. Perhaps he was a wealthy churchwarden?

Legend has it that on the dissolution of the monasteries, the silver belonging to Sele Priory was thrown down the well in the grounds. If it were true it probably does not amount to much as Sele was recorded as being a very poor house. Dangerous natural gases have prevented treasure hunters from reaching the bottom.

St Nicholas Bramber

One way of observing the past is by paintings, pictures and prints of earlier times. When one has access to pictorial records of a certain area that cover a long period of time, (allowing for certain artistic licence), a picture of the progress or decline of buildings and structures can be assessed. 1790 was a good year for worshippers at St. Nicholas Church, Bramber, as a major restoration was completed in that year.

St. Nicholas was built in the late 11th century. 'It had an eastern tower above the chancel, nave, and vest porch and vestry. The tower and nave with some crudely carved capitals, survive from the building built by William de Braose for his college of canons c1073, and formed part of a small cruciform building which had only a semicircular apse east of the tower. By the late 13th century there was a rectangular chancel, and in the 14th century, a new window was put into the north wall of the nave. Two new windows were put into the south wall of the nave in the 16th century. The north and south transepts were apparently demolished in the 14th and 15th centuries respectively, reflecting the lack of prosperity of the borough and the non-residence of its lords.'

The chancel and tower, the latter with a saddleback roof, both survived into the 17th century and a picture by W Hollar c1640/50 in the British Museum records this. Parts of the tower and chancel in a ruinous state are pictured in a print from F. Grose (*Antiq. of Eng. & Wales*) c1761. Around 1785 the newly installed rector (1783), Dr. Green, funded the demolition of the old chancel and the rebuilding of the tower as a new chancel. He was helped with donations from the future Lord Calthorpe and others. This major reconstruction was finished in 1790. A new font was provided and a three-light window was inserted into the east wall. In this window were three glazed panels of armorial bearings: Magdalen College, Duke of Rutland and Duke of Norfolk [SAC Vol 73].

In a later 'restoration' (1871) the window was removed. Many questions as to its disappearance have been asked. but its whereabouts, if it still exists, are not known. The rebuilding of Sele Priory 1787/90, when some windows were taken to Buncton chapel. Did another local chapel benefit? Look around!

7.9 St. Nicholas Church, Bramber, in 1785 by S.Hopper

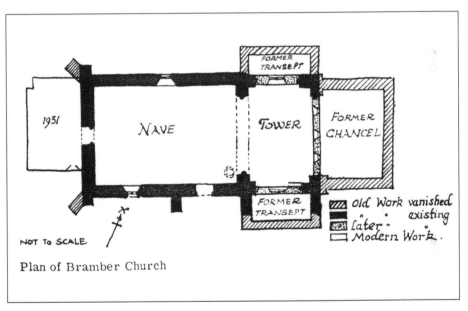

7.9a Revd. Arnold's plan of St.Nicholas Church, Bramber.
See 2.1a for a similar plan for St. Peter's.

Buzzing over Beeding

In the summer of 1911, an unusual sound was heard in the sky above these Adur Valley villages. It was the sound of an internal combustion engine propelling kite-like assemblies of bamboo spars held together with piano wire, covered with varnished linen. This was the year of the 'Circuit of Europe' air race. Shoreham was a staging post and a great number of the planes passed over Beeding and Small Dole. One lady, a pupil here at the time, remembers the event as being 'the most exciting thing I ever saw.'

The first 'heavier than air' flight is credited to the Wright Bros, at Kittyhawk, USA in December 1903. Flights were made in England from 1908, but were only short hops. S. F. Cody, an American employed by the army Balloon Section, made a flight of some 400 yards at Laffan's Plain in February 1909.

Louis Bleriot was the first to cross the English Channel in an aeroplane, but an attempt was made by Hubert Latham on 19th July 1909 which ended mid-channel when his engine failed. He obtained another plane and while preparing for another attempt, Bleriot made a successful crossing on the 25th July. He made a sporting offer to Latham by telegraph saying that he would share the prize put up by the 'Daily Mail' if he succeeded in crossing that day. Unfortunately, the weather deteriorated and it was two days later that he made his second attempt. Once again his engine failed, this time only one mile from Dover.

H. H. Piffard, an early aviator, is known as the first to fly from Shoreham aerodrome, then a dry saltmarsh or large meadow. Piffard built his first aeroplane, the 'Mayfly' and quite often got it into the air. An altitude of 30 feet was a major triumph. In 1911, O. C. Morrison flew from Hove Lawns to Shoreham in seven minutes, but it was the Pashley brothers who made the most impact. Before the First World War, they had a flying school at the aerodrome and we can be grateful to them for the early aerial photographs of this area.

Some of our older residents can remember a plane crash at Small Dole before the First World War. This was an aeroplane of the Naval Air Service; others remember an aeroplane landing in the brooks north of Beeding and taking off again.

The Train now standing in Church Lane!

Bungalow Town, on Shoreham Beach, was noted for its colony of people from the entertainment world. This settlement took off sometime in the early years of this century. Many of the dwellings were basically railway carriages, without wheels and bogies, topped by a corrugated iron pitched roof. Shipwrights and boatbuilders abounded in the area, and bungalows which survive today testify to their good workmanship.

Several of these homes have come to light. This is probably due to the enthusiasts of the many private railway companies seeking all sorts of restorable rolling stock for their lines. Queen Victoria's coach was discovered at West Chiltington by the 'LB&SCR Bogie Coach Fund' and will probably, after much rebuilding and refurbishment, be seen again on the Bluebell Railway.

Those keen observers who travel the Coombes-Botolphs road on a regular basis will no doubt have seen the railway coach between Lancing College and Coombes. It was once used as a dwelling but is now a store, or perhaps a chicken house.

The establishment of the Lancing Carriage Works by the LB&SCR in 1913 made redundant carriages more available locally. A comfortable home could be made for less than £100. The works no longer exist and the area is covered by the Churchill Industrial Estate.

One such bungalow existed in Church Lane, Upper Beeding, opposite the Primary School. Local intelligence has it that it was erected around 1915 and occupied by a Miss Cox. Later, the Sowton family lived there and are pictured in a photographic postcard probably taken between the wars. It was demolished to make way for two houses, 'Conifers' and 'Greenbanks'.

The picture shows an attractive looking residence with more than its share of front windows. Members of the family are seen tending the front garden which contained an extensive pergola. It was called 'Downsville'.

My thanks to Matilda O'Shea.

Charity

We have seen in past articles the harsh treatment of people under the 'poor laws' in earlier times, such as parish relief, means testing and the whipping of beggars. Life was very hard for most working folk in those days, but there was another side to their existence.

A footnote in a book titled *Magdalen Studies* mentions a Mrs Blackman of Beeding. 'Mrs. Blackman spent the whole of her long life in the Village and remembered Dr.Bloxam quite well. The Doctor was much loved by his people, to whom he was very generous in cases of sickness or of poverty. He had very large congregations at Beeding Church, and a large Sunday school'. The article goes on to say that Dr. Bloxam lent the children of the village warm red clothes every winter. These were returned to him in the summer in exchange for more suitable clothing.

Henry Allen was another person who cared for the less well-off in the village. He was vicar for forty years (1680-1720) and his will, proved by his wife, Anna, on 7th February 1720, left £5 per year for local people. The benefaction was on or about the feast of St. Michael and was to be distributed among four poor widows of the Parish, not having any public relief and who constantly kept their Church and who could read and say their Catechism. It appears that there were not always four widows to receive their £1.5s.0d.one hundred years ago. Bloxam records only those who received £1. 13s. 4d. each. They were Ann Nicholls, Jenny Stoner and Frances Weller. This was a generous sum in those days. A joint of beef could be had for the odd fourpence! The bequest is still in being as part of the Rector's Discretionary Fund.

St. Thomas' Day, 21st December, was popularly known as 'Gooding Day'. H. A. Lower records: 'The old women of every parish went from house to house to beg something wherewith to provide for the festivities of Christmas.' It is known that the Rev. J. R. Bloxam used to sit at his study window and hand a half-crown to any old woman who 'sold' him a sprig of evergreen.

See *The Early Years* [18.1(1)] for examples of
Vestry book entries regarding help for the poor of the parish.

Gnomonics

Trains and buses to catch, busy days full of appointments, make timekeeping necessary. Precise time to the second has only been around for about 150 years. Before the emergence of 'railway time' in 1850, there was no uniform time in the British Isles. Regions differed from London; Plymouth was 16 minutes adrift for example. This was accepted. People along the turnpikes would set their watches by the mail coaches, which were not always on time.

The first observance of the passing of time probably began in the Middle East. The Egyptians divided the 24 hours into 'night' (sunset to sunrise), and 'day' (sunrise to sunset). Each of these periods was divided into 12 hours, regardless of the season. so that the hours varied from 50 minutes in midwinter to 70 minutes at midsummer. Sundials are known to exist at least seven centuries before Christ. Ptolemy (circa 140 AD) provided all the details of this science in his 'De Analemmate'. Alfred the Great calibrated the candle, and it is recorded that a clock was installed at Westminster in 1288.

In the Navy, the sandglass was in use until Victorian times to regulate the watches at sea. Bells sounded as the glass was turned each half hour. Eight bells indicated the end of the four hour watch, one watch being divided into two 'Dog Watches' so that sailors did not have to keep the same watch every day.

Locally, the passage of time was recorded during the Middle Ages by a vertical sundial. One such dial still exists on the south wall of St. Botolphs Church, a little to the east of the porch. A 'gnomon' (a straight piece of metal) was driven into the wall and a plum line marked the noon position. Usually the Parish Priest provided calibrations to suit the Masses as he wished to take them. These incised divisions were known as 'Scratch Dials'. Perhaps they had more sun in those far-off days!

The 'Green' Farmer

Over the last decade we have seen a growing abundance of produce while many starve in the Third World. It is said to be uneconomical to ship the surplus. Many concerned people think that we should take out only what we need, which would appear to be a sensible idea.

In these modern times with agricultural technology studied at universities and chemical organizations manufacturing huge quantities of fertilizers and pesticides, one wonders how the farmers in earlier times managed their soil husbandry.

Listening to old Beeding inhabitants and researching early estate books, you appreciate the efforts made to keep the land fertile. One example was the use of animals. In the 19th century, a farmer kept sheep primarily for their manure. Mutton and wool were of secondary importance. Sheep were grazed on the Downs during the day, brought down and systematically folded at night in selected fields to enrich the soil. A breed of sheep was established that only dropped their manure at night in the fold. Power for the farm was provided by horses and oxen. The Sussex yeoman preferred the ox for ploughing, they were slower than horses but more sure, and while horses needed much stored hay and oats in winter, oxen could exist on hedge clippings and less grain.

To condition the soil, chalk was burned to make lime. This was carried out at Erringham (cement works), Castletown, and at Golding quarry, still in use for road materials. Sand from the seashore was used in great quantities on the claylands of the estuary. Much of Beeding would be flooded at high tides if it were not for the river banks.

Delving into 'Vestry' minute books, many entries record the use of unemployed poor for scraping the roads around Beeding clear of animal droppings. Cartloads were auctioned to farmers, the money being put to the 'poor rate'.

Now, using pesticides and destroying hedgerows and coppice, much of the food of small creatures and birds has been extinguished. With these gone and nesting places no longer available, the bird and wild animal population drastically cut, even more spraying is necessary.

8.2 A Sussex shepherd's smock. See 8.5.
(St. Mary's archive)

8.2a Sussex shepherd, George Bailey, tends his flock on the Downs

The Village Hall

The three main venues for village meetings in mediaeval times were the Manor House for Court Leet or Court Baron, the local inn and the church. The Manorial Court enforced the customs of the manor and was presided over by the Lord or his Steward. The inn was usually the centre of the local intelligence network. Sometimes the vestry meetings were held there. These were the forerunners of the modern parish councils which replaced the vestry in 1894. The King's Head and The Rising Sun (formerly The Star) were both used for this purpose. The early churches did not usually have any seating and parishioners stood for services, with the elderly and infirm resting against the sides of the nave, giving rise to the expression 'going to the wall' when people were in trouble. When it was necessary to hold public meetings, the body of the church was used as a village hall with the chancel being sacred and only occupied by monks and clergy. Later, meetings were held in the vestry, hence 'Vestry Meeting', the ecclesiastical parish council.

The village hall, a modern institution, was born out of the three meeting places. Small Dole was the first to have a village hall in 1911. Upper Beeding made do with a room in High Street (now demolished to provide access to Saltings Way). A new village hall was built circa 1930 on land acquired in two parcels from Arthur Wood: one piece was purchased in 1927 for £150 and an adjoining section in 1929 for £70. The present Hall now occupies this site in High Street. The title deeds were signed by the trustees on the 6th June 1931. They were: Thomas Horatio Fowler, Hatton G. Sugden, Thomas Daniel Cross, and George Thomas Hobbs. Mr. Cross, the founder of the Baptist movement in Upper Beeding, lived at Beeding Court from the early 20th century. Extensions and improvements were carried out over the years and now the building blended with the local scene. It hosted Horticultural Society shows, the WI (probably the first institution to be associated with the Village Hall), the Adur Players, a Playgroup and many public meetings including the Parish Council. Long may it survive.

The Wheelwright

I have often wondered how the world would have developed without the wheel. No one knows who invented it, if 'invent' is the right word. It more than likely evolved from the wooden roller.

The Egyptians knew all about rollers some 6000 years ago. The Great Pyramid was built by Pharaoh Khufu. It took twenty years and employed 100,000 workers. Nearly 500ft high, it was built on the inclined plane principal using rollers and levers. Within the structure, the wheel is depicted on their drawings of chariots. Some thousand years later, Stonehenge was constructed using the same system of transport. Many of the megaliths were brought from Wales by river and sea, and by roller overland to the site on Salisbury Plain.

The wheelwright was an occupation that may be older than the blacksmith. Wooden wheels on wooden axles were probably in use before metal was worked. Even when progress was made from the slice of log with a hole in the centre, the wooden wheel was outwardly a simple object, made up of many different parts.

The cart and coach wheel consisted of as many as twenty different pieces. First the hub, or nave, of turned hardwood, then the spokes, each tapered and shaped by a 'spokeshave'. The outer rim was composed of several felloes (fellys) – pieces of wood with a radius that fitted onto the spokes to form a circle. An iron tyre was prepared, smaller than the outer rim, heated then shrunk onto the wheel clamping the whole assembly together. This took the wear of the road.

There were several wheelwrights in our villages of Upper Beeding and Small Dole. One well known wheelwright William Luckin, recorded in the 1841 census, lived with his wife Sarah, daughters Silvia and Mary, and his apprentice Walter Turner in Beeding Street, probably at the old Bakehouse. William Luckin is recorded as a widower lodging with William Burgess at Phoenix Place, Upper Beeding in the 1851 census. William Weaver and George Weller resided at Small Dole.

The Smock

I wrote in an earlier article [4.5] that an area east of Pound Lane, some ten acres, shown on a map of 1733, was called the 'Flaxlands'. Whether flax was grown only for local consumption or some exported as a cash crop, we cannot say. Flax flourished in low lying water meadows. Linseed oil was extracted from it, but equally important, linen was manufactured from the plant. It required much water in processing, so the Brooklands of north Beeding were an ideal place.

Linen was the material which was used to make the smock worn by most agricultural labourers from the 17th to the early 20th century. The history of this garment is obscure. It is believed to have developed from a lady's undergarment (later called a shift or chemise). 'Frock' was a name given to the full skirted coat worn by men until the end of the 18th century. In the *Purefoy letters** of 1741, Henry Purefoy describes the clothes of a 'strange man' from Lincolnshire. 'Hee wears a blueish grey broad cloth coat and wast coat and a white ffrock over, buttoned at the hands like a shirt'. In a letter of 1746, Henry requests his tailor to 'bring the coachman a linnen frock to put over his cloathes when hee rubs his horse down'.

It appears that there were two main types of smock: that worn by the working agricultural labourer, with limited gathering (smocking) around the chest, whilst many tradesmen wore elaborately embroidered smocks for best over the 'Sunday' suits, and were tightly fastened around the neck and wrists. I believe the latter were dust-coats. As a young boy in these villages when many horses were employed in agriculture and as daily transport, I remember the dust and straw from dried horse droppings swirling around at the slightest breeze, stinging the eyes, bringing much discomfort on windy days. Water carts had to be employed on a regular basis in the High Streets around here. No wonder then, that people wore clothes that protected their better garments. Do any of our older readers remember 'Hoss' who used to drive the water cart?

*See M. Hall *Smocks* Shire Publications

8.5 An elaborately stitched ploughboy's blouse
(from Weldon's famous Practical Smocking)
(*St. Mary's archive*)

Entertainment

The village plays which were produced up to the war reflected the Sussex dialect as it had been spoken in earlier centuries. Looking at old scripts one can sometimes detect the regional differences by the spelling of the words. Many of the plays had been handed down by word of mouth from mediaeval times, gaining or losing in content according to the narrator. It was not until Victorian times that many of these obscure pageants were written down and so reflect the Sussex doggerel. Most plays featured tragedy, comedy, fantasy, magic, good and evil, with good usually triumphant!

Travelling players were often seen at fairs and markets, usually working their way around the counties. The village play was produced by the villagers, mainly from relics of old 'mummers' plays. Titles such as 'St. George and the Turkish Knight' and 'The Brown Pot' were adapted from early religious pageants. 'Barnaby's Brat' dates from the time of Edward II.

The 'Adur Players' were formed by Madge Cook, and the inaugural meeting attracted some forty potential 'thespians'. Their first effort was 'Loves a Luxury' which was staged in the present Village Hall. Before the hall was built in the 1930s, local events were presented in the old hall, which was over a boat repair workshop used by Mr. Adams. The site of this hall now forms the entrance to Saltings Way in the High Street.

Another venue was the Mission Hall opposite Dacre Gardens. This corrugated iron structure held services, Sunday school, magic lantern shows and many other events. The Towers Convent hosts local occasions, charity functions for the village, and produces many dramatic events which form part of the education of their pupils, with facilities which would be the envy of many small theatres.

Other local entertainment took the form of fetes usually staged for church funds. Mediaeval buildings need much maintenance. We are the custodians of three of these ancient structures and must pass them on to future generations in good order.

8.6 Village children dressed up for the annual Bramber and Beeding Fete 1927 – a popular event in the local calendar

8.6a Model train (⅓rd scale) in the grounds of Bramber Castle
(by courtesy of Gill Fox)

The Parish Magazine

Like many others, I am getting rather fed up with all the 'freebies' and junk mail that drop through my letterbox with alarming regularity. The dustmen are not amused either! Forests are disappearing to provide the paper that is probably unread and goes straight in the 'bin'. Not so long ago the parish magazine provided all the news and advertising needed by the communities.

In earlier times people were made aware of what was going on by information gathered at the local inn or church. Few could read or write, which was not a reflection on their intelligence, just the fact that learning was only for the most affluent.

The earliest announcements were made by the 'Town Crier', who was a literate man with a loud voice. Thanks to men like Raikes, Bell and Lancaster, who promoted education for the poor, the Victorian Age saw basic learning being made available to nearly all young people. As the population became more literate, the Town Crier faded into obscurity. Newspapers and information sheets as we know them today, emerged and gained popularity with the public exercising their new-found reading skills.

An ecclesiastical census in 1851 indicated that many churches were inadequate and from 1852 many were enlarged, as was our St. Peter's. From this time, as printing became less expensive, the parish magazine emerged to focus local attention on religious and other interesting information which concerned the rural communities without their own local newspaper.

The first known parish magazine in Beeding was produced in 1898, and reported on all church and village matters, results of fund-raising competitions, and who did what that month. It was also a calendar highlighting special days. The old parish magazine is one of the first things historians look at when researching a community as this information may not appear anywhere else and is of great value. In 1989 a set of six volumes of *The Villager* were sold by a bookseller for £25.

The Local Brew

Before Queen Victoria came to the throne there was little tea or coffee available. These were imported at great expense from India, China and South America. They were not for ordinary villagers, who would have to pay around half a year's wages for a pound of tea.

Cottagers usually made their own ginger beer. Inns and taverns provided refreshment to travellers and local drinkers who sought company. Farms usually had a brew-house within their curtilage, producing three main types of brewed beverage: small beer, ale beer and strong beer. Ale was a very mild table beer. It contained scarcely any alcohol and could be drunk to any extent without producing the least unpleasant effect. Small beer was less potent than this. It was made by adding a small quantity of fresh malt to that from which the ale had been brewed, fermenting the liquor with yeast. Neither this nor ale would keep for more than a month or so in hot weather, and had to be freshly brewed, but it admirably suited the purpose for which it was intended. The water it was made with, having been boiled for some time, was free from deleterious germs, an advantage to health in a society which often had cess-pits adjacent to wells.

Strong beer was a different thing altogether. Generally brewed in October, it was extremely potent, and was usually kept for a year. It has been described as 'Lunatic's Broth' and other choice names. N. P. Blaker, in his *Sussex in Bygone Days* (1906), said: 'A gentleman living in Henfield, always kept a good supply of this, and guests leaving the house found the road not only tortuous but much too narrow!'

A 'huckster' was a person who sold ale in the street. Hugh and Thomas Kidd of Beeding Street were hucksters. The Kidd family at one time owned Beeding Mill and were a well known Beeding family (1841 census).

Magna Carta (1215) laid down standard measures for wine and ale. The Assize of Bread and Ale (1267) allowed the civic authority in each locality to fix the price of bread and ale, based on the current prices of corn and malt.

Early Calculations

While surveying the grounds of St. Mary's Bramber for Miss Ellis, its owner, a local historian discovered what was at first sight a tarnished silver disc. This turned out to be a most important coin. It was a shilling piece of the reign of Philip and Mary (1553-1558) dated 1554. One may say 'What is so important? Other shillings from the same die must exist'. This is true, but numismatists know that this series of coins was a milestone in mathematics, being different from the established practice of the issue of minted coins by the Treasury. Interest centered on the date. This was in Arabic numerals. Usually it was put in Roman numerals. The date and place of manufacture was indicated by a mintmark. This was a small symbol within the design such as a leopard's head, a tun or an arrow, being a reference known only to the Royal Mint.

The fact that this date was in Arabic numerals indicated a revolutionary method of arithmetic had reached Britain and had been accepted by the government. Before this the Roman system of numbering was used in Europe. Counting was done on a 'chequer' board using counters mainly produced in Nuremberg. These were very thin with an engraved design, often being referred to as 'jettons' and were roughly the diameter of our present ten pence piece.* The person counting progressed up the board in a way that was similar to the use of the 'abacus'. Some operators were amazingly quick at this use of a 'chequer' board (hence Exchequer).

The modern way of numbering with the zero first followed by the digits 123456789 is known as the Arabic system, although the method was Indian in origin. Al-Kwarizimi, a Persian mathematician (circa 830), used this way of calculating, but it was the Arabs who introduced the zero, the lack of which had been a serious drawback to earlier arithmetic.

*The Florin [i.e. 2 shillings = 10p] was the first attempt at a decimal coinage in 1847 when it was introduced as one tenth of a pound. [KN-B]

Fishing*

The Compleat Angler (1653) was written by Izaak Walton (1593-1683). Its popularity indicates that river fishing had become more of a sport than an urgent need to catch food. Many landowners had created ponds and lakes for their fish stocks, but this was basically for the table. Rivers were valuable assets. Land adjoining inland water was at a premium if it had fishing rights.

We first hear of local fishing grants in a document of Sele Priory [2nd June 1438] in which John, Duke of Norfolk, confirmed an earlier gift to the Priory of Sele, of John de Brawysa (Braosa) of the mills and fisheries from the church of Old Shoreham to the place called 'Bedeney' (Bedney Corner, near St. Peter's) [Will, Lewes]

In 1624 Isaac Pocock is vested in the ownership of the fishing between Old Shoreham and Beeding. An entry in Dr. Bloxam's History adds: 'this privilege was afterwards inserted in the lease of the Priory of Sele, 'together also with the fishing of the river from Beeding to Old Shoreham. This addition has so continued through all subsequent leases to the present time'. Another entry says: 'The site of the ancient Priory of Sele with the remainder of the buildings, with a piece of ground computed at 6 acres, and the fishing of all the waters from a place called Beding to Old Shoreham church was granted by lease from Magdalen College to the minister of Sele (dated 1722)'.

In 1882, Mr. Long of the Beeding Company writes to the Revd. Bloxam DD to complain of men from Shoreham fishing the river with an immense net and 'cathing everything... nothing larger than a lead pencil escaping them, the net being so fine'. A newspaper report of 1890 records the appearance in court of Lewis Rasbrook of Shoreham and two of his family for fishing with a net in close season at Upper Beeding (30th May). They were fined 2/6 each including costs. So who owns the fishing rights now? I cannot find any reference to these being any other body, so can the incumbent give permission for the choir to drown a few worms?

* The first paragraph above is repeated in 17.9,
but the general subject-matter differs in each case. [Ed.]

What's in a Name?

In an earlier article [6.1] I tried to explain how names and surnames developed in mediaeval times, from locations and occupations. Victorians had Christian and surnames, but in many cases, especially in villages and farming communities, local characters were known by their nicknames. Some places had alternative names too.

Men with the surname White were sometimes called 'Chalky' or more likely 'Knocker', Miller was 'Dusty', whilst Lee was 'Tancy', Clerk 'Nobby', Martin 'Pincher'*, Wilson 'Tug'*, and so on. If a person was unusually tall he was dubbed 'Lofty'. Nicknames were not very often applied to the female gender.

In 1896 a book entitled *Henfield Folk 55 Years Ago – Gleanings About Henfield, by an Old Henfielder* was published. Written by Allen Davy (at the age of 65), he records, among other things, most of the residents along the Henfield Road in the 1840s. His area is from Upper Beeding (Horton) to Henfield itself. Horton Farm had the alternative name of 'Beggar's Fields'.

I only mention the residents with nicknames. He records that 'William Woolgar was called 'Dead Horse'. He lived next door to a chap named Whiteing, called 'Old Bad Job'. He was a very good hand at farming work, but whenever you saw him at work it was always the 'very worst job he ever had.' On to a place called 'Old Man's Neck'; there lived two Sayers: 'Sixfoot' and 'Old Tippy'. Another Sayer, Richard, was a resident of Nightingale Hall.

We get to know why Edwards, a thatcher, is called 'Fainty'. Alan Davy relates the reason: apparently when having a spree he would say "Now my lads, don't be fainty, let's have another quart." At times his old lady would go to fetch him home and he would offer her beer, but she would not take the 'sixpenny'. After a time Edwards would say 'bring my old 'duman a pint of eight-penny', landlord' and the old lady would sit down and make herself happy until it was time to fetch the cows.

* Naval nicknames

Sele - A Saxon Settlement

Beeding was founded by a Saxon chief, Beida, in 501AD (*Anglo Saxon Chronicle*). The mediaeval village was to the south of Beeding Court Farm. After the Norman Conquest Beeding extended north along the causeway (High St.), but in early documents Beeding was referred to as the hamlet of Sele. So where was Sele or Zelle? The original settlement was around the present church and priory. This area is a gravel mound or raised beach which extends south west to Coombes, also providing high ground for Beeding Court farm buildings. It was suitable for settling on - most of the surrounding estuary land was tidal, so buildings needed to be above high water level.

We first hear of Sele in *Beowulf*, the heroic poem of the Middle Ages. 'Sele' in this piece of Saxon literature means 'happiness'. It also meant a dwelling, large or small, and in our case could refer to a Saxon hall or large house which probably stood where the church and priory are now. The site was probably used for pagan worship before the entry of St. Wilfrid into Sussex at around 681AD when he brought Christianity to our county.

The first Christian church on the site was most likely a small two-storey wattle-and-daub-finished timber structure with a round or semi-circular apse. It may have been the Saxon hall. At different times in the year one can see in the grass of the priory garden, patterns of the earlier buildings. These can be seen quite clearly from the bell tower of St. Peter's, especially the half-round apse to the east.

The *Domesday* survey (1086) records two churches. This could mean that the original church had been replaced by a more permanent structure near by. The earlier one was still in use, perhaps by the monks who occupied the newly-built priory. All that remains of that early church is the base of the existing tower, which was repaired and rebuilt from 20 feet above ground around 1283. In 1308 there was a service to dedicate the almost completely rebuilt church of St. Peter and St. Paul at Sele. The apex of the nave is off-centre where it joins the tower, as it was widened at that time. There was a mediaeval south aisle, existing in 1627 but removed by c.1800. It was replaced in 1852.

Oxen

In 1989 Beeding and Bramber 'Twin Aid' provided ten oxen for third world villages. They cost £80 each. Tractors would have cost £5000, beyond our finances. Oxen at the end of their working life can still be a great asset.

Oxen are frequently recorded in the Bible. They were the motive power of earlier times. Without the ox and plough the population of the world would be much less than it is today. When the Bible records transactions which involve oxen, this being the basic exchange rate mechanism or early ECU, it did not always mean oxen in the flesh. From the Bronze Age onwards, ingots of metal, mainly copper, were used as currency; many have been discovered, impressed with the figure of an ox. These were believed to have been equal to the value of one ox.

For the observant, cast-off ox shoes can be found here in the fields and pathways of the Adur Valley. These are lozenge-shaped and look like half a horseshoe, two being fitted to each cloven hoof. Unlike the horse, the ox was not able to raise its legs. As a small boy I witnessed the shoeing of oxen in the fields here. The beast had to be pushed onto its side and the legs tied together while the smith did his work, the worn shoes often being cast aside on the spot.

Ox teams were used in our downland area up to the Second World War. They were patient beasts. A yoke of two oxen could do the work of a horse. In heavy claylands, their steady pull was preferred to the horse. Oxen were easier to feed in winter and could exist on leaves and hedge clippings, whereas a horse needed much hay and oats to survive.

The ox was used for pulling heavy wagons and other large objects. A Brighton man who was a known tippler said: "While wending my way home at dawn I met a windmill going the other way" (1797). This was quite true. The post mill was being moved from Belleview Field (Regency Square) to the Dyke Road by 86 oxen. It was later moved from there to Duncton Down above Clayton to become 'Jill', the companion to 'Jack'.

Great Storms

The great gale of October 16, 1987 will be remembered for a very long time. The devastation was far greater than any living person could recall.

Records of storms in the Middle Ages suggest that there are many parallels. The Anglo-Saxon Chronicle (that authentic voice of England, from Roman occupation to the 12th century) has an entry for 793 AD. It relates: 'In this year, forboding omens came over the land of Northumbria and wretchedly terrified the people. There were excessive whirlwinds, lightening storms, and firy dragons were seen flying in the sky. These signs were followed by a great famine.' On the morning of St. Laurence's Day in the year 1103 it is recorded that a wind did more damage than any man remembered before. There are many such entries in the 1100s.

The first recorded sea floods and catastrophic storms on the South Coast were in 1278 when the sea engulfed the ancient settlement of Brighthelmston (Brighton), a fishing village, and many other parts of Sussex. 1348 (the year the Black Death came to England through Shoreham) was another date of great storms in our area. Three and a half centuries later Daniel Defoe gives a graphic account of the damage done by the storm of 1700. He tells of the 'Dreadful Tempest' and mentions that 'Brighthelmston, being an old built and poor, tho' populous town was most miserably torn to pieces and made a picture of desolation, that it lookt as if an enemy had sackt it'. Two windmills were blown down and many ships and boats from Sussex were lost with the lives of many sailors.

Here in Upper Beeding an incident following a storm made headlines in a London paper. This is recorded in Dr. Bloxam's history of the parish. A man named Goddard*, aged 66, was killed by a falling tree by St. Peter's Church on what is today known as the Glebeland. The picture on the front cover of *The Penny Illustrated Paper* shows the falling elm tree with Goddard under it. The view is from the south and, apart from the gravestones, presumably the present churchyard. There appears to be a ruined tower with a Gothic arch east of the chancel. Maybe this is part of the old priory not removed in the rebuilding of the 1790s and still in being in February 1866, the date on the paper. It may just be artistic licence.

* Goddard owned the tea-rooms in Bramber Street.

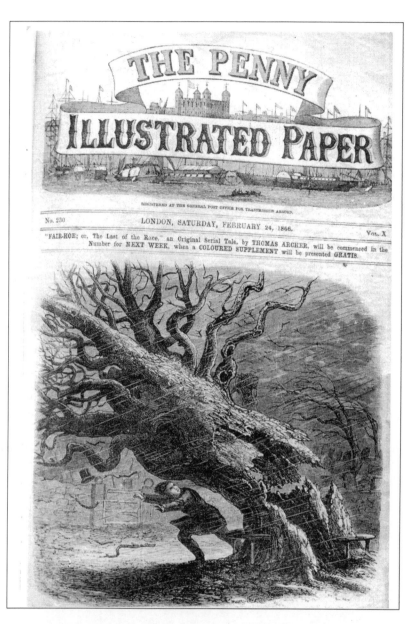

9.2 Dramatic drawing of a fatal accident when an ancient elm tree in the glebeland was blown over in a great storm, crushing a villager to death

Potter's Museum

Generations of families have been delighted by a visit to Potter's Museum. It was a popular venue for Sunday School and choir outings, so popular in fact, that the London Brighton & South Coast Railway had to extend Bramber Station platform until it was the longest in Southern England, to accommodate all the coaches and prevent excited children falling on to the rails.

As a youngster in the 1930s I spent many weekends with Edgar and Mrs. Collins, who were friends of my grandfather. Walter Potter had made models for my grandfather's medical lectures (he was a surgeon RAMC). When the museum contents were sold, I was asked if I would like to choose a momento. I chose a sawfish saw and a barbed wooden spear which I have shown to the children of Beeding School in chats on Victorian 'things'.

Walter Potter, born in Bramber in 1835, lived in the 'White Lion Hotel' which was altered and renamed the 'Castle'. As a boy he was very interested in natural history and preserved birds for his own pleasure. He started his museum when he was about 15 and, in 1861, the first of his specimens was on display in a summer house at the White Lion. This coincided with the opening of the railway. Later, in 1880, the separate building was in use, now part of a private house.

Many local people remember the museum with great nostalgia. Among the best exhibits was the 'Death and Burial of Cock Robin'. Other cases of stuffed birds and animals were presented to identify with nursery rhymes. Several of them came to life by inserting a penny in the slot. Other odd items of taxidermy were a four-legged hen (how did they catch it?) donated by Mr. Earle, butcher of Steyning, who reared it in 1908. Another well-known exhibit was the two-headed lamb. This had been given to Walter by Mr. Bailey, a shepherd, who discovered it in his flock on Beeding Downs.

Walter Potter died on 21st May 1918 and is buried in Bramber churchyard. His life work was sold at auction in 1972.*

*Sold at auction again in 2007 and dispersed [Ed.].

9.3 Celebrated Victorian taxidermist, Walter Potter,
seated outside his famous "Museum of Curiosities"

9.3a Walter Potter serving a customer in his shop

Dialect

The first people to use an alphabetic script were the Phoenicians. This was derived from the earliest known Semitic inscriptions c.1500 BC. We can sometimes discover how people spoke in the past by the spelling in old documents.

The modern English alphabet has 26 letters (earlier it had 24, there was no J or U). Scholars of the past wrote words, not to any nationally approved sequence, but phonetically. The same words could have very different spelling in Birmingham compared with East Anglia or Southern England. Spoken as spelt, words often indicated their area of origin.

Until the Second World War, most villages had a majority of residents who were born into that village, a legacy of the manorial system. Census material shows us that Beeding was populated by a great majority of agricultural labourers until the late 19th century. Modern Beeding has developed into a dormitory for people who work and shop outside the village. Many of the words and customs are now gone, and modern schooling has displaced earlier speech.

We are indebted to the Revd. W. D. Parish, Vicar of Selmeston (pronounced Simpson) who, in 1875, published a *Dictionary of the Sussex Dialect* [updated by Helena Hall in 1957] in which he preserved many of the old words and sayings of this county.

Flax was a crop grown on the east of Pound Lane. Parish says: "With the scutching and hitchelling or itchelling (hackling) to produce a carded thread called tire, which was then spun, woven, fulled and tented, by which various processes it became linen". The finisher was called a 'tainter'.

Asking the gardener why he is closing the gates early he replied: "Well I 'ears there's a couple of willocky (mad) bullicks about the village an' a bullick soon makes a tidy (considerable) 'avick in a garden". 'Going a gooding', is a custom well known in Beeding, referring here to a charity given by Dr. Bloxam. 'Donkey Tea' was a cool drink made from charred bread; tea was too expensive for 19th century workers. 'Tussie-Mussies' were small bunches of mixed flowers which children gave their mothers.

John Rouse Bloxam

The Parish Council and the District Council have decided to name the new housing development to the south of the extra-mural cemetery at St. Peter's, Bloxam Close, to perpetuate the memory of John Rouse Bloxam.

Dr. Bloxam was the vicar of Beeding from 1862 until his death in 1891. His photograph shows a spare figure but, in the Church of England, he was a giant. He lived at Sele Priory, which was the vicarage at that time. As a young man, he was curate to John Henry Newman (later Cardinal) at the Parish of Littlemore. Bloxam was to become a lifelong friend of Newman, even after Newman joined the Church of Rome. It was under Bloxam's direction that the 'Oxford Movement' revived ceremonial in the Church of England. The centenary of his death has been marked by the Church with a commemorative issue of a limited edition of an English bone-china mug.

Bloxam is best remembered here as the founder of Beeding School, a gift to the village in 1871 and still going strong 120 years later. I mentioned some of his other works in an earlier edition [12.7]. He was a most caring man who provided winter clothing for less well off families in the area and saw that the older villagers had coal during the winter months.

Bloxam was also a very good historian. He transcribed the parish registers and they are now available to researchers (copies are held by the Beeding and Bramber Local History Society). He kept a scrapbook entitled 'Rough Notices of Beeding Parish' which is a mine of information on the area from the earliest times, and is interleaved with letters, certificates and much interesting memorabilia from the past.

Richard Rouse Bloxam, his father, married Ann the sister of Sir Thomas Lawrence, President of the Royal Academy. Many of Lawrence's sketches were to be seen around the parish before the Second World War, as he gave many away to his pupils at the Priory.

See 11.12 for more about Dr. Bloxam

9.5 The Revd. Dr. John Rouse Bloxam
(*by courtesy of the President and Fellows of Magdalen College, Oxford*)

9.5a The tomb of Dr. Bloxam in Beeding churchyard

IN MEMORY OF
JOHN ROUSE BLOXAM D.D.
VICAR OF UPPER BEEDING
LATE FELLOW OF St. MAGDALEN COLLEGE
OXFORD
WHO DIED JAN 21st 1891
AGED 83 YEARS.
JESU! MERCY

The Automobile

There must be very few residents in these villages who do not know of, or have not observed, the rebuilding of Beeding Garage. Readers may remember the earlier articles [6.8 & 6.10] in which I wrote about the origins and early history of the Garage site, which developed from the old forge of blacksmith Harry Tribe. No doubt these improvements will remain in the present form for many years. The foregoing poses questions: who invented service stations? Who invented the petrol-driven automobile? Many will claim that they were Etienne Lenoir, or Karl Benz, Gottlieb Daimler, or Selden and the Duryea brothers from the USA. But who was the true inventor?

The first automobile to use an internal combustion engine using liquid petroleum as fuel was invented by an Austrian, Siegfried Marcus. He drove his first vehicle in Vienna on April 9th 1865, the same day that the American Civil War came to an end. Marcus was a Jew. When the Nazis invaded Europe they tried to erase mention of the fact that Benz and Daimler were not the true inventors of the motor car. This ploy did not work. The truth was too well documented.

At the turn of the 20th century many engineers were engaged in producing and improving automobiles. One of these pioneers was Harry Ricardo. Ricardo's engines were manufactured at Shoreham in a small boatyard next to the Bridge Hotel and initially were for marine use. Much of the fishing fleet was powered by his 9hp unit

He went into production of his 'Dolphin' motor car some time before 1908 as this was the date of the first advertisement for the car in motoring journals. The 15hp car was £400 and the 28hp £500. No doubt several were on the roads around Beeding in the first decades of this century.

Harry Ricardo, later Sir Harry, at one time lived at Tottington Farm. Matilda O'Shea remembers that she enjoyed the figs from the trees at the farm and recalls being frightened as a small girl by the turkeys which were kept there from time to time.

Issue No. C*

It seems no time at all that I was sitting at my typewriter composing an introduction for the history article of the first *Villager* magazine. It's hard to believe that this is my hundredth article. Friends and older residents have been most helpful with information on earlier village life, and I thank you all for your memories.

Another anniversary that occurs on July 3rd is the 10th year of the opening of the bypass for the three villages. What a splendid day it was with over 700 local schoolchildren marching to a point on the new road where the civil parishes of Beeding, Bramber and Steyning meet (between the two bridges). Tara Tysoe, a little eight year old pupil of Upper Beeding Primary School, set things in motion by cutting the red ribbon at Beeding Court Roundabout and planting a tree (still flourishing) with other children.

With the District Council elections resolved and strictly regulated, it is interesting to look back two hundred years to 1791 when Bramber was what is now known as a 'rotten borough', returning two members to Parliament but with only a handful of eligible voters.

The election of 1791 was so scandalous that it was investigated by a House of Commons Select Committee. Sir H. Gough-Calthorpe, Bart, was the Burgess at the time. All the leading members of Bramber Borough were questioned as to the methods of election procedure. One curious fact emerged: various persons, living outside the Borough, were in the habit of going to Steyning a short while before the election. They made a show of boiling pots and kettles in the street to make it appear that they were inhabitants.

At this time votes were bought by prospective members for large sums of money and landlords forced their tenants to vote as directed. Known as 'scot and lot', people inhabiting old houses or the sites of old houses were entitled to vote, and at election time had to vote openly so that all knew who they voted for.

Early Bramber boundaries included part of Church Street, Steyning. William Wilberforce was once an MP for Bramber.**

* Celebrating Keith's 100th (Roman numeral 'C') article for *The Villager*

** There is a much-quoted story of the great William Wilberforce, finding himself passing through an unknown village and, on asking its name and learning it to be Bramber, exclaimed: "Why, this must be the place I'm Member for!" See Picture Gallery for portraits of earlier Members for Bramber: Nicholas Barbon and Sir Richard Gough [Ed.]

9.7 Sir Henry Gough-Calthorpe, Member of Parliament
for Bramber 1734-41 & 1790-96

9.7a William Wilberforce, Member of Parliament for Bramber 1812-25

Superstitions

As I have related in earlier *Villager* articles, Beeding Hill lies on the route of the great east-west road from Canterbury to Southampton. Six roads met on the crest of the hill. Some were 'turnpikes' (toll roads) until the late 18th century, when the A283 to the coast was built under the title 'New Road to Shoreham avoiding Beeding Hill'.

Crossroads and hilltops have in the past been regarded as magical places. Fairy rings and fairies were believed to exist in these areas. Local superstition invested them with healing properties. Dead men and the gallows have also figured largely in cures for many ailments.

Mrs. Latham describes, in Simpson's *Sussex Folklore*, how, in her childhood, walks on Beeding Hill in the 1870s were spoilt by her terror of an ancient gibbet which stood there, and by the gruesome tales concerning it, related to her by her nurse. One of these was about a woman who was cured of a wen on the back of her neck by the touch of a dead murderer's hand. 'She was taken under the gallows in a cart and was held up in order that she might touch the dead hand, and she passed it three times over the wen, and then returned homewards'.

An amusing tale, popular in Sussex nurseries a century or more ago, is of two thieves who stole a pig. They put it in a sack and set off to carry it away, climbing the slopes of Beeding Hill. The day was hot and the pig was heavy, so half way up the hill they stopped for a rest....but they had laid the sack just on top of a fairy's hole. When they they set off again and before they had gone far, the man carrying the sack saw a tiny figure running along by his side and heard it call out in a shrill voice, 'Dick, Dick, where be you?' The man was startled, but then he was terrified to hear another voice from inside the sack.

> "In a sack,
> Pick-a-back.
> Going up Beeding Hill."

The thieves ran off as fast as they could, the fairies nipped back to their hole, and the pig made his way back to the farmer, who was a man always on good terms with the fairies.

Taxes (Part 2)

There are many people today who resent the present community charge and a small number who refuse to pay at all. It appears that this has always been the case with individuals. A form of personal tax had been levied since 1222 AD, but trouble was brewing in the 1370s when a tax of one groat (4d) was imposed on every person over 16. In 1380 this tax was trebled to one shilling (12d = 5p), which led to much unrest and tax gathers were attacked at Fobbing, in Kent, which led to the turmoil known as the Peasants' Revolt.[see 3.12].

King Ethelwulf (sometime of King's Barnes) legalised the lay taxes to the church, (tithes)*, around 855 AD. The main body of country clergy were supported by 'tithes'. Bishops, deans and chapters were endowed with manors and landed estates. The manor of Streatham was originally the stronghold of Earl Warbald, who in 770 AD presented 15 hides of land to Osmund, King of the West Saxons, for church endowments.

The following is from the registers of Bishop Robert Rede 1409 – a 'Monition' for the restoration of tithe retained together with a warning:

'It is reported by notorious rumour, with the assertion of trustworthy men, that certain sons of eternal damnation, parishioners of the Parish Church of Hurstmonceaux and other persons whose names we do not know, wickedly refuse to pay tithes of wool, lambs, sheaves and other things within that parish.....All who refuse to pay within ten days... will incur sentences of greater excommunication. If any obstinately refuse they are to appear before us in the Parish Church of Sele (Beeding) on September 9th to show reasonable cause, if they have any, why they should not incur this sentence, and to receive and do what justice may demand. Also to report what is due and the names of all who are rebellious. Given in our manor of Streatham. Aug. 24th 1409.'

The greater excommunication in those days cut off the offenders from all rites of the church, including Christian burial.

See also 5.1 Taxes (Part1)

*In 1836 tithes were commuted to a rent charge based on the current price of corn. The Tithe Act of 1925 abolished the rent charge and the Tithe Act of 1936 abolished them altogether. [KN-B]

Sanctuary

'It was yet early morning, and mists have scarcely lifted from the Downs above us when a woman hurried from the hillside into the town. Her hair was unkempt, her skirt bedraggled, she wears a hunted look. Isabel, wife of John le Chapelier of Beeding, has committed a crime. A hue and cry is raised and she knows that pursuit follows hard upon her heels. The Parish Priest, concluding his service at the altar, is disturbed by a commotion at the far end of the church. As he turns round, the panting, hunted creature runs toward him and falls exhausted at his feet. Isabel seeks refuge and claims the privilege of sanctuary. The good priest is familiar with such cases. It is not his duty to question this poor creature. In due time the Coroner will pay his visit, and then all will be enquired into. For the present she is safe.'*

Isabel's two children have been found murdered in Beeding. She has made no attempt to hide her crime, she is destitute and without money to buy bread and in the madness of her own hunger she has killed them. All night they have been hunting for her and, had she been caught, she most probably would have been executed on the spot.

Sanctuary was an attempt to ease the hot anger following a crime. A fugitive criminal had the right from Anglo Saxon times to take refuge in a church or churchyard. After 40 days he could confess before the King's representative and submit to banishment rather than face trial.

In 1486 it was decreed that Sanctuary should not protect persons charged with treason. Henry VIII reduced Sanctuary areas and designated the places where refuge might be sought to Derby, Lancaster, Manchester, Northampton, Wells, Norwich, Westminster and York. Sanctuary for crime was abolished in 1623 and for civil offences between 1697 and 1723.

Isabel was tried at a later time. The law was merciful to her for she escaped death, but was banished and could never return to England without the special grace of the King. It is not recorded if this was ever given.

*The Story of Shoreham, H. Cheal

The Screen

I wonder how many communicants pause to look up when leaving St.Peter's, Beeding? Above the south door leading to the porch is a piece of wooden tracery. This fragment is all that is left of an earlier 'Rood Screen'. Sometime before 1852 this screen, which was known to have been in place in 1830, separated the nave from the sanctuary.

On Sunday March 30th 1851, a church census of those attending and the number of sittings was carried out in England. As a consequence of this survey much building work was carried out in the 1830s to enlarge parish churches to cope with the increase in communicants who greatly outnumbered the sittings. In our area the number of C of E worshippers attending Sunday Services was as follows: Morning 4213, Afternoon 3790, Evening 615 (the population of the Steyning area was 16,867).

A faculty was issued in 1852 by Dr. Turner, Bishop of Chichester, for repairing and enlarging Beeding Parish Church. A new south aisle was to be provided to accommodate 80 children and 60 adults. For this it was necessary to take down the gallery at the west end of the church and also to remove the rood screen so that a new arch could be formed between nave and chancel. The faculty cost £12.18s.0d. Magdalen College promised a donation of £100 and a further £100 was provided by the vicar the Revd. George T. Calhoun. Voluntary contributions supplied the remainder.

The foregoing was most probably a result of the work of the 'Oxford Movement', 'the full tide of which was being felt throughout the country which not only produced a better type of churchmanship, but also led to the restoration and renewed beauty of our glorious old churches.' *.

With the removal of the old gallery, the harmonium disappeared and the musicians dispersed. The village shoemaker, named Edwards, was the flautist, a player of great talent and the last of the 19th century instrumentalists.

Perhaps sometime in the future it would be an interesting project to establish by carbon dating or dendrochronology the century that the screen was created. It may be that it was from the earlier rebuilding, recorded as being finished and dedicated to St. Peter and St. Paul on 24th February 1308.

*See Revd. H.E.B.Arnold

Revd. Thomas Hutchinson

Last month I wrote about the Rood Screen and the extension to the church. On consulting Dr. Arnold's unpublished works, further information has come to light. He records facts and figures relating to Dr. Thomas Hutchinson (1787-1812).

Dr. Hutchinson was a Sussex man. His father, also Thomas, was Rector of Cocking, Sussex where Thomas Jnr. was born in 1742. His father later became Vicar of Horsham, quite an important post, where young Thomas met and married a local girl. Our Thomas was described as a ready wit and of harmless humour, but with much talent. Three of his children are recorded in St. Peter's registers.

When appointed to Beeding he found the Revd. John Morgan in charge of the parish on a stipend of £30 per annum. A letter exists from Mr. Morgan, describing the vicarage at that time:

"Dec. 14th 1787. A survey of Sele Vicarage House in Archbishop Laud's time describes it in exactly the same state as Dr. Nicholas found it (1744); since which time he built an oven, new paved the kitchen, put in two new doors, and a very good well curb, and that it is now in good repair, except the garden fence....Dr. Nicholas is ready to pay the sum of £5 due on account of the bridge* at Lady Day 1786'.

It appears that the earlier vicars had not lived at the Priory, but at the 'Manse' in the village, the location of which is not at present positively known.

Soon after Dr. Hutchinson arrived, he had the ancient refectory and other ruined parts of the Priory building pulled down (without the consent of the College) and added three rooms with a cellar at the cost of £800. Perhaps because he did not have permission, the College only granted £150 towards the rebuilding. In 1790/1 a 'Gallile' (gallery)** was erected under the tower of Beeding Church at a cost of £40.... ' Arnold says that this 'Gallile' structure may account for the unusual height of the tower arch, which was often noted as somewhat peculiar.

*Beeding Bridge was rebuilt c.1785 and 'turnpiked'. Before that time the Vicar and Magdalen College, Oxford, were responsible for the upkeep of it.

** Perhaps a misprint for, or version of, 'gallilee', an architectural term applied to a chamber or porch at the western part of the nave. [Ed.]

St. Mary's*, Bramber (Part 2)

There has always been a romantic urge to discover secret passages and buried treasure. St. Mary's is a place where it is more than possible that these are likely to exist. During the last few months, unseen by the many visitors, excavations have been in progress under the stairs. Hopefully this will reveal underground rooms and passages that are known to be there, but the exact location has not yet been determined. During the occupation of Miss Ellis (1945 to 1979) persistent flooding of these cellars forced her to seal them off from the upper part of the building. These spaces once must have been dry and usable. Perhaps they were a part of the property that existed before Waynflete refurbished the bridge and house in the 1470s.

In May 1891 there was a review of Sir Arthur Conan Doyle's *The Musgrave Ritual*. Some of the illustrations from this text, in the Strand Magazine, show features that point to the location of the story being at St. Mary's, in particular referring to the giant trees which, for a hundred years or more, were in the grounds. He also mentions a 'lime walk', parts of which, until only a few years ago, could still be seen. There is also an illustration of a large stone discovered at the bottom of some stairs, but it has not yet been raised). Sir Arthur may have known of the Musgrave family and their connection with the house.** A Musgrave resided there in the late 19th century. Sir Arthur was also a Knight of St. John of Jerusalem (Hospitallers), who took over the estates of the Templars in the early 14th century. The Templars probably owned the earlier structure, the existence of which has recently been confirmed by archaeological evidence. Woven into the story is the legend that the royal Regalia of Charles II was buried there.

An American visitor, Mary Gibby, recalled that, in 1933, she visited an underground secret chapel in the house. This is also confirmed by the poet Anne Lewis-Smith, who married an RAF officer stationed at Truleigh Hill. While on their honeymoon at St. Mary's in 1944, the couple discovered below a 'chapel', with an altar and a flagged floor. Edward Colquhoun, a Shoreham author, said that, as a boy in the 1960s, he watched workmen filling in the cellars. He remembers that the rooms contained old oak furniture, ironwork and Sussex cast iron firebacks, which may still be there below stairs.

See 4.1 for Part 1 and also 5.9 *The Causeway*

*Following the gradual dismantling of the Great Bridge of Bramber, together with its chapel dedicated to St. Mary Magdalen, the Chapel House became known locally as 'St. Mary's' over time, though official modern-day requirements demand the more prosaic postal designation 'St. Mary's House'.[Ed.]

**The Conan Doyle connection remains a mystery and has yet to be proved. [Ed.]

10.1 Alfred Musgrave, Senior Probate Registrar, owner of St. Mary's 1899-1907. President of the Beeding, Bramber and Steyning Coronation Regatta 1902.

10.1a Miss Dorothy Ellis with her mother, taken soon after their arrival at St. Mary's House in 1944. She saved the house from demolition and sold to the lepidopterist, Dr. Paul Smart, in 1980

Castle Tales

No ancient place is without its legends. Our area possesses some that are well known, and some that are less so. There is a tendency in these days of technical education to dismiss legend as of no account; legend is part of tradition, and tradition is part of our heritage. Tradition is fast being stamped out, and if the pundits had their way, legend would share the same fate. (See Garratt)

When tales are passed down from generation to generation, there is usually a starting point somewhere that has some truth. Over hundreds of years narrators add or subtract details to enhance their story. As a young lad in Bramber, sometime before the last world war, I often listened to old inhabitants telling of a secret tunnel that went from Bramber Castle under the River Adur to Sele Priory on the opposite bank of the estuary. There is a story of the underground passage which told of a certain old man who just before his death related how as a boy he had entered a tunnel in the castle moat. It ran outward for a long way, but he became frightened and returned to the entrance without reaching the end. Unfortunately he gave no location. The tunnel probably existed in the form of an old culvert.

Bearing in mind that the area between castle and priory is a tidal flood plain, any underground passageway would have to be lined with water resistant cement or brickwork. The chance of any tunnel existing is extremely remote. However much logic you apply to an argument some local people claim they know there is a subterranean way to Sele from the Castle, although they have never seen it, nor can they point to any one who has. What faith!

On moonlight nights, a white horse is seen galloping around the moat and the undergrowth and fallen masonry seem to offer no barrier to its progress. Nothing else happens, but the legend was certainly known to the people of Bramber as recently as the 1930s. One ancient inhabitant told the author, Erridge: "We 'ears 'is 'OOFS too!" – which is just as it should be.

10.2 Bramber Castle. Remains of the keep.

Castle Ruins, Bramber

10.2a Bramber Castle. Remains of the guard-room.

Wartime Beeding (1942)

The last week in February is the anniversary of Warships Week (1942) in our area. Celebrations to commemorate that week used to take place in the schools of the Horsham District as a history project. On one occasion, Forest Community School hosted an exhibition to provide a 'window into the past' to enable pupils to reflect and research on life under wartime conditions in their towns and villages.

The Horsham District once raised £419,000 in National Savings in a single week, to purchase and adopt a submarine.

With the 'Battle of Britain' won, and the threat of invasion receding, Beeding and Bramber settled down to a wartime existence. Many fund-raising events for the war effort took place. The usual coffee mornings, church bazaars and no doubt the ubiquitous jumble sale; knitting circles fabricated 'Comforts from Home' in the form of socks, scarves and balaclavas for service men overseas.

There were little or no foreign imports of luxury items. Petrol was rationed and people were producing innovative recipes. These included vegetable pie, carrot jam, and concoctions which did not use fat, sugar or meat. Powdered egg was a useful product used in almost everything, especially in cake mixtures which had to be boiled before baking when butter was in short supply.

Beeding Primary School was reduced to part-time learning. Evacuees swelled the number of pupils, forcing the school to adopt a shift system. Some attended in the mornings and some in the afternoon. The corridors doubled as class-rooms and air raid shelters when insufficient warning was given of enemy aircraft approaching.

Gun emplacements near Beeding Bridge attracted the attention of the casual observer, including all the small boys in the vicinity. Scattered around the fields were concrete pill boxes; the remains of some still are to be seen in the south of the parish.

Surface air raid shelters and ARP (Air Raid Patrol) posts were also built at the same time. Many remained long after the war was over. One in Hyde Lane served as a store for many years. Remains of another can still be seen in winter on glebe land by St. Peter's Church.

Local Customs

Many of our local customs are dying out or have long since gone. Modern ways of entertaining have destroyed communal occasions and isolated families to a great degree. We gather around the television and are plied with the products of advertisers, thoughts of politicians and bureaucrats, and others who would have you believe their points of view.

Among our old traditions is 'April Fool's Day', beloved of all children; it is unlikely to die out in the forseeable future. One of the favourite tricks in Beeding was the parcel lying in the road. When a passer-by stooped to pick it up, it was jerked away by small children hidden in the hedge who had it on a long piece of string – an impossible thing to do with the level of today's traffic. Other catches were 'Mister your shoelace is undone', or in the days when some sort of headgear was worn by every one: 'Yer hat's on fire'! The unsuspecting would snatch it off in a great hurry only to be barracked by shouts of 'April Fool'.

Good Friday has always been, to the church-goer, the saddest day in the religious calendar, but to others a day of holiday in which to indulge in traditional games. Many from Beeding and Bramber walked down to Old Shoreham to the hill north of the church to witness the egg-rolling ceremony. It was known as 'Good Friday Hill'. Children and others went in procession to roll hard-boiled eggs, dyed in various colours, down the steep slopes.

'Kiss in the Ring' was another custom which ceased around the Second World War. Then, many girls were in domestic service, field workers or dairy maids. They were bound to their employers and seldom had time off for courting; therefore this was one opportunity to meet a boyfriend. Games often took place on an ancient site such as an old burial mound, usually singing 'Hey Diddle-Derry, Let's dance on the Bury.'*

One old Easter Day tradition followed by many was the wearing of a new article of clothing. Ladies, don't forget your 'Easter Bonnet'.

* *The Turning Year*, by J. Simpson

"Think only of the past as its remembrance gives you pleasure."
Jane Austen

The Water Supply

We in Britain have always had a good supply of water, especially in the South Downs region where the chalk filters the rainfall to provide hard, but pure water. The Ruskin stream at Fulking near the Shepherd and Dog Inn is one example of a supply of water that never dries up. John Ruskin was a one- time resident and is credited with instigating the installation of a hydraulic ram, turned by the stream to lift water higher up the village.* The ram is housed in a small building beside the stream as it discharges into the roadway. Verse 10 from Psalm 104 and verse 8 from Psalm 107 are spelt out on tiles at the side of this building.

In our area, as with many towns and villages, Brighton in particular, much disease was spread because of the unrestricted practice of having wells and cesspits in the same location where foul liquids seeped into the drinking water, causing many deaths. The 20th century has eliminated many of these problems by establishing proper waterworks and pumping stations.

Our water supply is drawn from deep wells to the south-east of Beeding where the road to Henfield turns sharply north. The Steyning and District Waterworks Company sank a well on this site c.1898. They also built a reservoir on the side of the Downs nearby to supply water to Beeding, Bramber, parts of Small Dole and eastern Steyning. Southern Water took over the old works and I am told that it now serves a much smaller area. Perhaps that is why we do not have a hosepipe ban here.

The daily authorised extraction of water from the wells is 499,840 gallons per 24 hours. Other boreholes were drilled in the 1970s, but several proved to be of little use. The Parish Council has been watchful as applications for tipping were filed, including Room Bottom – part of the watershed for the wells.

There are still wells around the villages. Noteable ones are at the Priory and in the garden of Pound House, but are no longer in use.

Every adult person in the UK consumes about 140 litres daily. This is as much as a family of 4 in the Third World villages of Somalia use in a fortnight.

See KN-B's article *Psalm 104 v. 10* [17.6]

Responsibility

Here in Beeding and Bramber, thankfully, we do not suffer crime and vandalism on the scale of larger towns and cities. There is vandalism of the unthinking and of the uncaring, the discarded drink can, the crisp packet or wrapper carelessly thrown down. Then there is the drunken yob weaving his way home tearing off windscreen wipers and wireless aerials from parked cars, actions of the permissive society and not a few magistrates describe it as 'a cry for help'. What nonsense! They would not dare to do damage to property in the full light of day; thieves and vandals work mostly under the cover of darkness.

Village elders and tradesmen in the last century had their own answer to crime and vandalism. This was the 'Felons Association' or 'Prosecuting Society'. The Henfield Prosecuting Society was formed in 1822. This included the Parishes of Cowfold, Albourne, Woodmancote, Shermanbury, Bolney, Keymer, West Grinstead, Hurstpierpoint, Horsham and Beeding (Upper and Lower were one Parish until 1838). They offered large sums of money as rewards for the apprehension of lawbreakers in general, particularly thieves. The scale of rewards had its oddities: for instance, 55 guineas was the sum for a case of sheep stealing. 'One ewe, the property of Mr. Henry Beckett of Beeding, stolen from the Ladybrooks' (north of the Driftway).* Murder only drew the sum of 10 guineas. 'A poster still exists (1947) announcing 25 Guineas reward for the conviction of some evil disposed person or persons who did on the night of the 8th of May 1835 break open the stable on Furze Field Farm Shermanbury....and maliciously cut off and carry away the hair from the tails of three carthorses.'

'Frankpledge', a Saxon method of law and order, involved inhabitants being formed into groups of ten men, known as a tithing. Representatives were known as tithingmen or headboroughs. They were responsible for good behaviour of each other and bound to produce offenders or would themselves be liable to make good any damage. Collective responsibility for apprehending offenders was dominant in early English life until police forces came into being in the 19th century.

Perhaps now is the time to reform the 'Tithing' in another mode?

* *The Story of Henfield*, H. de Candole

Gas

The recent arrival in Beeding of an old colleague and his wife, prompted me to mention another of the utilities we depend on – 'gas'. We both worked for the same construction firm in the gas and petro-chemical industry for many years.

Commercial use of gas was developed during what we know as the 'Industrial Revolution'. Roasting coal in a retort produced an inflammable vapour which could be used to heat and illuminate. By-products were extracted from a liquor drawn off which could be separated into naphtha, dyes and other chemicals. The residue of the coal was known as 'coke' and was used in blast furnaces to make steel in the Midlands.

Brighton used gas as early as 1819 when a design of the Prince of Wales Feathers over a shoemaker's shop in East Street was lit by gas. The Old Steyne was lit around 1824. The first gas works in the area was at Black Rock c.1818; coal was unloaded on the beach beneath the cliffs and hauled up there to avoid the duty that was charged to unload on Brighton beach. Later there was a works in Hove c.1835. In 1870 the role of these works was taken over by the new Portslade gasworks which remained until recent times.

Many people will remember the soft hiss of domestic gas lighting in their homes up until the Second World War. I remember as a boy being sent to the ironmongers shop to purchase gas mantles – fragile items needing careful handling with: 'Don't drop them!' ringing in my ears. In the days before automation, the lamplighter with his long pole lit the lamp posts at dusk and turned them off at dawn.

An entry in Dr. Bloxam's 'History of the Parish' records: '1888 Lighting at Upper Beeding: 'The village has just been supplied with public gas lamps; and these are found to be a real boon to the inhabitants. The cost of the lamps has been met out of the surplus from the Jubilee Fund, with the addition of some donations since received. The people of Upper Beeding are now happy in the light of the night; and are beginning to ask if Bramber is going to make up its mind and go and do likewise?' Presumably the supply came from Steyning.

'Friends'

I was approached by a lady whose name was Fry. She was researching her ancestors, particularly those that were sometime resident in the Beeding area.

Most of us know about the Society of Friends, or Quakers, founded by George Fox in the middle of the 17th century. Initially, they were seen as a most disruptive sect and caused much disturbance in the church services. Later they were to take a more passive role in society. Perhaps the best remembered of the latter era was the prison reformer Elizabeth Fry, who did much campaigning for the deprived in the early Victorian period.

Steyning was the centre of the local movement in the latter part of the 17th century. Penn House had been obtained for the sect c.1678. This may have been the focal point for their worship in the Adur Valley in the late 17th and early 18th centuries.

The Rev. Dr. Arnold noted an interesting item in an old document. He quotes: 'That same first day (24th April 1655) George Fox had a meeting at Ninian Brockett's house in Beeding.' It goes on to say that the Quakers living at Sele were accustomed to meet at Peppersgate, and were seldom less than 220. As the population was probably much less than this at the time it is possible that open air meetings for the whole of the Adur Valley took place there.

As I have pointed out in earlier articles, there were two crossing places across the river in mediaeval times – the Veteri Ponte (old bridge) at Botolphs, and the wagon ford at Sele. Sele was the village and area around the church and priory. West of the river there was a track from the place/farm known as 'Pepperscombe'. This crossed the Adur near where the 'White' bridge now stands and passed the church going east continuing down Church Lane where one road curved south and joined Hyde Street and up to the Bost Hill. The other forked east, passing Pound House and went towards Small Dole and Henfield. At one time this was a turnpike road and the toll was paid at 'Peppersgate' which was believed to be between Pound House and Ninian Brockett's house which was thought to be south and opposite Pound House. Today it is known as the west part of 'Smuggler's Lane', earlier known as 'Gypsy Lane'.

10.8 Elizabeth Fry, Quaker and prison reformer

10.8a George Fox, Quaker, who preached at Beeding

The Veteri Ponte (Part 2)

The earliest recorded bridge across the river now known as the Adur, was in our parish, somewhere in the locality of Botolphs. As I have mentioned in past articles, the great mediaeval road across southern England crossed the river in two places. There was a wagon ford near St.Peter's, located somewhere near the present 'White' Bridge, and another where the 25 foot contours come close together in the valley north of the cement works.

St. Peter de Veteri Ponte (Old Bridge) is mentioned in the *Chartulary of Sele Priory* in AD 1080. It must have been of great antiquity to have acquired the designation 'old', so we are back into the Saxon period or even Roman times. 'Ponte' or 'pons' can mean bridge or causeway, but it was a bridge, probably in the style of a pontoon crossing. These were constructed by laying wooden planks for a walkway across galleys of barge type boats. This form of structure is quite often seen carved into stonework on Roman monuments.

Before the 11th century the river rose much higher than it does now and was a very wide tidal estuary. A pontoon style bridge would allow for a kind of drawbridge to enable ships to reach the old port of St. Cuthman at Steyning. There was much speculation in the 1930s as to exactly where this crossing was located. Colonel Evans, who did much research here, was of the opinion that there was a causeway from south of Beeding Court near the site of the 12th century village of 'Beding' to a point near Annington.

Later in the 13th century, St. Peter de Veteri Ponte became known as 'St. Botolphs'. Probably renamed by the Normans, there is no mention of 'St. Botolphs' in the Domesday survey (1086), but a church is recorded in 'Haningedune' (Annington) . As no church or burial ground is known in the area of Annington itself, this must refer to the church now called St. Botolphs. If there ever was a pontoon bridge, it must have fallen into disuse around the time of the completion of the 'Great Bridge' of Bramber in the 12th century. At certain times of the year, a strange continuation of the South Downs Way can be seen in crop patterns from a vantage point on Beeding Hill.

KN-B returns here to the theme he developed in 1.2

Answers in the Soil

I mentioned in the last issue of *The Villager* that the Veteri Ponte was a pre-conquest river crossing. We must remember that High Street, Beeding, is built on a causeway and did not exist before the Normans arrived. Its formation was at about the same time as the building of Bramber Castle. I did remind you of the early hamlet of 'Beding' at the south end of the bypass and the theory that the Veteri Ponte was of the early Middle Ages or of late Roman origin and that 'Beding' was at its east end.

If you are a regular walker along the banks of the Adur, you will notice the changing pattern of the fields along what was once a wide tidal estuary With the October ploughing completed, much is revealed of ancient trackways, salt workings and evidence of lost mediaeval villages. The observer, from the higher ground, can see the different shades in the freshly ploughed earth which indicate well used tracks, the lines of grubbed out hedges and areas of earlier habitation. You can also see the field boundaries, marked by depressions where the ditches of the past have been filled in.

Many lost settlements are known in this part of the Adur Valley and can be located at this time of the year. There are several pointers for revealing them, paths apparently leading nowhere and old churches standing alone which would once have been the centre of busy villages. Before the turnpikes of the 18th century, this part of Sussex was impassable during much of the winter half of the year. Except for the maritime strip, Sussex was part of the great marshy forest of Andrede's Weald*, full of wolves, bears and bands of outlaws. No wonder, then, that travellers used the South Downs ridge as a safer way. This beaten highway had been used by people from Neolithic times and probably much earlier. The Romans, with their legions pushing to the west, passed along it, as did the Saxon settlers spreading out from the east coast. *The Anglo Saxon Chronical* records the coming of Beida, founder of Beeding, and his father, Port, in 501AD. No doubt it was used later in 681AD by St.Wilfrid, Bishop of York, when he came to convert the South Saxons to Christianity.

*Andrede's Weald (The Forest of Anderida) once covered the Weald reaching down as far as the coast. Possible connection with the Roman Fortress of Anderida at what is now Pevensey. [Ed.]

See also 5.12. See bibliography under John Burke and Cecile Woodford.

The Mills (Part 2)

I often sit by the fire in the winter researching odd items that may be of interest to readers of *The Villager*. On a shelf by my chimney-piece is the model of a windmill. There is a tale of great skill that produced the small replica of Beeding Mill. It was made for me by that great millwright, Frank Gregory, a friend and fellow researcher. It is correct in every detail, yet was made without any reference to pictures or photographs, for none were known at this time.

Though watermills existed before 1191, there were no windmills. The first windmill on Windmill Hill was recorded in 1384. The last to stand on the site was built c.1724 and was badly damaged in a gale of 1888. It stopped working around that time.

I have always been fascinated by windmills. My godfather, F. Branwell, wrote *The History of the Windmills of Brighton*. He left me a legacy which included his research documents and photographs. Some ten years ago I was given a 'For Sale' notice dated 1864. This is one of my prized possessions as it refers to the sale of Beeding Windmill with all the details of owner and occupier at that time, and of the workings: two pairs of millstones, a fantail, (to keep it into the wind) and a roundhouse for living or storage. During conversation with Frank, he said that, even with this limited information, he could make me a model of the original. It took him several months as he had much other work restoring full sized windmills in the county, but the result was superb.

The amazing thing was that, some years later, I discovered a photograph which was established by Dr.Tim Hudson (*Victoria County History*) to be of Beeding Windmill. The mill was in a very damaged condition and derelict but it was proof that Frank had got it right as it appeared to be the full-scale original of my model.

If you stand on Windmill Hill today, where Maines Farm road/track reaches the top, the careful observer can still see the remains of the mill. After ploughing has taken place, you can see a scatter of brick and tile to the north of the track. Go and have a look!

For Part 1 see 2.10

10.12 Beeding Mill c1891. Originally erected in 1343, but eventually caught fire. Mr Breach, the miller, can just be seen approaching on horse-back, and Mrs Breach standing at the doorway.

10.12a Sketch of a typical downland windmill

Field Names (Part 2)

This generation born into the emerging European Community has been forced to drop many of our old British measurements. I well remember as a young lad being told that Brighton lay three leagues east of Bramber (9 miles) by an old inhabitant. All good fairy stories used that term for distance. Shortly the 'mile' will disappear and be replaced by the kilometre. No doubt there is some sense in doing things by tenths, but all the old romantic terms are now passing out of our rich English language.

Furlong (as in 'a furrow long') indicated the length of the furrow which a pair of oxen with a plough usually made without turning. In past times the fields of the village community were divided up into strips, each one of which was 660 feet or 220 yards long (8 to the mile), and generally four rods wide, so making an acre. These acre strips were therefore 22 yards, the length of a modern cricket pitch. It was quite common for the youth of the villages to play ball games across these strips. It may have started with stoolball which eventually developed into cricket.

Many of our old fields had a prefix to the word furlong; 'Rake Furlong' was above and to the east of the water works on the Henfield Road. 'Cricketing Field' was near the top of Beeding Hill. Later in the last century, cricket matches took place at 'High Trees Corner' near the bypass roundabout and Shoreham Road. The trees have now gone. Cricket is now played on the Memorial Playing field, formerly known as the 'Ham'. To the north, reaching up to the church of St. Peter, was 'Sele Field' on which, in its south-east corner, the school was built about 1871.

The Saxons tended to name their settlements after a combination of local place features: 'ing', 'ingas', 'ham', 'ton', and importantly, in Beeding, the name of a worthy, Beida's 'ing'. The land to the north east of Pound House Cottage (corner of Pound Lane and Smuggler's Lane), known now as 'Cattle Copse', was, up to the last century, called 'Little Haven's Bye'. The Paddocks and the Driftway occupy what was 'Monk's Mead' and 'Middle Mead'. The area from Beeding Bridge, south of the High Street including Dawn Close and Crescent, was in earlier times known as 'Little Follies' and 'Great Follies' respectively, Dawn Crescent being in the 'Great Follies' area!

See 4.11 for Part 1

Chalk Pits

The decline of the Beeding Cement Works, on our southern border, has been a great blow to the community of this part of West Sussex. Many jobs have been lost, and revenue by way of rates to the District Council has fallen by many hundreds of thousands of pounds. In *The Villager* [2.12], I recorded that the works, established in about 1882, was at that time (1984) employing some 250 workers, mainly local, and manufactured 7,000 tons of cement each week.

The 'works' had been known for centuries as Erringham Chalk Pit and two early kilns for limeburning are known to have existed, but are now filled in. Lime was made by burning chalk in kilns and the lime manufacturing side of the pit was probably first established in Roman times.

Lime was a very important commodity to an agrarian society such as existed here in the Adur Valley before the last world war. In the days before the national road traffic network, it was used where it was manufactured. Soil was fertilised and conditioned by it. Builders used it to make lime mortar for bricklaying, plastering and limewash coating to weatherproof cottages and buildings. Lime was also most useful to the tanner for processing hides and other animal skins. It had peripheral uses when mixed with other elements, such as lighting of music hall stages, hence the term the 'limelight'.

Acts passed in Elizabethan times to conserve forest timber for shipbuilding put many furnace-based businesses out of operation as the cutting down of many tree species was forbidden. Without timber fuel, these industries moved to the Midlands where coal was increasingly being used. Local entrepreneurs gave the Erringham Works a dual role. It became a coal yard as well as a chalk pit. Coal was brought in by sea and distributed to the surrounding countryside as far upstream as West Grinstead, until the coming of the railways via the Baybridge Canal (Adur,1860s). There was a coal wharf at Beeding Bridge for the three villages.

KN-B introduced this subject in 2.12

Milestones

The age of the regular horse-drawn passenger coach went into decline in the 19th century, largely owing to the growth of the railway network. Before this, Sussex was notorious for its terrain. It was probably the most difficult county to travel through, especially the Weald, which was forest and marsh. Defoe recorded in his journal that in Sussex he met a lady going to church whose coach was being driven by six oxen, so deep was the mud!

The coaching era was a period that opened up England to county and countrywide commerce. Many small producers were willing to take their goods to places where the need for them was greatest. This was reflected in the better prices they could obtain from distant markets, allowing for the fare to be paid and still make a good profit. It was also a good period for surveyors and mapmakers. Many beautiful road maps were printed in the 18th and 19th centuries.

Milestones engraved with numbers recorded the distance of coach routes. In nearly all cases they radiated from London. Many were inscribed with a bow and three bells (Bow Bells) and the numbers were the distances in miles from the capital. Ours is marked 52. They also served to set the fares for passengers who were not travelling the full distance.

With the decline in coach travel, Britain, through the railway network, established one time for the whole country, 'Railway Time'. The origin of this time was London. Before 1850 there was regional time, which varied from district to district; Plymouth was 16 minutes adrift from the capital. This had been difficult for the coaches, so they carried chronometers set to gain or lose time, outward or backward to keep within their timetables.

Some years ago, the milestone at Beeding was removed from the grass bank in High Street at the corner of Hyde Lane, adjacent to the bus shelter. This was necessary as the top of the stone was being destroyed by grass-cutting machinery. It is hoped that it will be sited as near as possible to its original position.

In my younger days, 'tramps' were always referred to as 'Milestone Inspectors'.

Originally printed as 20.4

Smuggling

In the middle of August 1855 a celebrated Wild Beast Show visited Shoreham. It took up position next to the Custom House (later the Town Hall). Zoological shows aroused great interest in those days. While many of the coastguards, having been given free tickets for the show, were at the menagerie, a vessel laden with some 90 tons of stone for cement making entered the harbour and tied up at the Custom Quay. The Captain informed the revenue man on duty that he was trying to find a purchaser for his cargo. Concealed under the top dressing of stone was a substantial load of tobacco. The 'Show' proved so interesting that many of the revenue men, armed with their complimentary tickets, returned for the evening performance.

As the gloom of the evening crept over the river, so Henry Cheal relates, many bales of tobacco were quietly put over the side of the vessel into a barge, which went up the Adur as far as Beeding Chalk Pits (cement works) with the flood tide. Here three or four vans drawn by stout horses came along just in the nick of time. The bales were quickly unloaded from the barge into the vans, which departed. One was subsequently traced up through Horsham, and another through Hurst and Cuckfield, but there the trail ended.

A man, prompted by curiosity, had looked into one of the vans, but a sovereign stopped his tongue, at least for a time. One of the men concerned in the transit of the tobacco, who had been left behind drunk, boasted to an inn keeper that fourteen tons was about the quantity of the tobacco run, and from the size of the vans and the strength of the horses, it was estimated that this was not far short of the quantity. It was generally believed that the vans came from Horsham and that the drivers were advised by telegram from Brighton of the ship's arrival. As they could calculate the tide up the Adur to a nicety they did not appear at the chalk pits until wanted. The run was estimated as worth £8,000 to any officer who had stopped it. The captain of the vessel which had brought the tobacco to Shoreham left harbour next morning before the events of the previous night began to leak out, stating that he had sold his stone to a Brighton firm.*

*Henry Cheal, *The Story of Shoreham*

KN-B returns here to the subject he developed in *Owling* 4.12

Revelations

It is now ten years since I first started the regular series of monthly *Villager* articles. I have enjoyed putting them together, having learned a great deal from the research which was necessary for their production. I have drawn heavily on the work of John Rouse Bloxam, Vicar of Beeding from 1862 until his death in 1891. Dr. Bloxam was a man of great scholarship and a historian of vision. When I discovered in the 1970s that he had compiled a census of his communicants and other residents in the parish, I asked the permission of our Rector to withdraw his written records from the archives at Chichester, to make a copy for the Church.

In addition to the regular census returns, the record of Dr. Bloxam's perambulations around the parish gives us a 'window into the past' reflecting life in the Beeding area during the last half of the 1800s. What is so valuable to the local historian are his cross references and additional information that census material does not provide. He records that Harry Wells lived at the Malt House with his wife Charlotte and two children, Harry (born 1869) and Robert (born 1871). Harry Snr. was a wheelwright and Bloxam notes that he is the son of 'W'. Henry Wells is named as a wheelwright with wife Frances and child Emily, aged 9 years. They had a lodger, John Budd, a labourer. A new occupant, Clement Budd, a cow keeper, with his wife Ann and two children, William and Alice, take up residence in 1876. Clement Budd we know from other records was a churchwarden at St. Peter's Beeding. His name is cast into the new bells (1892) with two other wardens [See 3.3].

Some years ago whilst working on a book of Brighton History, I came across the Tattersall family who had helped Charles II escape to France in 1651. They were recorded as having two daughters named Sarah! It took some time to find out that the first had died and the second had also been named Sarah. Bloxam's census eliminates this sort of puzzle to some degree, as he names wives and mistresses, dating most children's birth years, noting the fact that some were born out of wedlock.

Historians owe much to the Reverend Dr. Bloxam.

The Chimney

When one looks at photographs, postcards and pictures of inhabited places in past times, one of the things that stands out to the observer is smoke from the chimneys. No matter what time of year it is, bare trees or ones in full leaf, summer or winter, smoke is always issuing out of chimneys.

There is a simple explanation. Before the beginning of the 20th century there was no local gas or electricity supply in rural areas such as ours. Residents of the last century back to primaeval times cooked on a fire. Wood and peat were probably the fuels used by our early ancestors, giving way to coal during the Industrial Revolution.

Chimneys did not come into use, or were not widely adopted, until the early 16th century. Smoke found its way out of the houses through the thatch on the roof. Chimney fireplaces from Elizabethan times were fairly large affairs; the 'inglenook' where everyone crowded round the fire was the social centre of the inn or big house. It was also the place where meat, bacon and sometimes fish were cured for future use in the days before fridge or freezer, and there was usually a place to keep salt dry.

In Victorian times most people cooked on a cast iron range. These were quite economical with soft coal as fuel. There was a fire box to fill with coal, and a hob at the top on which to boil kettles and puddings. At the side was an oven to roast and do all manner of baking. Usually one of the children of the household had the Saturday task of black-leading the stove - that and the daily scrubbing of the threshold or 'front step' were things that indicated the house-proud family.

Looking along the streets of any village with mediaeval origins one can see many tall chimney stacks on old buildings. These indicate that if they are not not now thatched, they once were. Many thatched cottages are now roofed with slates, tiles or stone slabs, but the tall chimneys remain. Stacks had to be a good distance from the roof level because of the danger of sparks setting alight the straw or reeds.

Charles Dickens drew our attention to the plight of young children who were forced to climb and sweep chimneys of large houses. His graphic descriptions of Victorian times are a history lesson of life in the 19th century.

Advertising

Students of local history who review census returns see that certain trades seem to run in families. Printing was dominant in ancestors on my father's side. One, Phillips, Printer, was located in Petworth.

A legacy of the old business left us with a collection of printed advertising notices along with ephemera of the 19th century. Broadsheets, auction notices, political handouts, for sale and to let information are valuable to local historians. Details, unrecorded elsewhere because they seemed commonplace, can be discovered on these flimsy sheets.

Reproduced here are details which appeared on a notice for the rental of Tottington Farm in May 1832.

Tottington Farm,
Beeding, Sussex.

To be Let,

And entered upon at Michaelmas next:

TOTTINGTON FARM, in the Parish of BEEDING; in the Occupation of Messrs. JAMES AND THOMAS LINGHAM:

Consisting of a Farmhouse and convenient Farm Buildings, a Cottage, and about 553 Acres of Land; viz.

	Acres.
House, Buildings, Orchards and Gardens, about	7
Arable Land	235
Meadow and Pasture	37
Sheep Down	131
Woodlands	143
Acres	553

For Particulars, apply to Mr. TYLER, Petworth; at whose Office a Plan may be seen; and to whom Tenders for Rent may be sent; and the Premises may be viewed, on Application to the Tenants.

Petworth, 21st May, 1832.

Phillips, Printer, Petworth.

A Beeding Hero

The memorial tablet remembering local servicemen who gave their lives in the the Second World War is set in the north wall of the nave of St. Peter's Church, opposite the main door. I often ponder on how they met their end. Top of the list is Albert E. Bousell HMS UNION and, knowing that UNION was a submarine, it prompted me to delve into the manner of his passing.

Albert was born on the 5th September 1901, the year the submarine service was founded. His father, William, married Ada from Southwick; his sister 'Bousey' was at school with some of our mature villagers. He joined the service in May 1927 as a telegraphist and became one of the first 'Trained Detectors' of the ASDIC apparatus. In times before the last war, for health reasons, time in submarines was limited, and Albert returned to Naval General Service in 1932 but by 1935 he was back in submarines, serving at various times in PERSEUS, PORPOISE, OXLEY, NARWHAL, SEALION, THAMES and UPHOLDER. All were subsequently sunk, except for SEALION, which survived a ramming in the Norwegian campaign.

Albert's fate was finally sealed when he joined HMS UNION. She left on patrol from Malta on the 14th July 1942 with instructions to attack a convoy of Rommel's supply ships reported by aircraft to be approaching Tripoli. When she failed to return to Malta by 22nd she was presumed lost and the 22nd was given as the date of the death of the crew. Being in control of a naval archive I have been in a position to research this Mediterranean incident. The Italian Embassy let me have a copy of their losses and action reports of the time, which reveal that UNION was sunk by the Italian torpedo boat escort 'Circe' on 20th July. 'Circe' saw a torpedo track aimed at the convoy and made for the firing point. She saw UNION's periscope through the clear water and dropped six depth charges. A large patch of oil was seen and an escorting seaplane dropped a bomb which produced more oil and air bubbles.

Give a thought to those 33 crew members who still lie entombed in UNION, now a war grave off Pantelleria.

'Born of the sun they travelled a short while towards the sun,
And left the vivid air signed with their honour.'
(*I Think Continuously of Those.*   Stephen Spender)

See also 19.9 for more Beeding heroes

Investment

At seemingly regular intervals one hears of the discovery of hoards of coins, mainly Roman, and other treasures unearthed by archaeologists and enthusiasts with metal detectors. When valuable collections are declared there has to be an enquiry as to how the valuables came to be where they were found. Were they lost, as most usually were, or hidden deliberately? Many of the caches found buried were put there by people during times of insecurity with the idea of recovering them at a later date. Sometimes they died before the location was passed on to their close relatives and dependants.

In mediaeval times the agricultural labourer did not use coins. Transactions were completed by barter: produce was exchanged for services, the miller working the mill owned by the Lord of the Manor took 'millsoke', a percentage of the corn being ground for villagers, the blacksmith may have required eggs or poultry for shoeing an ox or a horse. What money did exist in the area was owned by the Lord of the Manor or the Priory of Sele and was kept in a secure chest.

Until the 17th century there were no banking facilities available to the general population. Resident entrepreneurs who did have money could only enhance their fortunes by investing in the land. Old wills and bonds show that many well-to-do residents regularly loaned money to hard-up farmers and landowners, often at very modest rates. In Brighton up to three centuries ago, anyone with spare cash invested in boats. In fishing and other overseas ventures people would finance voyages in shares down to 1/64th of the cargo returned. Hence the term, 'When my ship comes in'.

A document has just come into my possession which reflects the moneylending element here in Beeding. Dated 1723, it records the loan of £348 to Thomas Haynes (Haines) the owner of Barrowhill Farm. The lenders recorded at the Manor Court are Ann Lancaster of Beeding at Seale, Spinster and her sister Jane, also a spinster. The bond is endorsed on the reverse with the repayments received by Ann and Jane.

The Way it Was!

"About 'old times' there always hovers a peculiar charm. A mellow atmosphere overhangs them. The present, as we battle along through it, seems full of friction and metallic clatter; but looking back, old days take on a rosy hue. The sharp edges are gone. Even the petty cares and worries which irritated us in the past seem very trivial compared to the difficulties which loom up in our paths as we grow older. Perhaps the modern appetite for speed and the things carried out on large-scale systems is responsible for this outlook on life." (so wrote Hopkins in 1928.)

This philosophy must also apply to the present time. As a young lad in these villages pre-war, I could walk down the centre of the road and have plenty of warning of approaching vehicles. Not so now. The speed of traffic through Beeding has increased tenfold since World War I: then it was mainly horse-drawn with the occasional traction engine and the odd car chugging by. Older residents will remember the excellent train service from Bramber station that took you to Shoreham in minutes and to Horsham and Brighton well within half an hour. There was also a regular 'Southdown' bus service for the outlying villages. One would be hard pushed these days, when most cars can reach a hundred miles an hour, to match these old railway timetables.

Before the 1960s, most children walked to school, some several miles from their homes. It would be difficult for many of them today, with the crowded roads and the threat of 'strangers'. Schoolchildren, who are bussed and carried by car to their places of learning, are missing much that was part of our general education.

As we walked, we watched the town and countryside through all seasons, observing the different birds nesting, workers 'hedging and ditching', harvesting, dallying at the forge to watch the blacksmith making a gate or shoeing a horse. Then there were the seasonal games, marbles played along gutters, conkers in the Autumn, whips and tops, hoops, and who today sees any youngster skipping to school? A former headteacher at Beeding Primary School recalled that her grandmother walked each school day with her sisters from Erringham to the newly built (1871) schoolhouse in Church Lane, Beeding.

Cater Rand

Cater Rand had a tremendous impact on the future of the Adur Valley. Born in 1749, he was destined to follow the family tradition of teaching, becoming a brilliant educator. When he took over the Lewes school run by his mother, c.1773, he advertised in the local press: "At Lewes, in Sussex, Youth are commodiously Boarded, educated, and Qualified for all manner of business, By CATER RAND and PROPER ASSISTANTS, Mr. Rand, with an ardent desire of opening the narrow confines of Youth, (which is too much neglected) intends going through a COURSE of LECTURES in EXPERIMENTAL PHILOSOPHY Three evenings a week with the first principals of religion, Taste and Learnings, and elevate their Minds, as they advance in Years, above the low Pursuits of sensual and tasteless Amusements".

Among the subjects taught were navigation, electric machines, slide rule, theodolite, map-making and charts and much else. Many of his pupils did well in engineering and shipping, but what happened to his school is not known.

Sussex was going through great change at the beginning of the 19th century. Population was growing fast. Arable acreage, especially of wheat, rose in response to the enlarged local markets. Fertile estuary land was reclaimed where possible, and here Rand emerges as a drainage engineer. The Commissioners of Sewers for the Rape of Bramber made use of his services. He drew up a map dated 29 September 1806, with his recommendations for improvements.

This map shows the river from Beeding boundary in the south to 'Bine' and Mock Bridges in the north. It features oxbows and meanders of the Adur with instructions to cut across to straighten the main course, and embanking to contain the resulting faster flow. An Act of Parliament was passed in 1807 to enable the river to be navigable for barge traffic. This map must be the survey document used for the Act. The 'White Bridge' near St. Peter's is marked as 'New Bridge'. There was formerly a wagon ford and a small wooden bridge there before that time.

The Changing Christmas

At the present time, no one in this country is likely to go hungry or be without the necessary comforts of life. Today's generation has different ranges of food all the year round. Before World War II, with the exception of the folk at the Manor House, and the 'well-to-do', very few ordinary working people saw a meal of chicken or turkey at any time other than Easter or Christmas. For the youngsters, an orange was only to be found in the Christmas stocking, along with a new penny and various trinkets and home-made sweetmeats. Preparations for Christmas festivities did not begin in October as they do now. It was in the last days of the school term that children made all their cards and decorations for the festival. This shorter period of preparation made the holiday more special; carol singing around the neighbourhood was, for many young ones the only way to earn money to buy presents for parents and family. Those of us who remember the old-time Christmas may feel that we have lost the true joy of the festival, but at least it is still a time of giving and receiving. For that we should be thankful.

The Revd. Dr. Bloxam, Vicar of St. Peter's for much of the last half of the 19th century, dispensed warm clothing to the poor in winter. At Christmas he sat at a window in the Priory (then the Vicarage) and gave half-a-crown to any old woman who brought him a sprig of evergreen. One of his parishioners, a Mrs. Blackman, late of Dacre Gardens, recorded that at the Christmas services, Bloxam sat at the fireplace near the pulpit in St. Peter's and distributed gifts.

The Journal of Councillor Timothy Burrell makes excellent seasonal reading. Timothy's first wife was the daughter of Sir Harry Goring of Highden, who was the brother-in-law of Colonel Bridger. Both were big land owners in this area. Timothy was an excellent recorder of everyday events in the years 1683 to 1714. He entertains his employees at Ockenden Hall at Yuletide and leaves us a recipe for 'plum pottage'. (1707)

See 9.5 *John Rouse Bloxam*

The Monks of Sele (Part 2)

"It has been well said that, if we would really understand the life of our forefathers we must not measure them by the standards of our own times. We must project our minds into the past and try, in imagination, to live as they lived. Material advantages have made gigantic strides within our own memory. We have gained much they never had. On the other hand, we may have lost something which made them a happy people – simplicity of manners, many homely virtues, good feeling between classes, and greater devotion to higher matters." So wrote the Revd. H. E. B. Arnold, former 20th century Beeding Curate, on the monks of Sele Priory.

The monasteries were a necessity of their day, when there was so much fighting between kings and local princes. Many people seeking a quiet life came to the religious houses. The great monasteries held most of the early records of learning. It was there, among the glories of church architecture, that they created their magnificent illuminated books.

The monks of Sele, who, for the first years, were of the Benedictine Order, did their work well. On any Sunday morning and at all great festivals of the church, they could be seen walking or riding on their mules to celebrate Mass in wayside corners, and villages for whose spiritual welfare they were responsible. They would return to the Priory in the late afternoon for their Sunday dinner, the only square meal of the week which their strict order allowed them to enjoy.

The Benedictines were not a closed order, as many later orders were. They were often mediators in local disputes and did much good work among the poor. One aspect of their existence was to labour; often they were given the most worthless lands, a practice which gave rise to the mediaeval saying:

"I was not good enough for man, so I am given to God."

We in Beeding and Bramber owe these monks a great deal. One of their primary projects was to recover land from what was a wide estuary in those far-off days, by embanking the river.

KN-B's original title was *Beeding's Monks.* See 5.4 for Part 1.

Sources for Beeding Studies

Readers of *The Villager* often ask me where I get the information to write these little 'windows into the past'. The answer is from books, manuscripts and some of the older villagers in our area.

The founder of our village, Beida (AD501), is mentioned in the *Anglo-Saxon Chronicle*. Translated by G. N. Garmonsway, this monumental work was edited by W. D. Parish in 1886 for the SAS, printed in Lewes by H. Wolfe, and published in 1953 by J. M. Dent. The text gives the original Latin text and translation, and, in particular, lists two churches in Beeding

Another important source is *The History of the Western Division of Sussex*, edited in the early 19th century by the Rev. James Dallaway and the Rev. Edmund Cartwright. Cartwright compiled the second volume himself in 1830, which made a specific mention of the Rape of Bramber. One very interesting feature of this part is the inclusion of a large folding map of the area, showing almost every house and barn, pond and forest. The map was drawn in 1824. It is estimated that only 90 copies were sent to subscribers before a fire in the warehouse destroyed the rest of the 250 printed copies, and thus must be considered very rare.

For studying the history of Beeding, the *Chartulary of the Priory of St. Peter at Sele,* is an essential source. It was printed in 1923 by W. Heffer, Cambridge, the work of L. F. Salzman, who translated most of the Latin documents of Sele. His introduction to the book is a useful history of our parish in medieval times, and is well worth reading before researching elsewhere.

A very interesting little book was privately published for Mrs. Edgar Collins (Bramber Museum) in 1973. It was edited by John G. Garratt. (See Appendix: Select Bibliography). His drawings and maps are especially interesting.

Former vicars and curates of Beeding were very good recorders of events. The Revd. H. E. B. Arnold produced many articles for earlier Parish Magazines, and the Revd. Dr. Bloxam was a dedicated historian. His 'Rough Notices of the History of the Parish' is a mine of information for any researcher.

Many 12th century documents have been translated and are available from Sussex record offices. Early tax subsidies give names of landowners and tenants in Beeding and Bramber. The census material up to 1890 is also invaluable.

The Moated Site

It is perhaps difficult to imagine the present day area of Beeding High Street, Saltings Way and The Street, Bramber as being part of an estuary, under water at each high tide. No building existed on the flood plain, only the high ground was built on. The old village of Beeding was to the south of Beeding Court. Apart from the churches, Beeding Court is the oldest habitation in the area for which there are records (from AD 1326). It is built on a moated site with the Adur forming the western boundary. The village of Sele, the monastic manor, was around the church of St. Peter and in linear form in a curve down to Hyde Street; one of the earlier river crossings in mediaeval times was forded at St. Botolphs (St. Peter de Veteri Ponte, pre-Conquest); and at the wagon ford at the site of the 'White Bridge' west of SS. Peter and Paul, Beeding.

The only buildings likely to have been in the flood plain itself were the Salterns (salt workings) which may have had garden-shed-like shelters for the workers. The late Eric Holden did much research on the mediaeval salt industry and extracts can be found in the journals of the Sussex Archaeological Society. Some of these mounds still exist north-west of the church and Sele Priory, and one can be seen just north of Bramber car park. Most of the others have been ploughed in the cultivated areas, but can be seen as light circles when the earth is bare.

The Normans constructed the first developments at Bramber: the castle and the 'Great Bridge' across the three courses of the Adur, slightly east of St. Mary's. This great bridge (rediscovered in 1829) was 170 feet long with a chapel on the central pier. Under St. Mary's (c.1477) there have been found earlier signs of human habitation. This may indicate the first 'wardens' residence', the collectors of tolls for de Braose.

Opposite and to the north of St. Mary's, behind Old Priory and Little St. Mary's, is a moated site. Eric Holden investigated this area in the 1970s when sewer trenches were being dug the length of Bramber Street. The site is 200 feet square and there is a raised platform of silt and rubble. Mediaeval pottery, roofing tiles, West Country slate and oyster shells were discovered. This mystery has not been speculated upon before and no one, to my knowledge, has done any research into what stood there in mediaeval times.

See 2.4, 12.8, 13.1 *Salt Pits on the Adur*

The Little Chapel on Bramber Bridge

In the year 1440, the monks of Sele were severely reprimanded by Bishop Praty for their neglect of the services in this little wayfarers' chapel. In 1459, the old Benedictine priory of Sele, which had been established in the time of the Conqueror, practically ceased to exist, and its buildings and endowments were acquired by William Waynflete, then Bishop of Winchester. He hoped they would serve as a part-endowment for his new College of St. Mary Magdalen in Oxford, but the College did not come into full possession until circa 1490, some thirty years later.

Meanwhile the condition of the bridge and chapel had become truly deplorable. Towards the end of the fifteenth century a noble benefactor, one Richard Jay of Crawley, (Bewbush, Crawley, was part of Upper Beeding) left in his will, amongst other gifts, ten Marks* (1466/7). 'To the workes (at Bramber Bridge) and to the Chappell on the brigge by even porcions and ten Marks for the poor and to amend the foule weyes next to Bermbre and Craweley.'** He also bequeathed 'xiid' (12 pence) to the almes people of the hospital of St. Mary Magdalen in Bridlington [sic] (Bidlington , a manor in Bramber).

Doubtless it was soon found that these monies were not sufficient for the work to be done, but help was at hand. In the following year 1468 John Arundell (Bishop of Chichester 1459-78) granted an indulgence of 40 days to all who would assist in the repairs of the bridge and causeway 'now in so bad a condition that they cannot easily be repaired without the help of the alms of the faithfull'***.

A book published in 1893 by Max de Trenqualéon, titled *West-Grinstead et Les Caryll*, is a story of the life of the Caryll family, a cadet branch of the de Braose. In it is an account of the rebuilding/repair of the bridge and chapel with the mason's bills and source of his building materials.

---

*The Mark at this time was not a coin but a value of 13/4d– a unit of accountancy equal to the value in early mediaeval period to 128 silver pennies, later to 8oz silver [KN-B].

**Sussex Records* xli, pp.197-8

***SAC xxii. p222

12.4 The chapel on the bridge at St. Ives, Cambridgeshire, a smaller version of what the Great Bridge of Bramber might have looked like.
(*by courtesy of Cambridge Newspapers*)

Flint Tools

One Sunday in April, Doreen, busy with the choir, said to me: 'Keith, is this a flint implement?' What she showed me was a very nicely made leaf shaped arrowhead. It was almost certainly of the Neolithic (New Stone Age) period which ended not so long ago in terms of world history, (c.1800 BC). In Biblical chronology this would be the time of the patriarchs Isaac and Jacob).

There were three main stone age periods, the Paleolithic, when single crudely-fashioned stone tools were used, the Mesolithic (Middle Stone Age), with less primitive methods of tilling and harvesting, and lastly, the Neolithic period, ending c.2500 BC. Tools were used in greater varieties and had better form. The Neolithic Age was notable for its flint mining.

Early man discovered that flint, newly dug, was more malleable and could be worked into shape much better. Flint, exposed to the elements, gets case-hardened, so if it is allowed to harden after it has been fashioned into an implement it makes a much better tool. Many beautiful artefacts can be seen in museums testifying to the skill of these early fabricators. Flint was mined on Cissbury Hill and also worked there [see 6.7]. Hundreds of these worked flint pieces can be picked up in this area. As a young lad in the 1930s, I took part in the archaeological dig on these mine shafts with the doctors Curwen, father and son, and others from the Sussex Archaeological Society. I still have nice artefacts from that time. It could be said that Cissbury was a centre of an earlier industrial revolution, manufacturing tools for a wide area.

The arrowhead, chipped from a larger struck flake, was probably finally fashioned with a hard piece of wood. This was then fixed into a cleft shaft that had been straightened and smoothed with a flint spoke-shave (a flint blade with a crescent shaped piece removed). The head would be bound with animal sinew and glued with an extract of boiled hide and bone. This concoction was made by dropping heated stones (potboilers) into clay pots of water and the animal remains. A feather for the flight would be attached in a similar way. The bow would be smoothed and shaped, and strung with sinew or plaited fibre.

D-Day

One of the biggest naval operations of all time took place along the south coast of England in preparation for the invasion of Europe. Creeks and harbours on the Channel were full of shipping of all sorts: landing craft for tanks and infantry, supply ships, tugs and escort vessels. Other mystery objects were being brought to the surface: these were parts of the 'Mulberry' prefabricated harbours, which were to be towed across the Channel and sunk to provide jetties and harbours for unloading supplies. The sections were known as 'Phoenixes', made of reinforced concrete; they had the appearance of a block of flats floating on their side.

Submarines had been busy in the months leading to the invasion, first by landing reconnaisance parties to inspect the landing beaches for defensive objects and, secondly, to test the shore for the bearing of tanks and heavy weapons. Small submarines also played a part in the operation: X20 and X23 were stationed there to surface as beacons to guide the huge fleet to their correct positions on the French coast. They had been secretly in position there for some time before D-Day, as the operation had been postponed several times due to bad weather.

So what happened in our area? Prior to the landing, there had been a great build-up of troops and ammunition dumps, tank parks, big guns and all the paraphernalia of modern warfare. Sele Court (now part of the Towers Convent) played host to the Regina Rifle Regiment, a part of the 3rd Canadian Division. They left here in March 1944 to practice landings on the Isle of Wight and Stokes Bay in Hampshire. The 15th Scottish Division took their place at Sele Court until D-Day. Burletts on Clays Hill was the temporary home of the Artillery. Four 25 pounders were lodged there with their crews. Castletown also had four 25 pounders as residents. The ammunition for these guns was stockpiled in Castletown Pit; St. Mary's House was the CO's HQ.

40,000 men died or were casualties in the first few weeks after 6th June 1944, while the 'forgotten' armies were fighting on in Burma and the Far East. Do read the names on the war memorials in our churches and churchyards and think of those who lost their lives, enabling us to have our tomorrows.

My thanks to Len Sanford for local knowledge [KN-B]

12.6 Councillor Len Sanford, whose encyclopaedic knowledge of wartime Bramber and Beeding was unequalled. Seen here on his retirement with Sheila van den Bergh, Chairman of the Horsham District Council, and Joyce Shaw (left), at a tree-planting ceremony in honour of his 55 years of service to the community.

12.6a Canadians of the 3rd Regina Rifles, outside St. Mary's House, just before D-Day, 1944.

St. Peter's Bells (Part 2)

For some people one of the most pleasant moments of the week is lying in bed on a Sunday morning listening to the sound of church bells, but how many spare a thought for those who are actually ringing the bells high up in the tower? I have previously related [3.3] the history of St. Peter's bells, describing the two mediaeval (1307 AD) and six Victorian bells now hanging, and the 9cwt. bell cast in 1613 which was removed c.1892 to be recast into four Victorian ones.

It is necessary to go back to the mid-1600s to understand what bellringing is about. A fundamental change took place in the manner in which church bells were hung. Up to that time bells in almost every country were hung on a spindle with a rope attached. In England from the 17th century, as new bells were installed, they were attached to a wooden wheel with a rope running round the rim of the wheel, down to the ringing chamber below. This method allowed a far greater degree of control, so that any one ringer could, by retarding the rope slightly as it went up or down, slow his bell and let another ring before it. The bells could therefore be made to change places in the order of their ringing, so change-ringing was born. No other country in Europe adopted the wheel method so, except for a few isolated cases, 'change-ringing' is a particularly English sound.

In 1688, a Cambridge printer, Fabian Stedman, published a book on the new method of ringing. He classified change-ringing and took as his basis the number of changes possible on seven bells; this is 5,040, a full peal, which takes over three hours to ring. St. Peter's has eight bells and would therefore have 40,320 permutations.

Apart from Sunday and practice, bells are rung at weddings and funerals. At burial services the bells are half muffled to give a distinctive sound; one man, Thomas Nash, who died in 1813, reversed this practice. In his will he left instructions that on the anniversary of his wedding each year the bells should be muffled, "& solemn and doleful changes rung" in token of this calamity, whilst at his funeral, as John Camp relates, there should be rung "a merrie, mirthful and joyous peal to celebrate my release from domestic Tyrrany and Wretchedness". What a cynic!

See also 3.3 for Part 1

Saltings Field

Before the 11th century the river, now known as the Adur, stretched from the steps below St. Peter's Church to the ditches at Bramber Castle and as far as St. Cuthman's port at Steyning. From the late 11th century, man-made drainage systems caused the sea to recede, leaving the port high and dry. With the decline of the height of the tides more land became available for agriculture. William Camden, in his work, *Britannia* (1586), mentioned that in the past ships with full sail came up river as far as Bramber.

The land immediately east of the river between Beeding Bridge and the Priory Field (some seven acres) is not defined on an early 17th century map of the area (See Gotham), but is shown as a saltmarsh on a later (Terrier) map dated 1733 (Mason). This area must have been unusable until the 18th century. The land on each side of the river is studded with salt workings except for this stretch. Beeding has, as far back as it is possible to research, been predominately arable, most of the land being used for growing wheat, oats, barley, legumes and fodder. Tithe records reveal that there were three or four times the amount of grains produced as there were fleeces or hides. Sale (Sele) Croft has a long record of being a place for fattening sheep and cattle so has not been used for anything other than feedstock. The land is low-lying and would flood at each tide if it were not for the banks of the Adur which were last built up in the 1950s. It has been designated as a flood storage area by the river authorities. There would be real danger of local flooding if it were built upon.

In the last 'Local Plan' (1978-1988) Policy 48 states: "A public open space to be laid out adjacent to the river Adur and the south of Priory Field, Upper Beeding (to be acquired by the Horsham District Council when restraints on government spending (1978) are removed) However until this land can be acquired, the existing use will remain undisturbed."

KN-B returns to this subject in 13.1

12.8 A saltcote, made of wattle topped with a turf roof, and pillars of salt in the Adur valley,as portrayed in the 16th century Painted Room at St. Mary's, Bramber

The Glebeland

The application by the Parish Church Council to Horsham District Council for a new Church Room* to replace the existing structure set me thinking. One of the conditions for planning consent was that an archaeological inspection would be imposed on builders during the course of construction. What would any archaeologist expect to find on this site that would be of interest? Perhaps the foundations of former dwellings or barns as this was relatively high ground above the flood plain of former times before the embanking of the river took place. A church does not usually stand alone; if it does, it is often the site of a deserted village. There is evidence that St. Peter's was once the centre of a village known as Sele/Sela. Could the Black Death of 1348 have led to the depopulation? Or perhaps it occurred during the Commonwealth period of the 17th century?

We know that there was a church and priory on the site of the present one. A church is recorded as existing before 1066, and at the Domesday survey twenty years after the Conquest, two churches are entered into those books. The earlier, possibly Saxon, building can be seen in crop patterns from the tower of St. Peter's. This may date from the time of St. Wilfrid, who came to Sussex around AD 681. The present church structure dates from the early 14th century, dedicated to SS Peter and Paul on February 24th 1308. In the 1850s, a south aisle was added after a national ecclesiastical survey of worshippers (1851) indicated a need for more places. A 14th century chapel to St. John existed to the north of the chancel. It is thought that the square column in the north-east corner inside the chancel is a relic of that chapel. The south aisle is dedicated to the Blessed Virgin Mary, replacing an earlier aisle removed before 1802, as seen in drawings of the period.

The Priory dates from the late 11th century and was an impressive building. Roman roof tile fragments were found under the chancel floor in 1983. I do not think there will be anything of importance on the glebeland, but you never can be sure. It was rebuilt in the 1790s with an addition (1838) to the south. At the bottom of the steps to the river there is much dressed stonework which could be remains of a jetty or foundations of a watermill recorded in the vicinity.

*The Bevan Hall, now built.

The Coach Wall in High Street

Some years ago I wrote an article on the roads [2.3]. Sussex roads up to the 18th century were almost impassable during the winter months. I quoted the Revd. H. E. B. Arnold's quaint reflection on the highways as 'The Foul Ways of Sussex People'. Sussex women, it is said, have been credited with having the longest legs in England as a result of having to pull their feet out of deep mud at every step!

A statute of 1555 imposed the upkeep of the highways on the parish, which was not very well received, and tended to be ignored. In the 18th and 19th centuries many Turnpike Acts were passed. Turnpike Trusts were set up and the roads were built and paid for by tolls which laid the costs, rightfully, on those who used them. The building of these roads caused the disappearance of many old disused structures. Acts of Parliament allowed the Trusts to use the materials from mediaeval castles. Much of Bramber Castle is probably under the streets of our villages.

The coaching period really took off in the late 18th century. The Prince Regent led the way by making Brighton his seaside residence. Coaching gave way to the railways in the middle of the 19th century. Rail travel was much cheaper and quicker, so coach proprietors were unable to compete. The coaching era was a romantic period and opened up the country to those who, formerly, had only been to the next market town. They were the main carrier of news from the capital and elsewhere. Our High Street was part of the coach network from the late 18th century, Beeding Bridge was rebuilt in brick in 1785 and the old toll road past Dacre Gardens was the result of an act of 1807 and was titled 'The New Road to Shoreham avoiding Beeding Hill'.

The high wall opposite April Cottage is a relic of the Turnpike period. Some landowners were incensed that coach passengers sitting atop a mail coach could see over their walls intruding on their privacy. Many raised the height of walls to restore their seclusion. Our 'Coach Wall' is a very good example, and one of the few still standing in Sussex.

See also *The Turnpikes* 12.12

A Hundred Years of Parish Councils

There can be very few communities in this world that can call themselves totally 'free'. Ever since man has lived in groups there has always been tribal administration and justice to regulate at varying degrees the lives of social groups.

The Romans were great civil administrators, and they brought to our country the first proper government of England as a whole. Laws were passed in the Senate in Rome and the legions saw that they were carried out. Sadly, perhaps, the Roman Empire declined and early in the fifth century they packed up and left.

The fine roads were allowed to fall into disrepair, isolating communities. The Jutes, Angles and Saxons came in to fill the void. In our part of the world the Saxons followed the Romans around AD 490. They administered their laws from small kingdoms. Under the Saxons each village or area was divided into 'tithings' (ten men). These men had to stand security for the good behaviour of the others. This was known as the Frankpledge. Collective responsibility for securing offenders was a dominant part of English life. The larger areas known as the Saxon Hundred were thought to support 100 families. We in Beeding were in the hundred of Burbeach, which used to stretch as far up country as Bewbush near Crawley. It is recorded that the Hundred Court for 1788 was held in the King's Head in the High Street.

Courts Leet and Courts Baron were held at Beeding Court – the main Manor of Beeding. Some of the earlier meetings were held in the Church. Although the chancel was sacred, the body of the Church was used as a parish hall. It was often the only sheltered meeting place. There was very little seating until after the Reformation.

Later on the Vestry was used and the term 'Vestry' came to mean the group of elders who ran the village. They appointed the 'Overseer of the Poor', established by the Poor Law act of 1597 and Poor Relief act of 1601. These guardians had the power to levy a rate, to pay a dole to paupers and help with medical aid. They also found work for the idle in the parish. Minutes of meetings from 1826 to 1853 exist. Our Parish Council was established in late 1894 under the Local Government act (1894) which allowed elections to take place in rural areas where the population exceeded 300.

KN-B dealt substantially with this subject in 1.9
but here revives the subject to celebrate the Centenary

The Turnpikes

Recent reports indicate that the Government is proposing toll roads in the UK. This is nothing new. All roads were private before the first Turnpike Act of 1663. Some would say that it is right to get the users to pay for the upkeep of these routes, but everyone benefits from their existence. I have written before about our early roads and how they declined when the Roman occupation ceased in the 5th century. This period was known as the 'Dark Ages'. Communities became isolated because of the absence of proper highways. The pack horse was often the only outside link.

Earlier turnpikes connected us with London. Post coaches came via Steyning, through Bramber and Beeding, over Beeding Hill and down to Shoreham east of Erringham and on to Brighton. An Act was passed in 1807 to build a road east of the Adur from Beeding to Shoreham (now A283). I have copies of the Trust's minutes from the 1860s to the winding up in 1885. (County Councils assumed responsibility for most roads c.1888. Trusts were wound up at this time). The title of this new road was 'The New Road to Shoreham Avoiding Beeding Hill.' The right to levy tolls was auctioned yearly by the Trust. The following extract from the minute book refers to Beeding Toll Gate between Beeding Court and the Rising Sun Inn. 'At a meeting of the Trustees of the 'Horsham and Steyning and Beeding Road Act 1860' held by adjournment at the Chequers Inn at Steyning on Wednesday the 22nd day of September 1869.'

Present...The Revd. T. Medland, T. F. Wisden Esq., Messrs. Thos Wisden, W. Stanford Jnr. and George Michell; the Revd. T. Medland is elected chairman.

They ordered that the tolls arising at the gate called Beeding Gate, which were let for the year ending 29th of September inst. for the sum of £130 be put up at that sum which was done, but not let (there being no bidder), but afterwards let to Mr. George Smith at £130 (George Smith built 'The Towers' in 1883). 'The Trustees present do declare that the road under their care and superintendence is in a good state and condition.' It also resolved to accept Mr. A. S. Elliott's tender for 'supplying 80 loads of good clean land flints of 60 bushels to the load at 8/6 per load be accepted.' The last entry, 19th December 1885, deals with the winding up of the Trust and records that the Gate House was sold for '£17.10.0 and that £315.19.9 be distributed proportionally to the Bondholders.'

See 2.3 and 12.10

Salt Pits on the Adur

The news that there may be salt pits in Saltings Field was greeted with joy by many conservationists and concerned people who would like the area preserved. In earlier *Villagers,* I have on several occasions mentioned salt workings and have been indebted to Eric and Hilda Holden for local information. I think it was they who coined the term Saltern for the raised salt workings.

In the past, rent and other debts were paid 'in kind', that is by some produce of the soil or other article of commerce. Ambers of salt, weights of cheese and pounds of pepper were common payments in Sussex in mediaeval years. The Adur and other river valleys produced much salt. Many agricultural labourers worked the salterns in any spare time they were allowed.

14th century documents show that salt was a flourishing trade at that time. In the years between 1323 and 1329, the recorded shipments of salt from Sussex were fifty-eight. We do not know the size of each ship load, but it may have exceeded one ton. There appears to have been a decline in this work as there are only 3 shipments in the years 1395 to 1399. This may have come about by wars at the time, or the Black Death which decimated this area in 1348/9 and reduced the population by 70% in some places.

The *Chartulary of the Priory of Sele* records gifts of land and other items the monks received from various kind donors, including salt pits. These they let out to tenants who paid their rent in salt. It is noted that as early as 1153 [*Chartulary* 148] that Ralph de Sancto Audoeno had given to Sele: 'My salt pit which is near Anningedon'. In 1180 [*Chartulary* 26] Sir William de Braose gave 'All his bridge of Brambre and five salt pits and three men with their lands at the head of the same bridge on the east... and also mills or fisheries... for the support of the convent'. In 1230 [*Chartulary* 5] we read that these pits lay 'at the head of the lesser bridge [Beeding Bridge] towards the east and that the land was west of the greater bridge of Brembre' (opposite St. Mary's).

See also *The Moated Site* 12.3

For more on saltings see 2.4 and 12.8

Earlier Views of the County

History was one of my favourite subjects at school. We had a particularly good and enthusiastic master, Mr. Patching, a youngish veteran of the First World War trenches, who was a storyteller of the first degree. Not for us just the reciting of key dates; his interesting lessons were very much looked forward to by his pupils.

As a lad in junior school my hobby, overseen by my grandfather, was collecting old guide books of Sussex. A ten-year-old these days could not do this as most of them are too expensive. When I started, nearly sixty years ago, you could pick up a 19th century guide book for around a penny, anything of the 18th century was usually twopence, with very few exceeding one shilling (20 to the £). Later in life, I added the published editions of many of the old Sussex diarists to the growing library that was accumulating in my bedroom. All this was put on hold in 1943 when my assistance was required to overcome the Third Reich!

History is the evidence of the past; the written word is more reliable than events passed down by word of mouth. These can be distorted and enlarged upon by the narrator to suit his audience. Kings and Parliaments provide the main events of national history, but it is the county and village diarists who tell the true story of everyday life in their localities. They relate their own way of life and of those around them and are a good reflection of long gone lifestyles. Much can be gained from accounts written by visitors. These provide a supplement to the local diarist by recording what may be trivial customs locally and so commonplace as not to be commented upon. The visitor marvels at certain things that would escape the local scribe.

Deterrents – Law and Order

In several past issues I have mentioned local law and punishment from early records. Saxon 'frankpledge' involved collective responsibility for the apprehension and punishment of wrong-doers in the parish. The 1285 Statute of Winchester affirmed the obligations of a parish to keep its own law and order with a system of 'watch and ward'. The Statute also introduced 'hue and cry' in which a person or persons wishing to make an arrest could call on any resident of the manor or parish to join them in pursuit. Everyone was obliged to join the hue and cry, and literally cry aloud to attract the attention of others.

In the early 19th century, before there were proper policemen, village elders and businessmen formed and funded 'Prosecuting Societies' or 'Felons' Associations'. Murder seemed to be of equal worth to sheep or cattle stealing: one could be hanged for either. Mail robbery was also a capital offence.

Beeding's first policeman was appointed shortly after 30th November 1837, following a proposal by Richard Goddard, the parish chairman. Three (unpaid) inspectors were appointed to oversee him.

On the south side of Windmill Hill, a part of Tenantry Down, there are terraces of cultivation. Some are named furlongs of land on old leases. On this slope there is documented what is known as 'Hangman's Acre'. It is said to be the place where a gibbet was erected following a conviction for robbery of the mail near Erringham in December 1775. The area has a long history, as the Hundred Court (Burbeach) has been held in the valley west of the waterworks from mediaeval times.

Felons convicted of capital offences were, upon being executed, hung in chains or iron cages till they rotted, to deter others. It is well recorded that one robber, executed at Shoreham, was hung on a gibbet and his mother visited the site regularly to pick up the bones as they fell so that she could secretly bury them in a churchyard. The sad tale inspired Lord Tennyson's poem 'Rizpah'.

Knepp Castle and the Carylls

Knepp Castle was, from some time after the Conquest, built and owned by William de Braose. His main residence was of course the newly constructed castle at Bramber. Each of the five 'Rapes' of Sussex, (later six) had a river, a port, a castle and a forest. The port and castle were in the maritime part with the forest to the north of the Rape (St. Leonards in our division). The forest provided many of the things needed to sustain life: timber for building and fuel for heating and cooking. It was also host to bear, wolf, boar, and many types of deer. The main recreation of the nobility was hunting, which also provided food and clothing. Some hunts lasted for several days and Knepp was intended to be a hunting lodge being halfway between the forest and the castle at Bramber.

On the 8th April 1202, King John visited Knepp Castle in the parish of Shipley. He visited again in January 1215 and stayed three days. Originally de Braose supported John, but he later quarrelled with him and had to go into exile. In 1216 King John ordered Knepp to be razed to the ground and sequestrated Bramber Castle. That it was not fully destroyed at the time is supported by the Caryll family being in residence in 1341 ('Nona Returns').

The Carylls were a cadet branch of the de Braose line, as were the Bruces in Scotland. The Carylls are recorded in many of the documents locally from Bosham to Sompting and up to West Grinstead. They were in residence or in ownership of many of the Knights Templar lands after 1309* and they may be connected to St.Mary's, Bramber as an account of the rebuilding of Bramber Bridge in the fifteenth century is recorded in the published records of the Caryll line.**

In Shipley Church there is a magnificent monument under which lie the remains of Sir Thomas Caryll who expired on 30th January 1616 aged 49. The prose inscribed thereon is worth reading. There are no Carylls in the current phone book.

* Templars arrested by order of Edward II in 1308

** See Max de Trenqualéon in bibliography

13.4 The remains of the original Knepp Castle,
destroyed by fire during the time of the Carryl family

13.4a Knepp Castle today, now the home of the Burrell family
(by courtesy of the Daily Telegraph)

Forget it Not!

V.E. Day (Victory in Europe) is the day when World War II came to an end in our part of the globe. I have been told many tales of what happened locally on that day. Most people remember what they were doing at the time. Others like our resident George Clark, were probably not aware of it: he was in a Japanese prison camp in a poor state.

When war came, everyone did something to help the war effort. Those too young or too old for the armed services joined the L.D.V. (Local Defence Volunteers), nicknamed the 'Look, Duck and Vanish'. They held the fort until the Home Guard evolved from their ranks. Other residents became Air Raid Wardens and Civil Defence rescue workers on top of their day jobs.

Beeding and Bramber were not too badly knocked about as some front line south coast villages were. Nearby Shoreham Airport attracted the attention of the Luftwaffe and our two villages were bombed and machine-gunned from time to time. A bomb fell at the back of the Rising Sun, another fell at night in a duck pond near the Towers and we heard tell that the residents of Sele Gardens awoke in the morning to find many of the houses covered with a thick layer of mud! Several aeroplanes were brought down in the area. One German plane crashed near 'Tin-pots' and some dead crew members were buried at Botolphs. Later, on July 4th 1944, a Flying Fortress* crashed in Tottington Wood. The crew baled out.

Early in the war there were several bombing incidents. Three bombs were dropped at Stretham Manor Farm on August 28th 1940. September in the same year was very busy here, with many high explosive and incendiary bombs and parachute mines locally. October was also a bad month for residents. The 13th saw three bombs fall on Small Dole with one fatality. Flying bombs are recorded in the Beeding School Log as passing over. Pupils were herded into the corridor until the danger had passed.

November 5th 1944 is the last recorded attack on the villages, when a flying bomb (Doodlebug) fell 200 yards west of New Hall Farm. Nineteen houses were damaged but happily there were no casualties. The last air raid warning was sounded at 25 minutes to midnight on December 11th 1944.

*The 'Flying Fortress' bomber

Coins

It is generally accepted that the English 'penny' was originally a silver denarius from either Tiberius or more probably Augustus, as the latter's coinage had been in circulation for a much longer time. These coins from 2,000 years ago are, considering the time when they were produced, some of the most beautifully struck, with excellent portraits of the head's of state. These were unlike the mediaeval currency of Europe, which portrayed almost caricature portraits of the kings and bishops of the period.

Coins were a very necessary exchange medium, especially small change. If a person wished to purchase a penny article and the trader could not give change for, say, a shilling that was offered, it restricted the transaction. In time of a dearth of coinage entrepreneurs struck their own, redeemable at their business address.

In the 1930s, an advertisement appeared in the window of a Bramber shop. It was put there by a collector who wished to purchase a 17th century Bramber halfpenny trade token. The evidence of the coin's existence was first noticed in a list of Sussex tokens in 1888. At the time it caused much amusement; people searched through their old boxes and attics as the price offered increased at regular intervals. Unfortunately the coin did not exist; the catalogue mistakenly said: 'Robert Higgins... his halfpenny...1666'. When the worn specimen was properly examined it was found to be from Ellesmere (Shropshire)!

See 14.9 *The Penny*

The Lord of Bramber's Hounds

At the present time, fox-hunting is in decline, being, as it is, a bloodsport. In earlier days, hunting was vital to the survival of ordinary people, who had little means to preserve meat and game for any length of time. The huntsmen did not wear the hunting 'pink' and quite often they hunted on foot.

"About the year 1260, William V, Lord of Bramber, placed his horses and a pack of hounds in the care of the monks of Sele Priory, with board and lodgings for his grooms. The dull monotony of the cloister was broken by the tramping of hunters and the baying of dogs. We may even picture the monks gathering up their habits and following the hunt as fast as their legs could carry them, tumbling over mounds and ditches with such laughter and enjoyment, whilst the good Prior perchance rode his sorry nag in their midst. For a few hours they were not merely monks, but simple country folk," as the Revd. H. E. B. Arnold, sometime Curate of Beeding and Bramber, relates.

We might not have known of these occasions had it not been for our cautious Prior of Sele, Walter de Colvile. He got a little anxious lest his Lord of Bramber might thrust too much responsibility and expense upon his narrow resources, so he obtained a 'Letter of Indemnity' from Sir William as follows: "Whereas the prior and monks of Sele of their mere courtesy have often taken care of our young horses and have brought up our young hounds or harriers for us; and have also given corrodies or liveries to certain of our men, we do not wish that their courtesy, so shown to us of their mere good will and grace, and not of due nor right, may be turned to the prejudice or damage of the said house of Sele.* Wherefore we acknowledge by these presents for ourselves and our heirs that the said prior and monks are not, nor ever were bound to do us such service; wherefore neither we, nor our heirs can ever in future claim such services as of due right." **

*In a similar incident, Queen Matilda, whilst hunting in Kent, left her pack of hounds behind at a monastery and never reclaimed them, to the complete impoverishment of the monks. Perhaps the monks of Sele suffered a similar fate. [Ed]

** *The Chartulary of Sele* [Ch.63]. See bibliography.

The Mace

Early man had to devise weapons for his own protection and to kill the wild animals he needed for food, clothing and his general sustenance. These primitive weapons were most likely to be hand-held flints. As time progressed he may have obtained a stone which had a hole to which he attached a rude wooden handle to extend his reach, or just as likely a wooden club as depicted by artists drawing prehistoric scenes.

Neolithic man made great improvements in the tools he fashioned from flint and bone. This period was a manufacturing era. Cissbury had flint mines and was a manufacturing and trading area for stone tools.

Beautifully fabricated axes, spears, knives, sickles and all manner of stone implements were produced. Palaeolithic man had used roughly shaped knapped flints but, in the 'New Stone Age', Neolithic man shaped his tools to give them form, then ground and polished them into well-finished articles. These were treasured by their owners and were buried with them, along with a whetstone for use in the afterlife. It is certain that some of the larger artefacts were more than just tools; they also indicated status in the tribe.

These early axes and clubs were the forerunners of the mace. 'Mace', as a word, seems to have appeared in documents around the time of the Norman Conquest; no doubt the mace was used at Senlac, and probably for centuries before. One can see many of these lethal-looking weapons in the armoury of the Tower of London. They could inflict terrible wounds in the hands of armoured knights on horseback. The mace carried by the mediaeval knight was also a badge of office: it was his authority from the monarch. At the end of the mediaeval period and the beginning of the Renaissance, gunpowder emerged and the pistol superseded the mace as a sign of authority. To this day, Speakers of the House of Commons take their authority from the mace, which lies in front of them.

In St. Nicholas at Bramber, one can see a mace belonging to the Constable or Headborough of Bramber. This is not a weapon; it dates from the time of Queen Anne, bears her coat of arms, and was for ceremonial use. The Constable was appointed by the Duke of Norfolk, Lord of the Manor.

13.8 Retrieving the Bramber Mace

Chairman of Bramber Parish Council, Mrs. Gillian Fox, with (from to left to right), fellow-councillors, Vivienne Hines, Len Sanford, James Armour-Milne (Secretary), Boyd Pendennis and Geoff Fox (13.8)

The Mace (later restored by Jacqueline Fox) was in possession of Walter Potter's Museum of Curiosities and was eventually under threat when the collection was auctioned. Tremendous efforts were made by the Parish Council to bring the Mace back to its proper home in Bramber, where it now resides.

(Photograph by courtesy of Gillian Fox)

The Ecu

I have just received the first of the cupro-nickel Ecu's, which may become our pocket change in the future. It is the size of a 10 pence piece. On the obverse, there is a female bust wearing a Greek helmet with the visor lifted as on early coins of Athens. It has the words: BRITANNIARUM DEI GRATIA 1995. On the reverse is a likeness of the Pilgrim Fathers' 'Mayflower' with the legend: UNITA TAUETUR DEUS, much in the style of the old 'Ship Halfpenny' of George VI.

The Government has been involved in discussions over the name by which the new coinage will be known. I have seen in newspapers that the name FLORIN is favoured. 'Florin' was first used on a gold coin of Edward III (c.1344). Because of its design, it was also known as a 'Double Leopard'. It was worth six shillings then. Later in the reign of Queen Victoria, the silver florin was introduced as the first decimal coin. It was inscribed ONE TENTH OF A POUND. Worth two shillings, it circulated from 1849 until 1967 when it became the ten 'new pence' coin.

These days, the coinage is not worth the metal it is made from. It was all different before the Second World War and up to 1946, as many senior citizens will recall, when the higher denominations were silver. The intrinsic value was there in your hand. Melted down, it was still worth its value. There is no coin today to replace the magnificent silver crown of five shillings (25p). Some lucky children had them for their birthdays. I had to make do with a silver sixpence, but what a lot one could buy with it.

The 'copper' coins of my childhood were made of bronze. The 'Saturday Penny", which had to be earned, bought quite a lot of sweets, and strange things such as 'Tiger Nuts', 'Spanish Root (an aromatic fibrous tick that could be chewed until it looked like an old paint brush), 'Everlasting Toffee' and many other sweetmeats.

The silver penny exists today in the Maundy Money set, but the first silver pennies were the standard unit of currency from Saxon times c.AD 775. It was cut in half for the halfpenny and in quarters for the 'Farthing' (fourth thing). Copper for the low denominations came in around the time of Charles II, replaced by bronze c.1860. A bronze farthing can be seen embedded in the flint wall above the window at the east end of the nave of St. Peter's.

Church Mysteries

Most people have inquiring minds and want to know the inside and outside of most things. I class myself as an inquirer, and I hate to leave puzzles and mysteries unsolved. As Christmas approaches and as I sit in my pew at St. Peter's before the Sunday service, I try and imagine how things would have been in the last century at this season. In these winter months, the fireplace in the north wall of the nave would have had a fire going to warm the parishioners. Did those who sat nearest have to stoke it during the service, I wonder?

One thing drew my attention above all others. This is the curious wall mounting beside the pulpit. As you will note, it is a shallow depression in the chancel wall with no immediate apparent function. It has a lead or pewter surrounding collar in the shape of a diamond with trefoils at each angle. Was it something to do with the carved rood-screen, which in earlier days divided the nave from the sanctuary? A fragment of this is mounted above the entrance door inside the south aisle.

The church has gone through many changes since 1073. The oldest remaining part is the bottom half of the tower which dates from 1283. The early structure of the church was rebuilt c.1307 on the original tower. You can observe that the axis of the nave is not central to the tower by looking at the ridge of the roof where it abuts the tower. The present south aisle is from the 1850s. An earlier aisle was known to exist in 1627 but was gone by 1800.

Inside the church many alterations have been made. There once was a minstrel gallery at the west end. In Bloxam's day, the pulpit was on the opposite side of the chancel arch and was most likely moved to its present position during the 1850s. This may be the answer to the origin of the collared recess. One theory suggested that it was formed to accommodate the door knob of an earlier pulpit door when it was in the open position. The pulpit has been lowered and reduced in size over past years.

Villages

The present civil parish of Upper Beeding is a collection of mediaeval and earlier villages and settlements. There were until 1984 seven villages within the parish of Upper Beeding. In 1984 the Boundary Commission ceded King's Barn area to Steyning civil parish to establish our western boundary at the River Adur. This part of our parish was the some-time home of King Alfred, his father Athelwulf, and three of his brothers, so five Saxon Kings.

Mediaeval Beeding was in the area of Beeding Court Farm and in the fields to the south, where evidence has been found of habitation. This place was thought to be the east end of the bridge or causeway (Veteri Ponte in documents). Beeding High Street did not exist before the Conquest (1066) as a built up area; it was still estuary. SELE, or SELA, was the ecclesiastical settlement around the church of St. Peter and the priory which probably included, as a linear village, part of Hyde Street.

Small Dole was most likely the largest of the other settlements; its name recorded from Elizabethan times, referred to as 'Dole Green' in 1808. Edburton was joined to the civil parish of Beeding in 1933 (1000 acres). The eastern part of Edburton (1552 acres) had been included in Fulking civil parish when West and East Sussex had been divided for administration in 1889. Tottington, another small settlement, was known as the manor of Tottington Wood, including Hoe Wood, supporting a few farm workers.

Upper and Lower Horton was a scattered settlement. The manor of Horton-Maybank or Horton Horsey stretched down to the coast. This brings us to 'Thundersbarrow'. A collection of settlements usually had a defendable gathering place in times of unrest. After the Conquest, Bramber Castle would have been the place where inhabitants could take their possessions and some animals to safely. Before that time a defendable area was necessary for periods when roving bands of lawless men, and small armies under regional warlords, needed supplies. Thundersbarrow, south of Beeding Hill, was the gathering place for our forebears. Corn-drying ovens, and other artefacts have been discovered there, but there seems to be no sign of permanent habitation within the earth walls and embankments of this 'Iron Age' fort.

Fifty Years of the Memorial Playing Field

Why so named? Memorial Playing Fields? If one looks around the village of Upper Beeding there is no large war memorial except for the small cross with bronze plaques at the entrance to St. Peter's churchyard; this commemorates the local men who fell in the First World War. The Parish Council, meeting in 1942, decided that the village needed a playing field which would also be a tribute to the dead of both world wars. Very little was done about this until the Second World War ended. There was a place to play cricket at High Trees Corner near Beeding Court roundabout, but no designated football or stoolball ground. Matches were played on fields with the permission of local landowners.

The Parish Council entered into an agreement with West Sussex County Council on the 14th January 1946 to rent, with the option to purchase, the 'Ham', a seven acre field which was once part of Pond Farm. Permission to buy and applications to acquire grants and loans took all of two years. A grant of £2,155 was received from the Ministry of Education, £720 was raised in the district and £950 was borrowed by the Parish Council. A mortgage was obtained and payments began on 1st July 1946 with the final payment of £998 10s 7d being made on 1st July 1950.

Having been in use for some time, the field was officially opened during the summer of 1948 by the MP for Arundel/Shoreham division, Mr.W. N. Cuthbert. He remarked upon the splendid example that Beeding had set the whole county. He said he preferred to see a living memorial to the war dead: 'Your people are going to enjoy this field,' he said, addressing the Chairman of the Council: 'This is money well spent'.

Entertainments during the afternoon included cricket (tip and run), stoolball and football matches, and a dance at the Village Hall later, attracting some 140 local residents.

The Memorial Playing Field owes its existence to the efforts of two parish councillors: Frank Lucas, a Parish Council member for 25 years (15 as Chairman). He was owner of Lucas Stores (later the Pharmacy), a Royal Flying Corps man of the First World War and keen to remember fallen comrades. The other founder was the vicar, the Rev. R. de Mowbray Young, a Parish Councillor from 1939.

14.2 Ladies' committee – 2nd Annual Welfare Sports, Beeding, 1926

14.2a Men's committee – 2nd Annual Welfare Sports, Beeding, 1926

Weathervanes

Most of you know that I rake the gravel path leading to St. Peter's Church nearly every week of the year. During the spring and summer it is a very pleasant task in the stillness of the churchyard, great for meditating. From September to February the job gets difficult because of the trees shedding their leaves, and on a dry day with a puff of wind, they get unmanageable. My wife, Margaret, helps load the leaves. My other aid in this autumn period is on the church tower, our refurbished weathervane. This is of great importance to me as it determines the way I get the leaves together to remove them.

The earliest weathervane is thought to be in the form of a golden Triton, which was mounted on the Tower of the Winds in Athens c.50BC. Before that time, streamers had been used to indicate the direction of the wind. Weather-cocks appeared in England around the 8th century. The cock was used as a pointer as it was a noted symbol of vigilance.

Why would a church need a weathervane? In the 9th century, the Pope decreed that a weathercock must be placed on all church steeples to signify the Church's sovereignty and to remind Christians they must be vigilant. In the 13th century, only the nobility were allowed to have weathervanes. Vanes come in all shapes and sizes, usually surmounting a horizontal cross, having the cardinal points NESW to indicate the direction of the wind. This indication is considered unnecessary on church buildings as the nave and chancel stretch from west to east. Sometimes a fish is used as a pointer, an early Christian symbol. The Greek word for fish is formed by the initial letters*, standing for 'Jesus Christ, Son of God, Saviour'.

* ICHTHYS

Semaphore

In 1925, James Dunning published a book about the Roman road to Portslade. This interesting book reviewed the Roman roads in our part of Southern England and the author's theories on the routes of those roads. Dunning also speculated on the position of Roman encampments on the South Downs. As a former pupil and follower of I. D. Margary and George Hollyman, I was lucky to be included in the band of young workers available for the 'digs' in the 1930s. It was the opinion of George Hollyman that the castle/fortified stockade just to the east of Beeding Hill, erected by the Normans at the time of the Conquest as a vantage point while the castle of Bramber was being constructed, was built over an earlier Roman station.

The Romans were great communicators, keeping in close touch with all their outlying camps and settlements. This site could have been a signal station in a chain of such positions across the maritime south.

A typical fort of this type would have been a square walled enclosure with turrets at the corner, surrounded by a shallow ditch. In the centre of the enclosure stood a wooden tower built on a stone foundation. The tower would have been up to 100 feet high and probably had semaphore arms which could have been seen for many miles. It is thought that each tower station would have been manned by some 40 soldiers/operators. Remains of other Roman signal towers can be seen at Castle Hill, Scarborough, and another near Whitby.

Some thirteen hundred years later during the Napoleonic wars of the late 18th and early 19th century, the navy and army were to some extent controlled by the same Roman method of signalling. Semaphore towers from London to Portsmouth and other naval ports sent messages from the Admiralty to ships of the Royal Navy in just a few minutes. It is recorded that the chain of semaphore stations was still transmitting orders in 1893. Marconi invented wireless telegraphy in 1897 and developed his discovery over the next few years. By 1905, it was widely in use and brought about the demise of the semaphore.

The Beeding Higgler

As a youngster, I often met an old lady who had lived in Beeding all her life. She told me she was the wife of a higgler. Asked to explain, she told me that 'higgler' was a Sussex term. In early-times, the higglers called on farms and smallholdings and bought up eggs and poultry, selling them on at a small profit around the markets, to innkeepers and those who catered to the public. As the 19th century approached the roads became easier to traverse and the higgler gave up his traditional wicker basket carried on foot, adopting a small cart. Before the 1800s, London markets were very difficult to reach from places like Beeding, where there was no direct access. Fat poultry was imported from the continent for the London markets through ports like Newhaven and Brighton, which had direct links to carriers who made daily journeys to the capital.

The advent of the railway opened up London markets to many small, formerly isolated places like ours. The higgler was then employed by poultry producers to roam the countryside buying up all lean chickens to fatten. When the railway came to Bramber a small industry was built up here in poultry fattening, because the principal markets in Leadenhall and Smithfield were now within hours of the producer. Many agricultural labourers and their wives raised a few fowls for a bit of pocket money, but the main suppliers were well organised in cramming or force-feeding the birds. The higgler was now supplied with a cash float and bought chickens for the fattener on commission (usually 2 shillings a dozen). Many travelled to a radius of some 40 miles.

Fattening was then a three week task. Fed on oats and barley for the first week and force fed by machine for the last two weeks, they were then killed and dressed for the market on the day of dispatch. The machine used was like a portable sausage-maker operated by two skilled men. The fowls even seemed to look forward to the procedure during the last stages of fattening. They were fed on barley meal, mutton suet, treacle, sugar and milk, with linseed oil added in the winter months. Good fat chicken could fetch as much as 5/- each, a good sum in those days of the last century. Small feathers were also used, sold for about 6d a pound. A feather mattress could take up up to sixty pounds in weight and was much prized by the owner.

Dovecotes

In former times, the salt pits in the estuary were used for gathering salt for the preserving of meat during the winter months. Until the practice of growing root crops was adopted, large numbers of cattle had to be slaughtered at the commencement of winter because of the lack of feeding stuffs for them. Beef and pork were pickled in brine and stored in tubs. The naval coopers were always busy fabricating barrels for this purpose.

In the past, the owners of large estates constructed ice pits where ice gathered from frozen lakes was stored. This method of storage was not satisfactory for preserving food for any length of time. The ice was used for cooling drinks and making desserts for the well off.

This resulted in there being little fresh meat in the winter. One way of overcoming this was to use the birds and eggs available, such as pigeon and dove. These could be made to lay eggs all year round in proper nesting sites. This was virtually free food. Dovecotes were set up to ease the task of egg-collecting. These structures (usually of flint or brick) were, in the mediaeval period, only allowed to be owned by the lord of the manor or the local priest. They were usually circular, but rectangular ones are recorded and could accommodate five hundred birds or more. Some of the circular ones were fitted with a device called a 'potence' which consisted of a ladder fixed to a revolving frame to enable all the nests to be reached from inside without difficulty.

Records show that eggs were used as part of rents to the crown and ecclesiastical establishments. Regarded as an important possession, a dovecote is recorded at Beeding Court in the year 1326.

Watermills

Power sources for agricultural work in early times were provided by men, oxen and horses. It is not known when man first used the power of water to grind corn, but it is certain that there were water mills in ancient Greece. Cereals were then squashed rather than ground. Fine flour was made by pestle and mortar and stone querns. It was most probable that the Romans introduced water-driven corn mills into England. In AD 395 laws were made in Rome for the protection of their watermills, which indicated their importance to the community.

Although the Romans must have brought their mill technology to the British Isles, the first mention of a corn mill was in an Anglo Saxon charter dated AD 664. In the following century and onward, frequent reliable references occur to charters for mills.

The Domesday survey, completed in 1086, although not covering all of the counties, noted that there were 7,500 watermills in England. If a mill was recorded in the 1086 survey it was exempt from ecclesiastical tithes and it is fairly certain that places mentioned continued to possess mills on the same site for centuries. A windmill replaced a watermill on the 'Millfield' site north west of Beeding Bridge.

There were three main types of watermill, as there were with the later (from the 12th century) windmills. The water cornmill types were known as undershot, breast and overshot. The undershot had its centre shaft above the level of the stream. The breast wheel was fitted with buckets and usually enclosed in a culvert beneath the water source. The overshot wheel is beneath the source and gets the benefit of the full impulse of the water, but its speed may be retarded by the level of water below it.

There was a watermill recorded at Sele Priory in mediaeval times. Local mill historians believe it was fed from a stream from the Henfield - Small Dole direction. There is a mill pond to the north of St. Peter's; the site can be seen from the tower. The mill was located west of the Priory. Dressed stonework at the bottom of the steps leading down to the river from St. Peter's has been recorded in Victorian times, but appears to be overgrown at present.

'The Rising Sun'

Inns and alehouses, from early times, were situated where they would attract most business, usually on the main street of the village. News of foreign wars, happenings in the capital and local intelligence was passed on through the local hostelry. With the mailcoach era and the building of the turnpike roads, many small premises were enlarged or rebuilt to take advantage of the increasing trade. They were often staging posts for the changing of coach horses as well as victualling passengers.

The Kings Head, the main inn in Beeding from the 17th century, was the only inn on a coaching map of the late 18th century at the time when the turnpike went through Beeding High Street, through Castletown, and over the top of Beeding Hill. Things changed after an Act of Parliament (1807) which allowed the new turnpike road to be built along the east side of the Adur. The company survived until c.1885. There was a toll booth just south of The Rising Sun. In the early 19th century, it was recorded as an alehouse, which later became an inn under the name of The Star. Vestry meetings (early parish council gatherings) were held there from the 1850s, the first being held on Thursday 2nd March 1854, which indicated the growing importance of the place (from the 17th century they had been held at the King's Head). On that day, the Parish Constables were elected, among them Richard Kidd the miller. This was the first time the name Rising Sun had been used for what was formerly The Star.

There is a story of a later miller of Beeding Mill. His name was Jack Cruley. Cards, dice and drink parted him from his house, mill, money and friends. Finally his wife, unable to endure his ways, deserted him. Returning one night from the 'Rising Sun' somewhat mellow with ale from the horn, he wandered into a thicket and walked in a circle for some hours. Unable to find his way out he cried for help. An owl flying by questioned "Whoo? Whoo?" 'Jack Cruley' answered the miller. "Whoo? Whoo?" cried the owl mockingly. "Jack Cruley, I tell 'e," answered the bewildered miller. "Poor old Jack who's lost his mill, money and wife an' who's now lost his way".

14.8 The Rising Sun c1914, once a tied property run by the Steyning Brewery.

14.8a The Rising Sun 2010
(Photograph by courtesy of Barry and Sue Snell)

The Yew

The best place to see a mature yew tree today is to visit an old churchyard. It has, since early times, been associated with ecclesiastical premises. It has for a long time been a symbol of sadness. The yew may have come from Spain in mediaeval times, since it was known as the Spanish Yew.

Before the Industrial Revolution, the tree must have been the source of much of the armaments of many armies; no doubt the yew bows were the secret weapons of the archers of Agincourt (1415).

English poetry is littered with references to the yew bow and arrow. 'With Spanish yew so strong/Arrows a clothyard long,' as Drayton wrote in 1619. And Sir Walter Scott in 1817: 'When from Wulfstane's bended yew sprung forth the grey-goose shaft.'

Reading E. Woodman's *The Seaboard and the Downs* recently, I came across a reference to Upper Beeding. The book was published at the turn of the last century. The author remarks on the parish, noting that it is untouched and not developed in the manner Steyning has!

One thing that caught my eye was the mention of the avenue of yews that line the pathway leading to St. Peter's Church: Woodman claims these were planted some ten years before. I have always believed that these were planted by Dr. Bloxam and his helpers as there are other references to this being so. As the book was written c.1901, this puts the date of planting around 1890/1 which must have been during the last year of the Reverend Bloxam's life, as he died in January 1891. These are a fitting living memorial to this man's work. He played his part in the Oxford Movement, which among other things helped to beautify our churches.

The storm of 1987 took its toll of the yews and many other trees surrounding the church. Sadly there is only one large ancient yew left; perhaps this one witnessed the building of the church in 1308. As a reminder of October 1987, I have two large yew logs each side of my stone fireplace – all that is left of the other yews.

A Penny

We will soon be hearing the cry 'a penny for the guy'. I was recently going through old school books and ephemera from Upper Beeding School. An essay I came across, from the last century, reminded me of one I was set as a schoolboy in the early thirties. It was entitled 'The Adventures of a Penny'. This appears to have been a title which has endured for many years, given to children to exercise their minds and to show them the movements of an ordinary bronze penny as it passed from person to person, was lost and found again, and what it purchased along the way.

In the days before decimalization the 'd' in '£.s.d.' was a relic of the Roman occupation: 'd' for denarius, a silver coin of the time. Some, though I am not one of them, believe it comes from the French 'denier'. The first of our silver pennies was made by hammering a design onto a not too round flat piece of silver. Know as 'hammered' coinage, the silver penny was the standard coin in England for about 500 years. The first recognisable portrait of a king was of Offa. The inscription REX ANGLOR means 'King of the English', first appears on the coins of King Alfred, who sometimes lived at King's Barnes, then part of Beeding.

It was not until William I came to the throne that a king was truly king of the English. The coinage at that time was better than the French 'denier', so William wisely did not interfere with it, but he did introduce a cross on the reverse side to deter 'clipping', which plagued early coinage. Fraudsters shaved off the coin edges to accumulate silver to be melted to their own advantage. The cross also enabled the coin to be cut into half-pennies and into quarters for farthings (forthings). In 1275 a gold penny was introduced to the value of 20 silver pennies.

The silver penny still exists in the English coinage and is still legal tender. I refer to the Royal Maundy Money, a silver penny, twopence, threepence and fourpence (groat). The early Maundy services saw the monarch washing the feet of the poor, paralleling the washing of the Apostles' feet by Jesus at the Last Supper. This act was redeemed by the gift of coins.

Police

There has been some interest locally in the return of the village policeman, a person who knows all the local villains, where they live, and often their movements. Prevention is better than cure.

Until the early 19th century there was no regular police force. Order was kept by the Militia, a much hated practice that resulted in affrays such as the Peterloo Massacre. In 1829 a regular police force was established in London by Robert Peel. Three thousand 'Bobbies' or 'Peelers' replaced the old Bow Street Runners, who were few in number. This force was controlled by the Home Office and was unarmed except for wooden truncheons. This new system drove the criminal out of the big towns into the countryside so other towns had to employ the same methods. Finally in 1856 every county and borough was obliged to maintain a police force.

In our parish records I came across two entries in the vestry minutes: 'On April 1st 1831 it was resolved that a pair of handcuffs be purchased for the use of the parish.' At a later vestry meeting in The King's Head on November 30th 1837 a proposal was put by the parish chairman Richard Goddard: 'It was agreed upon that a man should be appointed to act as a policeman to watch the parish of Upper Beeding, in respect of the property of every description. There shall also be appointed three inspectors for the district (more chiefs than Indians!) Mr. Joseph Morris of Beeding Court shall be one.'

'The said policeman shall every day call on one of the inspectors to know his destination for his nightly watching and an assessment shall be made according to act of Parliament to defray the said expence.' The first mentioned as a policeman was John Carter on February 13th 1839, but it was unclear as to whether he was the first appointed. It was probably no coincidence that the Beeding inspectors were farmers, as they were most of them likely to be robbed of their livestock. Penalties were very harsh. Stealing an animal was a capital offence and if caught it was an advantage to the thief to try and murder his captor rather than face the death penalty. The old saying was: 'You might as well be hanged for a sheep as a lamb'.

KN-B has more to say on this subject in 3.9

Early Inhabitants

When I first came back to Beeding, I was quite surprised to find an abundance of Neolithic flint implements in and on the soil in my garden: arrowheads, axes, scrapers, fabricators and many other tools used by early man. These flints were probably mined at Cissbury, the nearest flint mines, and shaped locally for use by the people of the Adur valley area.

Those who patronise Beeding Garage, should, perhaps, pause and give a thought to what this site may have looked like in the Neolithic period, which ended some 1800 years before the birth of Christ. Its position was at the eastern edge of a wide estuary. There was no Beeding village, no High Street causeway, probably just a fording place for the early hunter/gatherers who resided on the garage location at different times.

During excavations for the installation of petrol tanks at the garage around the end of the First World War, remains of mammoths, aurochs, woolly rhino, red deer and other food sources were found in the clay. Early hunters would most likely have butchered their kill on the spot where it fell, so we might speculate that the garage now covers a watering place for animals. The melting ice would have made the river less saline than it is at the present day.

A mammoth was a large hairy elephant with deadly tusks much bigger than an elephant's and lived during the Ice Age. The last ice age dates back to about 8,000 years ago, when ice covered much of the British Isles. Remains of mammoths can be seen in parts of northern Europe and Asia, frozen into the tundra. Now and again, the ice melts and we can have an opportunity to study these prehistoric elephant-like creatures.

Old Church Music

The main kind of music in English churches is for the organ, for majestic ones in Cathedrals down to the manually operated varieties in the small parish churches. One relic may be seen at Botolphs with the handle still in place.

Among the many things that Oliver Cromwell was blamed for *was* the demise of the church organ. A law was passed by Parliament in 1644 abolishing it. The method used to carry out the law was often riotous and sacrilegious, and not always to Cromwell's wishes. The ravage of Chichester cathedral and the destruction of its organ is described by Dean Ryves: 'The next day their first business was to plunder the Cathedral Church. They left not so much as a cushion for the pulpit, nor a chalice for the Blessed Sacrement, The commanders having in person executed the covetous part of the sacrilege they leave the destructive and spoiling part to be finished by the common soldiers. As they broke down the organ and dashed the pipes with their pole axes they cried out in scoff, " Harke how the organ goe"!' "

Many of the small village churches remained without their organs until the latter half of the 19th century. Direct evidence of this is furnished by the Selsey collection of -Psalmes, where the preface makes this statement: 'The organ adds much to the effect of church music, and now by ready made construction it is now brought within the range of economy (however limited) of every parish; its general adoption is therefore strongly recommended and earnestly hoped for, 30th September 1842.'

From the middle"of the 17th century until the end of the 19th, church music was performed by a choir, sometimes with an instrumental band. These bands used many instruments that the average person will never have heard of...Barrelorgan, Basshorn, Flutina, Pitchpipe, Seraphim, Serpent and Vamphorn along with violins and oboes.

Local communicants made up the bands and were usually self taught and very proud of the fact. It is recorded that one such church band after adverse comment from the Vicar whitewashed all the outsides of his windows during the night. Older residents may remember the Serpent that hung on the wall of Potter's Museum of Curiosity in Bramber. This was used regularly in St.Peter's, Beeding, until the early 19th century.

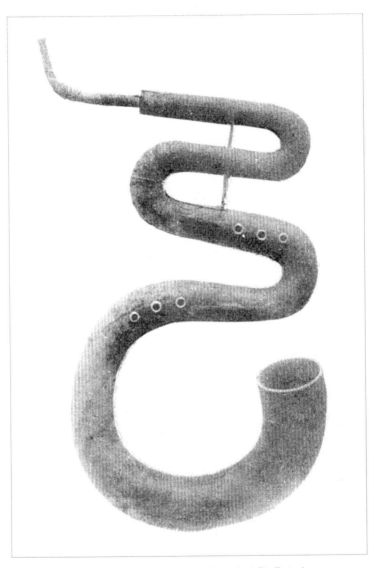

15.2 The Bramber Serpent, played at St. Peter's
Church, Beeding, until the early 19th century

The Wandering Minstrel

In the past, I have written about church music. 'Lay' music developed out of early music, rather as talking newspapers and history articles have today. The name Harper, or Piper, takes us back to the Middle Ages, for they will almost certainly have been the kin of minstrels of the past. The *Chartulary of Sele Priory* mentions Nicholas the Harper [*Chartulary* 127] and William the Piper [*Chartulary* 13] as witnesses to documents for land tenure.

The Revd. H. Arnold describes for us the scene at Bramber Castle in the time of de Braose: 'The gate porter with a profound bow would suddenly announce: "A minstrel is at the gate!" Immediately, all work ceased. The ladies left their tapestries, the grooms the stables, the maids the scrubbing; all rushed to the Great Hall, and the minstrel, often an old man and in many cases half blind, would be assisted to a warm corner by the log fire. He would strike a few preliminary chords and then launch out into some ballad of the great deeds of the castle's family, or of the Crusades and battles of love and adventure'. These men had wandered over half of Europe and even as far as the Holy Land. Many of our old ballads were composed by them, and rank high among the beautiful songs and prose in our literature.

Because most people were tied to their area and were illiterate, the only source of outside knowledge of happenings were from these nomadic musicians, who brought them news of the great battles, and the victories won. In the year AD 878, a former resident of King's Barnes, King Alfred, being a good musician, disguised himself as a minstrel and ventured into the invading Danish array's camp, where he learnt all about the enemy forces. Next morning, he gained a crushing victory over Guthrum's fighting men, who then promised never to invade Wessex again.

Some three hundred years later, another minstrel wandered through central Europe, searching for his master, Richard I, the Lionheart, who had been imprisoned by Leopold of Austria. After a year in captivity, Richard was located by his minstrel, Blondel de Neste. The captive king answered by singing from his cell window the ditty which they had composed together in happier times. Ransome was paid and he returned home.

15.3 King Richard I
(*St. Mary's archive*)

A Bronze Age Hoard

Just recently, I have been pointing out to developers the risks to Beeding Bridge as a result of building upstream. This has led me to ponder the possible fate of the Bronze Age settlement that was situated west of Bramber Castle in what is now known as Clay's and Fever's fields, between 900 and 700 years ago.

The site was part of a very early 'Industrial Revolution' in Sussex. Bronze weapons and implements were cast there at this encampment nearly three thousand years ago. Fuel and water were vital to metal-making and, as was known from other mediaeval industries (glass and iron) when the supply of trees ran out for fuelling this work, whole villages were moved on to other places where wood was more plentiful.

We know a little about the Bramber 'settlement' because in 1981, a hoard of bronze artefacts, spears, knives, chisels, socketed axes and other items, probably for agricultural use, were fou founder's hoard. Most of the tools and weapons were damaged in some way or another and it was assumed by the archaeologists that they were gathered together for melting down and recasting. Thanks to two Steyning men, these were saved from being reburied. There were over one hundred items and most are now in Worthing Museum.

That there was a workshop for this foundry operation is supported by the discovery of pieces of a crucible 'glassy', vitrified from superheating, and burnt flint which could be used as pot-boilers. Crushed flint was also used with other materials to make crucibles. That this hoard exists perhaps points to the fact that the site was evacuated rather quickly during flooding, as it was on the very edge of the flood plain at that time. It is speculation that this is the answer, as the finds were excavated from five feet down in the estuary clay.

The Swiss Gardens

Until the latter years of the Industrial Revolution in the 19th century, most outside pleasures were only for the wealthy. In due course, industry put more money in the pockets of the workers and artisans. Coupled with this was the development of the railways which liberated many of the labouring classes for short breaks from the place where they lived and worked. Prior to the 19th century, very few working folk managed to travel more than a few miles from their birthplace.

I have written before about the attractions in Beeding and Bramber, Potter's Museum and the amusement park in the grounds of Bramber Castle, which from the mid-Victorian period entertained generations of Sunday School children. The Tea Gardens drew to Bramber those shopworkers and young people in service who would take a boat ride up the Adur to Beeding Bridge. To accommodate these outings, the platform at Bramber station was lengthened until it was the longest in the south of England.*

James Britton Bailey, a shipbuilder from Shoreham and something of an enterpreneur, decided that this area should have something to rival the Vauxhall Gardens in London, and Ireland's pleasure grounds on The Level at Brighton. The result was the construction of what came to be known as the Swiss Gardens. Only the Swiss Cottage public house remains of what was the greatest attraction in this whole area. The gardens boasted the largest ballroom on the south coast (150' x 54') and a refreshment building for upwards of 1000 people. This site, opened in 1839, also had two boating lakes, and a tower thought to have been 100 feet tall, with an observation gallery at the top. This could be seen from as far away as Beeding Hill.

The Brighton-Shoreham line of the London, Brighton and South Coast Railway was opened in May 1840. Such was the attraction of this new form of travel that 1750 passengers were carried on the first day, almost all destined to spend the day at the new gardens. Train fares were one shilling First Class, ninepence Second Class and sixpence Third Class. James Bailey died in 1863 and was succeeded by Edward Goodchild, who increased the attractions with balloon ascents, firework displays, archery, and bowls. The Gardens ceased to attract people in the early 20th century and were closed around 1908.

*Bramber Station enabled crowds of weekend sightseers to enjoy any of the eight tea gardens in the village, model train rides at Bramber Castle, as well as river walks and boating at Beeding. See PG3

15.5 The Swiss Gardens, Shoreham-by-Sea

The Bramber Shot

Many of you may have attended the Summer Fete at 'Tinker's Court' and perhaps a few of you attempted a 'go' at the 'Bramber Shot' contest. Others will have pondered the wisdom of trying to hurl an iron ball weighing nearly half a hundredweight further than your neighbour can.

Where did it all start? In the early 1980s, Beeding and Bramber joined together to adopt the village of Yobe, in Somalia, as an alternative to twinning with a European town. Our commitment was to raise £2000 per annum for five years to get Yobe on its feet again. The parishes raised money in all manner of ways. One was a biennial fair at Bramber Castle which included a mini 'Highland Games'. The event was sponsored by Beckett Newspapers and became known as the 'Steyning Herald Bramber Shot Contest', with trophies for team and individual winners. A lady's trophy was added to the last two contests. When the Yobe adoption ceased in 1988, the contest carried on the 'Tinker's Court' fund-raising for the ecclesiastical parish, with part of the money going to the overseas missions.

The Shot Put* is a contest, developed out of boredom, by the Royal Navy and Army in the days when muzzle-loading cannons were used and the cannonballs were available for recreational use when not being fired at the enemy. The Scots, from early times, also used large round river-rolled stones in their clan games, probably long before the cannon was invented. The one used at the Newtonmoor Highland Games weighed 60½ lbs.

The Bramber Shot itself is thought to have been used as a mortar shell by a Royal Navy 'bomb ketch' in the Moray Firth, some time during the Battle of Culloden in April 1746. For a century and a half it was put to use as a chimney counterbalance in a house near Drummossie Moor. It was given to me by a Mr. and Mrs. McQueen, who said it was from her grandmother's house, and that Mrs. McQueen's great-grandmother had been on the moor at the time of the battle. The shot had been used in the local 'games' from time to time.

* See the biographical introduction for more about KN-B and the Shot Put contest

Bath Tubs

The Adur Bath Tub Race has been regularly staged by the Shoreham and Southwick Round Table for many years. The Adur river race raises a lot of money annually for local charities and worthy causes. With each passing year, it seems that there are more entrants than ever, lined up for the start from Beeding bridge, where competitors are sent on their way with a hail of eggs and flour 'bombs'. Everyone joins in the spirit of the occasion.

Early postcards and photographs show that flooding occurred regularly in the area of the bridge, Beeding High Street and The Street, Bramber. The flooding was checked in the early days (1950s) when the river authority dredged the river and built up the banks to abate the nuisance of the streets being awash at very high tides, and ruining the furniture and carpets in low-lying dwellings. In some of the early pictures, you can see adults and children paddling tin bath-tubs up and down the flooded streets, but it is unlikely that they ever tackled the River Adur itself for their sport.

Beeding was the lowest crossing until the tollbridge was built in 1781. The earlier bridge was timber, a smaller version of the old tollbridge at Shoreham, and it would have been here that the young Charles II crossed on his flight in 1651.

Beeding Bridge, rebuilt 1785, has seen much local history in its two hundred and fifteen years of existence. The river was made navigable as far as West Grinstead by the Baybridge Canal Co., through oxbows, allowing the passage of barges upstream. It also speeded up the outgoing tide, making it one of the fastest flowing rivers in the south of England. As new housing was built up river as far as Burgess Hill, Coolham and just south of Horsham, the run-off drains into the Adur were inadequate. When high tides and long periods of rain coincided with adverse winds, this was a threat to Beeding Bridge, as the whole of the Weald to the north drains through this narrow opening.

15.8 The Beeding and Bramber Bath Tub Race: "They're off!"

15.8a Crowds gather to watch the spills and thrills

The Right Lines!

Many of you will now be aware of the plans to develop the old cement works quarry for leisure, by installing a ski slope, ice rinks, hotels and all the paraphernalia that goes with this sort of entertainment and sports complex.

If the project goes ahead there will be a new system of transport such as a tramway, or some people-moving trackway. This will take passengers from massive car parks in Shoreham or from the railway station or airport. A journey back into the past.*

Railways have been in existence for over a thousand years. Mining in central Europe used railways from the Middle Ages onwards. These were very primitive affairs, the rails being squared timbers and the wagons were small wooden hoppers pulled by man or horse. In the 17th century, the early years of the Industrial Revolution, horse-drawn wooden railways proved their worth to the collieries of the Midlands. Overland journeys, carrying coal and raw materials to the emerging canal system were increased fivefold by the trackways. As production of iron increased, plateways were laid. These were flat, interlocking pieces of cast iron with a flange on the inside edge which enabled ordinary carts to be run on these tracks.

The invention of the steam engine about 1820 called for much stronger rails. John Birkinshaw invented a method of rolling wedge-shaped wrought- iron rails. These were a tremendous improvement on the earlier cast iron permanent way, which was brittle.

Here in the Adur valley, the railways came late, as did many other rural lines. The Brighton to Shoreham line was opened on 12th May 1840, Shoreham to Partridge Green on 1st July 1861, and continued on to Horsham on the 16th September of the same year. The London Brighton and South Coast Railway became the Southern Railway in 1923. Bramber was a much-used station for Sunday School outings and excursions. One attraction was the castle, another the hire of boats on the Adur at Beeding and nearly all visited Potter's Museum of taxidermy. With hindsight, the museum was a rather morbid place, but the 'Death of Cock Robin' and other displays delighted generations of children.

*This project was abandoned [Ed.]

KN-B also wrote about the railways in 4.7.

15.9 The tea kiosk at Bramber Castle

15.9a Boys joy-riding in the Bramber Cart

Underpinning the Chancel Arch at St. Peter's

Many of our regular church goers will remember the upheaval in the Sanctuary on St. Peter's back in 1983, when the chancel arch had to be underpinned, along with other parts of the church. I was called up to the church early one evening by the Rector to see the excavations. Apparently the contractors had left the work in a hurry. The reason was quite evident: a skull and several bones had been revealed in the pit adjacent to the north chancel arch. In the dim light and with the sun's rays shining through the window in the south wall, the skull took on an amber luminescence!

Between us the remains were reverently removed to a temporary place of safety and we explored the pit. One skeleton appeared to have been buried with ceremony but parts of two others looked as if they had been thrown in carelessly before the top burial. What at the time we thought were the remains of a pair of gloves atop the complete skeleton, turned out later to be hazel bark, pointing to what is known by archaeologists as a 'Hazel Burial', where hazel wands are laid herringbone fashion over the body. Looking through the Church records and other documents, it is thought that the remains of the complete skeleton were those of John Snellying, who was recorded as being buried within the church in the year of 1494.

Among the debris in the pit was early stained glass, floor tiles which were almost certainly from the earlier Priory of Sele, and odd pieces of stone damaged and discarded, some still bearing masons' marks. In the mediaeval period there stood a chapel dedicated to St. John abutting the north wall of the chancel. It is thought that the pillar in the north east corner of the sanctuary we see today is all that remains above ground of that old building. Perhaps much of the debris in the pit came from that source?

Food for thought is also provided by the spoil heap which was deposited outside the church. On examination by Eric Holden, pieces of Roman roof tile were discovered. *The Domesday Book* records two churches in Beeding. Crop patterns of an earlier building with a round apse can be seen from the bell tower in the Priory garden. Was there a Christian church of the Roman period here long before St. Wilfrid?

John Snellying was reinterred with quiet reverence.

Beating the Bounds*

Being present at the funeral service of Edgar Collins last week brought back a host of memories. My mind wandered back to all the walks that he had organised for us in the past with a great deal of pleasure. The most memorable for me was Easter, when new life in the countryside was awakening.

When I suggested, a few years ago now, that the church should carry out a 'Beating of the Bounds', Edgar was the first to offer help with the trial run. It took us two days to complete. These were the days when King's Barns were still part of the civil parish; they are still a part of the ecclesiastical boundary.

What was the object of 'Beating the Bounds'? This ancient custom dates back to the 9th century. These processions took place at Rogationtide and were traditionally led by the Vicar and churchwardens with most of the locals taking part.

Today you could ask any child in Beeding where the boundary of their parish was and it is very doubtful if any could answer that question! A child of the last century knew exactly where the limits of the parish he lived in were, it had been pointed out to the child at each 'merestone' or boundary mark. A meresman usually joined the perambulation to make sure that all the marks were established in their right places and in the minds of children. The last meresman that we know about, was William Mills a farmer and tenant of Pond Farm.

William Mills and Charles Woolgar, meresmen for Bramber, perambulated the villages for several days with John Stirton, a corporal in the Royal Engineers. This was to record the boundaries of those villages for the new Ordnance Survey Department. The results are contained in the meresmen report books which are still available to researchers.

Apart from village perimeters there were also the borders of the different 'manors' within or overlapping the villages. The manor was the unit of administration in early times.

This article is presented as a tribute to Edgar, who in his eighties could walk the legs off most of us. I will miss him.

*Prompted by memories of his friend, Edgar Collins,
KN-B has returned here to a similar theme from 2.9

Sussex Bell Teams

Transport throughout the Weald of Sussex in early times was by packhorse along narrow tracks and across shallow fords sufficient to allow the progress of a string of laden horses. We have lost some of the old names for these tracks and pathways. One such track remaining is 'Bost' hill' or Bostel, a pathway up a hill along which the traveller could proceed unobserved. The term 'Hollow-way' means a narrow track where the trees and hedges cover the path and almost join overhead. One 'Hollow-way' exists along the north of the Downs from Horton to Edburton, Fulking and Poynings, but it seems to have grown wider every time I use it.

Up to the general use of the motor car in the early 20th century, these tracks were wide enough to allow the passage of a farm wagon. Nathaniel Panie Blaker describes how in his time the traffic was regulated: 'You will find here and there, where it has not been altered and made wider, and remains wide enough for one wagon only, that at certain intervals the bank curves outward on each side for a few yards, and leaves a space sufficient for two wagons to pass.' The bells were used to give notice when two wagons were approaching in opposite directions, so that one could stop in the recess and allow the other to pass. In my younger days a bell team was by no means uncommon (before the turn of the century) and the sound on a bright summer morning was perfectly delightful. The bells, which were in perfect tune, were fixed in a frame and carried on the collar of each of the four horses and the carter took the greatest pride in the peal of his bells.

In former days carters took great pride in their horses, looked after them well and enjoyed seeing them in good condition with glossy coats. When they went on a journey away from the farm, especially if it were into a town, they used to put the bell on the shoulders of their teams, rosettes on each side of the bridle, the forehead plate, (a plate of ornamental bright brass) on their foreheads and plait their manes and tails with bright coloured ribands. It gives a pang of sadness when one sees the bells used as dinner gongs, and forehead plates as room ornaments.

The Tinder Box

There are many ways to obtain a naked flame these days. One can take a box of matches, a cigarette lighter, or even light a flame from a gas stove that has automatic ignition. In prehistoric times, the source of a fire was precious and tribes carried around their own pots containing burning embers. In dry countries, before the match was invented, fire was made by friction, using two pieces of wood. This was a difficult and tedious task achived by revolving and rubbing by hand a stick onto the indentation in another piece of wood. After much effort, the friction generated enough heat to start fine wood shavings to smoulder, a few puffs from the operator bringing them to flame. In damp conditions things were much more difficult.

In the time before the general use of gas or electricity, Beeding folk relied, summer and winter, on wood or coal stoves and ranges for cooking and heating. Stoves were kept going overnight by banking up with ashes so that one did not have to relight them each morning in winter. Before the Victorian age and the invention of the match that could be struck, the main source of fire was the ubiquitous 'tinder box'.

Up to the turn of this century, almost every household possessed a tinder box. As a boy I saw one in Potter's Museum in Bramber among the curios in that splendid collection. Flint, steel and tinder made up the tinder box. The tinder consisted of linen rag which had been ignited and allowed to burn until it was dark brown and then the flame was extinguished. It was kept in a round tin box a few inches in diameter and a couple of inches deep: this was to keep the tinder dry and was weighed down by a piece of lead the same diameter as the box to keep the linen compressed. The flint was an ordinary garden flint, knapped to provide one or more sharp edges. The steel was a piece of flat steel about three inches long, in the shape of a 'U', with one limb longer than the other. The method was to hold the steel by the short end and strike with the flint so that sparks fell onto the tinder rag and started to smoulder. A thin sliver of wood dipped in brimstone was then applied to the glowing part. This was the forerunner of the match that could be struck on another chemical substance and ignited by friction. The tinder box from the museum was given to me when the contents were sold in the 1970s.

Village Signs

At the present time, there is a lot of activity around the village by residents to get their gardens and frontages in good order for the inspection party of the 'Best Kept Village Competition'.

The village committee of 'Beeding in Bloom' has been very busy, led by Keith Lucas, erecting and maintaining hanging baskets of flowers, ensuring grass verges are trimmed and generally seeing that all is tidy for the visit. Earlier in the year, planters were constructed and filled. An earth bank at Beeding Court roundabout has been supplied by WSCC and Keith, with the help of Cllr. Grinyer, has spelt out the name of the village with bedding (beeding!) plants.

Another way that the village will be enhanced is by a sign depicting a view or legend associated with this locality, to be erected near the earth bank, with the village picked out name in flowers.

Village signs were thought to have developed out of the inn signs. These were a focal point of any small village or inhabited area. No one knows when these village signs were first used. In the past, gibbets were sometimes erected at crossroads, or at the entrance to small communities to deter the lawless and to show that the residents were able to dispense their own justice. In the 18th and 19th centuries many of these gruesome posts were replaced by village signs.

A pictorial representation of the name of the village is a common form of sign. Others depict scenes from village history or saints and worthies associated with the local past. At Bently in Hampshire, a village sign was erected by the first Lord Baden-Powell. This displayed an open book on which were recorded prominent events in the history of that village, much like the battle honours that accompany the crests on ships in the Royal Navy.

The Parish Council has commissioned a sign for Upper Beeding. Should it show our founder Beida c.AD 501, in full Saxon armour? Or some dominant feature in the area such as the humpback bridge? The bridge has existed since just after the Norman Conquest as a timber structure. In 1785 it was rebuilt in brick at the expense of the vicar and Magdalen College. It was so strong that it was able to support tanks during World War II.

Twin Aid

As we approach Christmas, news has arrived in Beeding and Bramber of renewed contact with our adopted village Yobe in Somalia. The country is now divided, with Yobe in the north.

For those readers who were not here in the 1980s, Yobe was adopted by the parish council and the local community. 'Bandaid' and other organisations did much of the initial relief, but we wanted a more lengthy commitment and adopted Yobe on a five year plan.

The amount of money raised exceeded £20,000 with which we upgraded a well by installing a new water pump and storage facilities. Six tons of cement donated by Blue Circle, shipped free by an anonymous donor, paid for the rebuilding of the school house and provided half the wages for a teacher. School materials and uniforms were also provided, so that Yobe pupils wore the same clothing as Beeding Primary School children.

The former Archbishop of Canterbury, Dr Runcie, and the Princess Royal, commended us for inspiring other villages, putting into practice Dr Runcie's message, 'Help is better than handouts'. In the late 1980s contact was lost when Action Aid had to withdraw from this war-torn country.

At that time we funded other projects in Africa but set aside a further £500 for the time that we were reunited with our twin village. Now, ten years later, I have received a letter from the parent charity, saying that they are now back in the region. We will hand this money over at the parish council meeting on the 2nd November, when Action Aid will be present to receive it.

Having mentioned in passing that we were inducting a new Rector, Father Timothy L'Estrange in October, the Somalis sent a gift of frankincense to be used at the induction. Incense is about the only cash crop from this region.

16.11 Keith, Chairman for Upper Beeding Parish Council, and Gill Fox, Chairman for Bramber, presenting the donation to members of the Somali Embassy representatives.

16.11a Peter Thorogood (left) hosted a reception to celebrate the Yobe Project. Peter seen here with guest of honour, Mrs. Beryl de Clare Richards and ceremonial piper.

St. Peter's Corona

Looking at and admiring the magnificent *corona* in the nave of St. Peter's, I have often wondered what the connection was between the Rev. John Rouse Bloxam and Augustus Welby Northmore Pugin. This enamelled brass Gothic styled centrepiece that embellishes our church was designed and made by Pugin.

Pugin lived from 1812 to 1852 and spent his last year in Bedlam, dying it is said through overwork. He is known to have done many of the drawings for Sir Charles Barry in his designs for the new Houses of Parliament. Pugin was also a writer, publishing books on Gothic and ecclesiastical architecture.

The Rev. Dr. Bloxam was curate to the Rev. John Henry (later Cardinal) Newnian when he was the vicar of Littlemore. Bloxam was born in 1807 and died in 1891 at Beeding, where he was vicar from 1862 until his death. He is buried in the churchyard to the west of the lamp on the gravel drive.

Dr. Bloxam is best known in ecclesiastical circles as the co-founder of the 'Oxford Movement', which endeavoured to revive ceremonial in the Church of England. It was under his direction and inspiration that this movement led to the beautifying of our churches, which has endured to this day.

Bloxam's mother Ann, was the sister of Sir Thomas Lawrence, president of the Royal Academy. Bloxam gave many of Lawrence's sketches to his pupils at the Priory, as prizes for good work.

It is not known when St. Peter's was endowed with the corona, but with his artistic connections, it is possible that Bloxam could have commissioned Pugin to produce the treasure that is above our heads. Next time that you are in the church, look up and enjoy it!

Pugin died a decade before Bloxam became vicar of Beeding. Is it possible that the corona was intended for Littlemore? We know that some of the candlesticks came from there. Perhaps one day, research will provide an answer.

Godless Decimal

My great grandfather (1802-1879) had an interest in numismatics. On going through some of his papers, I happened upon some correspondence that referred to the unrest caused by the issue of a new coin.

Many of us older residents thought the conversion to decimal currency was a 'con' to raise prices by stealth. I am still of that opinion! Many were saddened by the loss of the half-crown, shilling, sixpence and threepence, also the comfortable bronze penny, halfpenny and farthing. They felt like real money! The truth is that we were prepared to go decimal one hundred and fifty years ago.

In 1847, Sir John Bowring advocated the striking of coins of one tenth and one hundredth of a pound. The former was struck to test public opinion. Much discussion ensued as to the name of the proposed piece. Suggestions were *centum, decade* and *dime,* although eventually the committee settled *for florin.* This was an old English coinage term, like the earlier *mark.* The florin found favour because coins of a similar value and size circulated in several European countries.

The first adopted design of this new two-shilling piece was in 1849, with the crowned head of Queen Victoria on the obverse and a 'Gothic' pattern cross on the reverse. The coin was stamped 'one tenth of a pound'. It had been some two hundred years since a monarch on the coinage had worn a crown. It was thought at the time that this coin would perhaps replace the half-crown.

The new florin proved to be much disliked by the public, as its size was so near the half-crown. Religious leaders spoke out against it because of the design of the obverse. Around the Queen's head were the letters, *Victoria Regina 1849.* The omission of *Dei gratia* (by the grace of God), dubbed the coin the 'Godless florin'. All two-shilling pieces minted later had the inscription restored. When Potter's Museum in Bramber was dispersed, the widow of the owner kindly gave me a 'Godless florin'.

KN-B returns to the subject of coins and currency at 18.6

Psalm 104 v 10

He sendeth the springs into the rivers: which run among the hills.

The sexton was a lay officer of the church who was in many cases the local grave-digger, an office which made him a suitable candidate for the occasional job of well-sinking. The well-digger was probably, with the exception of the deep-sea diver, the only one who started his work from the top and worked his way down! In deep wells, courses of bricks were laid a few feet at a time as the work progressed. This was to line the shaft and prevent the inward collapse of the soft patches of soil sometimes encountered.

Life is not possible without water. Before the advent of water companies and the luxury of piped water, all users had to have access to a clear stream or a well. Some would have their own; others would use the communal water supply where it existed. This was the village well, or after the Industrial Revolution, the village pump. This was, apart from the local inn, the focal point of the day for the women. Information or gossip was exchanged as they waited their turn to draw water.

Our water is drawn from deep wells in the eastern part of Beeding, where the road to Henfield turns sharply north. The Steyning and District Waterworks Company sank wells on this site around 1898. They also built a reservoir on the side of the Downs nearby, to supply water to Beeding, Bramber, parts of Small Dole and the eastern area of Steyning. Southern Water took over the old works and I am told that it now serves a much smaller area. Perhaps that is why we do not have a hosepipe ban as often as others do.

The daily permitted extraction of water from the wells is about half a million gallons every twenty-four hours. Other boreholes were drilled in the 1970s, but most proved not to be worth the yield they delivered. The Parish Council has been most watchful in recent years, as applications for tipping in our area have been filed. There are still many wells around the villages, perhaps the best known being the ones in the front gardens of Pound House and the present 'Candytuft'. Others exist in the grounds of Sele Priory and elsewhere. Some are dangerous, owing to natural gas collecting at the bottom and there is the danger of collapse in the unlined ones.

KN-B dealt with other aspects of this subject in *The Water Supply* 10.5

Land Measures

The local name 'Hyde' probably has its origin in the Hyde Farm estate, which is much of the eastern part of Beeding. So what was a hyde (hide)? The hide of the 'middle ages' was a land measure. It was the area of land that could be ploughed in a year with one plough. It was generally believed to be sufficient to support a family unit and also known as *husbandland*.

The hide was part of the Saxon *hundred*. The Normans continued to use this term after the conquest. We live in the hundred of Burbeach. The hundred was thought to have been made up of one hundred hides or family units and was the subdivision of the 'rape'. There were originally five rapes in Domesday Sussex, which were increased later to six. Each rape had a castle, a river, a port and a forest.

The hide varied considerably, much depending on the quality of the soil. Generally, it was between sixty and one hundred and eighty acres. The hide was subdivided into quarters known as *virgates or yardlands*. Yardlands were known in Sussex as *wista*. A quarter virgate was known as a *farthingdale*. Below this was the standard English *acre*. The acre was the area of land that could be ploughed by a yoke of oxen in a day.

The acre was standardised by Edward I as forty *rods* long by four rods wide. The English *furlong* was one 'furrow' long and is now one eighth of a mile. In ancient law a Saxon *Ceorl* had to possess five hides, a chapel, a kitchen, a book and a bell before he could become a *Thane*.

Going metric may have made things easier for the scholar. I mourn the passing of the *inch* (three grains of wheat end to end), the *foot* (the length of Henry VIII's foot) and the *yard* (from nose to outstretched fingertip). The *pole, perch* and *chain* have now disappeared along with the *league* (three miles). The latter was a well-loved measure of the writers of 'Once upon a time' books.

Very Fishy*

Izaak Walton (1593-1683) wrote *The Compleat Angler* in 1653. Its instant popularity indicated that river fishing had become more of a sport than the urgent need to catch food. Most large landowners had created ponds and lakes to breed fish stocks primarily for the table. Rivers were valuable assets; land adjoining inland water was more desirable if it had fishing rights.

In 1882, a Mr Long of the Beeding Co. wrote to the Rev. Dr. Bloxam. He complained of men from the Shoreham area fishing the River Adur with an immense net and catching everything... 'nothing larger than a lead pencil escaping them, the net being so fine'. A newspaper report of the 1890s records the appearance in court of Lewis Rasbrook of Shoreham and two of his family, for fishing with a net in the closed season in Upper Heeding on the 30 May. They were each fined a halfcrown, including costs.

We first hear of local fishing grants in a document of Sele Priory dated 2 June 1438. In this, John Duke of Norfolk confirmed an earlier gift of John de Brawysa of the mills and fisheries from the church of Old Shoreham to the place called 'Bedeney' (Bedney Corner near St. Peter's) to the Prior of Sele, William Lewes,

In 1624 Isaac Pocock is vested in the ownership of the fishing rights between Old Shoreham and Beeding. An entry in Dr. Bloxam's history adds...'this privilege was afterwards inserted into the lease of the Priory of Sele, together also with the fishing of the river from Beeding to Old Shoreham'. This condition has so continued through all subsequent leases to the present time. Another entry says...'the scite of the ancient Priory of Sele with the remainder of the buildings with a piece of ground computed at 6 acres, and all the fishing of all the waters from a place called Beeding to Old Shoreham church was granted by lease from Magdalen College to the minister of Sele' (dated 1772).

So, who owns the fishing rights now? I cannot find any reference to these being with any other body. Can the Rector give permission for the choir and servers to drown a few worms?

*The first paragraph above is a repeat of the one in 8.10,
but the general subject-matter differs in each case [Ed.]

'Black' Beeding

No one today would think of Beeding as the 'Black Country' – a term that conjures up pit winding-wheels, tall chimneys and the 'dark satanic mills' of Victorian literature. In earlier times, *Beding* consisted of our village, part of St. Leonard's forest (Upper) and Bewbush tithing, which is now part of Crawley.

Some people may be surprised to learn that many of the cannons that were used by and against the Spanish Armada were made in Sussex. Some were smuggled out of the country by way of the River Adur. The iron masters and entrepreneurs acquired tax-free Spanish gold. Cannon and shot were made in our area from the fifteenth century.

An extensive forest was situated between the North and South Downs of Sussex and Kent, providing an abundance of timber for charcoal, in order to fuel the furnaces of the iron and glass works. Large areas of water, called hammer ponds, were created to power the bellows and 'trip' hammers that produced and fashioned the metal.

In 1587, Sir Edward Caryll recorded the names of forty-nine miners working in St. Leonard's Forest, which point to large quantities of ironstone and limestone being mined in our locality. It is mentioned that at this time Sussex had some fifty thousand iron workers, but I have seen no written proof of this.

If one goes back further into the past, Sussex may have been even more productive of iron. It is recorded that in the thirteenth century, Henry III (1254) ordered the Sheriff of Sussex to supply thirty thousand horseshoes and sixty thousand nails. Perhaps many of these were used in the Battle of Lewes in 1265, when Henry clashed with Simon de Montfort.

In mediaeval times, glass was also produced in large quantities in the Sussex Weald, the two industries consuming huge areas of forest for fuel. This led to the Elizabethan laws restricting the use of timber. Luckily, coal was being mined at that time in the Midlands and with the spread of the canal system in the seventeenth century, the later 'Industrial Revolution' took off. This left Sussex to return to an agrarian economy. Names like *Cinderhill, Furnace Green* and places with *Ash* in the name remind us of relics of past ironworks.

Tenuous Links with the Past

One of our best-known carols, *Good King Wenceslas,* was written in Sussex by the Rev. John Mason Neale, who was a historian and a friend of Dr Bloxam of Beeding.

King Wenceslas (1361-1413) was king of Bohemia and reigned as Wenceslas IV. We know that his sister was married to King Richard II of England (the only surviving son of the 'Black Prince'). Richard was born in 1367 and reigned from 1377-1399.

The young King Richard II was said to be delicate, effeminate and stubborn, although he confronted the leaders of the 'Peasants' Revolt', Wat Tyler and others of the 'rising'. It must be remembered that on the previous day, the rebels had occupied the Tower of London and its environs and had killed Sir Robert Hales, who was the Grand Master of the Knights of the Hospital of St. John.

After receiving demands and insults from the rebel leaders, the Lord Mayor of London, Sir Robert Walworth, killed Wat Tyler and the rebellion failed. The Rising was the last straw in a chain of events which began in the 1300s. Famine in 1315, and in the years that followed, reduced the population almost as much as the Black Death of 1348 was to do. Known earlier as the 'Great Pestilence', the Black Death continued to occur regularly until the late 17th century. Medical men and historians now agree that it may have been anthrax rather than bubonic plague.

A former Lord Mayor and MP, Nicholas Brembre, was later knighted for his services to the King during the Peasants' Revolt. Sir Nicholas was a descendent of Philip de Brembre, whose name appears on many of the documents recorded in the *Chartulary of Sele Priory.* This indicates that he was a man of some stature as a landowner in this area. Around 1387, Sir Nicholas was involved in a plot and accused of treason. Denied the right as a knight, to defend himself in single combat, he was hanged.

So there you have it, tenuous links indeed!

Christmas Past

At this time of the year, most children think that 'Rudolph the Red-nosed Reindeer' pulls Santa's sledge. What nonsense! Years ago, before television and radio, mothers read the story *The Night before Christmas* to the young ones on Christmas Eve. Today, many older people can still remember the exciting names of Santa's reindeer...*Dasher* and *Dancer, Prancer* and *Vixen, Comet* and *Cupid, Donner* and *Blitzen.* They'd leave Rudolph far behind!

The count-down to Christmas starts sometime just after the summer holiday. Before the Second World War, it was usually only a week or two before the 25 December. Now the real meaning of Christmas is being lost and revolves around large amounts of cash.

Child benefit probably started with the church. A footnote in the book *Magdalen Studies,* mentions a 'Mrs Blackman' of Beeding. She had spent the whole of her long life in the village and remembered Dr. Bloxam, vicar of Beeding for the last half of the nineteenth century, quite well. Voices filtering down from the last century are most interesting. She records that Dr. Bloxam was much loved by the congregation, which was quite large. Mrs Blackman goes on to say that Bloxam lent the children of the village warm red clothes every winter. These were returned to him in the summer in exchange for more suitable clothing.

It is also recorded, that on St. Thomas's Day (21st December), the good Doctor sat at his study window and used to hand a half-crown to any woman of the parish who 'sold' him a sprig of evergreen. This was known as 'Going on Gooding Day', when the old women of the village went from house to house to beg something wherewith to provide for the festivities of Christmas.

Henry Allen, was another person who cared for the less well off. He was vicar for forty years (1680 - 1720). In his will, proved by his wife Anna on 7 February 1720, he left £5 per year for local people. The benefaction was on or about the feast of St. Michael and was distributed among four poor widows of the parish... "not having any publick relief and could read their catechism". It appears that there were not always four poor widows to receive their gratuity. Three are recorded...Ann Nichols, Jenny Stoner and Frances Weller. It was a generous sum in those days, when a joint of beef could be had for the old fourpence. The bequest is still in being as part of the Rector's discretionary fund.

The Early Years

At the end of the first millennium 1000 AD, Aethelred, named the 'Unready', was on the throne. He gained power at the age of ten in AD 978 and, through taking bad advice allowed the Danes to plunder the country.

The *Domesday Book* is probably the only reference that we have to the population of Beeding around the time of the last millennium. It was compiled in 1085-6 and lists the landholders and principal tenants, but does not account for the wives and children. The next proper census was in 1811, which began a series continuing every ten years until the present day. In those early years of the 19th century, Beeding had a population of some 460 inhabitants. There was a poor rate of one shilling in the pound, a church rate of twopence in the pound and life for the common man was very hard. I list below extracts from the 'Vestry' minutes of the first decade of the 1800s, clearly not a time to be unemployed:

Resolved that J.Best, his wife and 7 children receive £60 for there expences to go to Van Diemen's land [Tasmania].

That sick people be allowed a pint of porter a day.

That Dame Foster is allowed 20s. for doing for Welling Wheeler and family and 2s. 6d per week for the time to come if required.

That all those accepted for the highway are to work 12 hours a day.

Resolved that Thomas Winton is to receive a pair of half boots, a pair of trowsers and a round frock.

William Sharp is to dig 2 loads of flints a week at 2s. a load.

Men that have got a wife and 2 children that works on the road to receive 10s. a week.

Resolved that John Roberts to work on the road for 1s. a day.

Resolved that Wm. Winter be bound an apprentice to Henry Hodges, cordwainer [boot and shoe maker].

Hodges to receive £5 when he is bound and the other £5 at the expiration of 3 years and he is bound for 6 years.

That all those who frequent the Publick House shall have their pay taken off.

That Wm Slaughters son Fredrick is to receive £1 at his going into service and if he comes back he is not to receive any pay for 10 weeks.

That £1 5s. be paid for coffin and laying forth J. Sharp.

For more about the poor of the parish see 5.2 *The Poor Law* and 7.12 *Charity*

Beeding's Fifteen Centuries

This is the 18th year of the *Villager* and also these little articles, so it may be appropriate to mention this anniversary. The village and community of this name is 1500 years old this year; I quote the *Anglo Saxon Chronicle* which records: 'The year 501. In this year Port and his two sons, Bieda and Maegla, came to Britain at a place called Portsmuda (Portsmouth, Hampshire) and slew a young Briton, a very noble man'(*The Parker Chronicle*). *The Laud Chronicle* adds that Port and his sons seized land as well as killing a young noble. Bieda is recognised as the founder of Beeding by most historians. It must be remembered that the Romans had left Britain a few decades before and much of our land was up for grabs. The Jutes occupied what is now Kent. The Angles and Frisians settled mainly on the east coast and names like Axholme had Scandinavian origins. Ine, King of Wessex, first mentioned 'Sud-Sexia' (Sussex, land of the south Saxons) in the year AD 678. Many of the continental tribes had served as mercenaries for the Romans and were not strangers to Britain, but the poor indigenous peasant carried on working for whoever the landowners were. The soil had to be tended in this agrarian society or starvation would surely follow.

Records show, and historians agree, that the name Beeding evolved from the term BIEDA'S ING or INGAS; Ing was Saxon for 'meadow' or 'the people of'. By 1086 the name entered in the *Domesday Book* was Beddinges – it also recorded that we did not pay geld (taxes or 'Dane geld'), which may indicate that the area was impoverished. At this time Lower Beeding and Bewbush Hundred at Crawley were part of our lands; these were detached in 1838.

Until the end of the 19th century, Beeding was spelt with only one 'e'. From several early documents it appears that our area was used for all types of agriculture and the growing of flax.

Beeding can boast of a few worthies: Owen Oglethorpe was a former vicar, who went on to become Bishop of Carlisle and crowned Elizabeth the First when no other clergyman would. Dr Bloxam was an architect of the 'Oxford Movement' with Newman and Keble. Bloxam was curate to John Henry Newman at Littlemoor. Newman stayed at the priory before he went to Rome.

Bieda's Ing*

In the past, I mentioned that Beeding was founded by a Saxon chieftain called Bieda. *The Anglo-Saxon Chronicle* records the year of establishment as AD 501, but does not give us any clues as to his residence in the area.

When the Romans left these shores in the 5th century, the country attracted the Saxon tribes, who were a rather insular people. The fine roads and highways of the Roman occupation fell into disrepair and swift communications with the other tribes/areas declined. A curtain of darkness known as the Dark Age (AD 450 to 580) descended on Britain. The Germanic tribes were flooding into Britain and were not checked by the indigenous population until the battle of Mount Badon c. AD 515. We know so little of this age that the life of Beida and his followers is somewhat of a mystery to us.

To get a picture of the early 6th century landscape, we must try to visualise a scene, very different from that of today. North of the South Downs was a dense forest of Anderida, which included the forest of St. Leonard (dragons were recorded in this place). South of the Downs was the maritime part of Sussex. Beeding and Bramber with Botolphs were astride a tidal estuary and salt marsh, which was probably devoid of standing timber. *The Anglo-Saxon Chronicle* mentions that Beida had two ships, so it's likely he would reside not too far from them.

There should be no doubt that the Romans left at least one substantial dwelling when they departed. Sele/Sela was a Saxon name (happy/hall). Could Beida have lived at this raised site? Saxon remains are known to exist in Hyde Street, but there is not enough evidence so far to say it was more than agricultural farm buildings. Beeding Court is the main manor house in Beeding, just north of the mediaeval village site of Beding – .earlier called the hamlet of Sele. This village may have been the east end of the Veteri Ponte (old bridge). Records of the present manor go back to 1326, but it was probably used much earlier as an inhabited site

One place I favour is Thundersbarrow, a British Roman Saxon encampment which lies to the south of Beeding on the east side of the river. It is not far off the great east-west road across southern England from Canterbury to Winchester via Southampton, crossing the Adur at Botolphs/Annington and at Sele via Hyde Street and the church, where a wagon ford is recorded.

Perhaps Beida* (our founder) is buried up on the South Downs in one of the tumuli that abound upon Beeding Hill!

*In several instances 'Beida' has the alternative spelling 'Bieda'.

3,840 to the Pound

Soon, if no one complains too much, the last vestige of our traditional currency will be phased out. I am of course referring to the pound sterling, a miserable coin now, but once a powerful world currency in gold, silver and banknote. Only our more mature residents will remember the great purchasing power of the pre-war pound.

Before World War II, a daily newspaper could be bought for a *penny.* Children's pocket money, a weekly *halfpenny* or 'ha'penny' for the younger ones, could buy several ounces of sweets and other delights. Even ounces are now long gone! The old-age pension was *ten shillings* (50p), which was enough to purchase a week's supply of groceries. I seem to remember that the train fare from Bramber to Brighton was three pence. This was possibly half fare. Does anyone remember?

I have mentioned in earlier articles that I have artefacts from the old Bramber museum. When the contents of the museum were sold, the wife of Edgar Collins, the curator, invited me to take some items as keepsakes. I chose some small African artefacts, plus a small collection of Victorian coins and tokens of the 1840s.

Leaving aside the penny, twopenny, threepenny and fourpenny pieces of the *maundy* money, there were fifteen other denominations within the pound: the gold *sovereign* and *half sovereign,* the silver *crown* (4 to the £), the *halfcrown* (8 to the £), the *shilling,* called a 'bob' (20 to the £), and the *sixpence,* a 'tanner' (40 to the £). A coin, nicknamed the 'joey', was a tag given to the silver *fourpence* (60 to the £), the silver *threepence* (80 to the £) and the silver *threehalfpence* (160 to the £). In copper, there was the *penny* (240 to the £), the *halfpenny* (480 to the £) and the *farthing* (960 to the £). Half, third and quarter fractions of the farthing were also produced mainly for use in the Colonies. I noticed that a recent numismatic catalogue valued a *quarter farthing* (3,840 to the £) in extra fine condition at £40. Based on a pound's worth, this would be some £153,600 today!

See 17.5 *The Godless Decimal*, about the Victorian attempt to decimalise.

History of Names

The area called Castletown in Beeding has always intrigued me. I discovered some time ago, when first preparing to contribute history articles to *The Villager* in 1983, that people here thought that the name came from the Towers Convent. Before 1911, the Towers had been castellated, with the tower on the south-west corner being eighty feet high. Photographs from around 1890 show the building impressively standing alone. Castletown, I later found out, is recorded as such on Ordnance Survey maps as far back as 1868. As the building was erected about 1883, clearly the name is not derived from it.

It seems too far from the site at Bramber to have been the town below the castle. On Truleigh Hill where the power lines now cross the Downs, there was a mott and bailey defensive building, established about 1066 after the conquest. Was this the castle of Castletown? The Bostel (Saxon for 'bost-hill') indicates that it is a hidden path or road up a hill that one can ascend or descend without being seen. In an earlier *Villager* I mentioned the existence of an old Roman signal/semaphore station on the same site as the mott and bailey. Perhaps long use of this as a place of defence with a garrison could have endowed Castletown with its name. Who knows?

In his census of 1870, the Reverend Dr. Bloxam recorded new houses at 'Nell', called 'Castletown'. Later, his notes in the 1880s say that many are empty. A wall and some doorways can still be seen opposite Castletown chalkpit.

A story about the Reverend William Stukeley, who was interested in all things Roman and died in 1765, shows that one has to be careful with research. He made several journeys to different parts of England looking for Roman remains and artefacts. An uninterested bystander informed him that there was a certain stile that was known locally as 'Caesar's stile'. Taking directions, Stukeley set out to locate this stile, no doubt assuming some Roman connection. On reaching the stile, he saw an old chap in smock and gaiters and asked him. "Is this Caesar's stile?" "Lord love yer, yes," said the yokel. "I helped old Bob Caesar build this as a boy, nearly sixty year ago!"

The Map*

Did you know that there is a Parish Millennium Map being assembled now? This is to illustrate the many points of interest within our boundaries, as a time record of the area. Apart from village appraisals and local plans, the last time this was done was in the tithe maps of the mid-Victorian period.

Travellers, landowners, military men and historians have a need for maps of different kinds. Travellers needed them in order to seek the best routes. Stewards and bailiffs of the great landowners need to know how much land the lord owned and who occupied it. The ecclesiastical authorities required similar information in 1836, when their tithes were commuted into annual money rents instead of the former tenth of produce that had existed since the time of King Ethelwulf. So, the tithe map was added to our store of records of the past.

Gerhardus Mercator (1512-1594), the Flemish geographer, is probably the best known cartographer. He was a pioneer of navigational maps and charts. Christopher Saxon (born 1542), John Speed (born 1552), with Noren, Morden and John Ogilby, are among the best known cartographers to produce early English county and road maps. Perhaps the most famous series of maps is that produced by the Ordnance Survey, founded in 1791. They established the one inch to one mile national scale for maps.

A few maps of our parish exist as estate maps. One of the earliest (1627) by John Gotham, shows oxbows in the Adur that were removed by the Navigation Act of around 1807. This act provided for barge traffic on the river. Perhaps the most beautiful and informative local map is the 19th century one of the Rape of Bramber, surveyed in 1824. Engraved by Davies and published by Edmund Cartwright in 1830. This shows the geography of our area with every house, park, woodland, pond and watermill. Sadly, only ninety copies ever reached subscribers to the edition, as there was a fire in the printer's storeroom. No one knows how many copies remain today.

*The Beeding Millennium Map can be seen in Beeding Village Hall.
The Bramber Millennium Map can be seen at St. Mary's House, Bramber [Ed.]

Records of the past in Beeding and Bramber

Wliile discussing with a resident the history of flooding in Beeding and Bramber, he posed the question, 'Where do you get all your information from on this area?'

Most of you readers know that I am a collector of books on Sussex and have written several myself. Of the many sources I use, the prime item of local knowledge in this area is titled, *The Chartulary of Sele Priory,* by an old tutor of mine, L. F. Salzman. This book, compiled in the 1920s, transcribes and lists every charier and conveyance then known from AD 1080 to about 1480.

The Adur is well banked now, but in early times flooding at high tides was necessary, as it supported the salt making trade In the 1300s, we exported many shipments of salt to the continent, but the trade declined some time after the Black Death about 1348. In the years 1323-29 recorded shipments were fifty-eight. From 1395-99, only three are known.

Before the windmill, watermills were dependent on a store of water from the millpond, which, in our area, refilled on every tide. There was such a mill at the bottom of the Glebeland steps, where there is much dressed stonework*.

'We, Walter de Coleuile prior of Sele and the monks, have granted to William Painter (Palmerio), vicar of Sele, a salt-pit with all its appurtenances which Swetman de Bedinges sold to him; namely that salt-pit which is situated between our watermill on the south and between (sic) the salt-pit which William Henri at one time held of us on the north; to hold to him and his heirs and assigns of the said Swetman and his heirs freely and quietly in fee and inheritance, paying yearly to us and our successors 6 reams of salt and to Swetman and his heirs a halfpenny at the feast of St. Thomas the Apostle.'

The field below the Priory at this time was known as 'Les Denier' (tenth). A century later it was known as 'Diggoners'.

Chartulary No. 16 1254AD [KN-B]

Beeding's Dark Age

Following on from the last two issues we continue to study Beeding in the period when our founder BIEDA occupied the land. The formal end of the Roman rule was c.AD 410 when Emperor Honorius withdrew the legions from the Roman province of Britannia, which they had ruled for nearly four centauries. The kingdom of Sussex came into being in the six centuries from that time until the Norman Domesday survey in AD 1086.

What we now know as Sussex was invaded by the Saxon chieftain/king, Aelle, sometime around AD 460. The place name 'Sussex' is a contraction of 'South Saxon' but it would have taken a long time to evolve under that title. Very little evidence remains in script of these early years. Legends passed down by word of mouth (times immemorial) are only as good as the narrator who added or missed out parts to suit his storytelling.

Bieda, as we know from the *Anglo Saxon Chronicle*, arrived in AD 50l, probably resided here [in Beeding] and also at Beddingham, near Lewes, another village credited to his list of property. He would have lived until around the middle of the sixth century, had he lived his three score and ten years. There is direct access from Beeding to Beddingham via the Adur, sea and Ouse.

In the future, archaeologists will peel off the layers of history and we may then know how villagers lived in Bieda's time. Agriculture was the main occupation and it is likely that Saxon fanning was similar to the practices worked up to the early 20th century here, the exceptions being, there were no root crops (potatoes, turnips). Forms of wheat, oats and barley, with legumes, were grown; cattle and sheep were husbanded; oysters and fish were harvested from the river and estuary. Fowl was also part of the diet. Without sugar beet, honey was the sweetener for cakes and the like. Oxen were the main power for ploughing in the deep clays, horses were faster workers but needed oats and hay, while oxen could exist in winter on hedge clippings and the like.

The area around Botolphs supported a small Saxon settlement; sunken-featured huts have been excavated in the extra-mural cemetery (virtually thatched pits). Hyde Street also has evidence of Saxon settlement as has SELE. Under Bramber Castle there is probably much evidence of Saxons, a defensive mound such as this would have attracted the earlier tribes as it did the Normans. Known burial sites have grave goods which indicate pagan worship. Some missionary priests preceded St. Wilfred who arrived here in Sussex c.AD 681, but the period in Beeding from Bieda until ecclesiastical records begin* is a blank at the present time.

* The first known writing was by the English monk, Gildas, in his work *De Excidio et Conquestu Britanniae* AD 547 [KN-B].

Beeding's Heroes*

As a result of my appeal for information in *The Villager,* we have received first-hand recollections of the men of our villages who are named on the war memorial in St. Peter's church; stark official records tell us when they died, but it does not usually tell us how. Local intelligence can create little 'windows' into the past to give a picture of their pre-war youthfulness; many joined up in their teens.

Dacre Gardens is the former home of our hero, Frank Gaston, as was Ernest Searle. Frank Edward Gaston was the son of Albert Edward and Charlotte Gaston, sometime residents of 26 Dacre Gardens, Beeding.

Frank was married to Winifred Theresa of Rosyth, Fife. We do not know when he joined up but, as he was a volunteer reservist, it was probably sometime around the eve of the Second World War. He was a leading aircraftsman (No. 976285) and a member of 242 Squadron, a fighter squadron flying Spitfire Mark IX's, engaged in escorting bomber raids on the Italian mainland during the invasion. This Royal Air Force Volunteer Reserve squadron was based at an airfield somewhere near the village of Poretta on the French island of Corsica. Frank was killed in a motorcycle accident while doing dispatch rider duty, taking orders to an ammunition ship on 12th July 1944. He was 23 years of age.

Frank's older sister, Miss L. Gaston, who lived in Old Fort Road at Shoreham, assisted me with some of the information on his early life. He worked locally before the war, sometimes as an odd-job man, but he wanted to fly and aspired to be a rear gunner; he joined the R.A.F. Volunteer Reserve. Unfortunately, owing to eyesight problems, he was unable to be air crew and became an aircraftsman as ground crew. Frank is buried in the Biguglia War Cemetery, Haute-Corse, France, [ref. Grave 2.c.8]. Biguglia is a small village 9 kilometres south of Bastia, which is a town and sub-prefecture of the department of Corsica situated on the coast north-east of the island. The cemetery lies 7 kilometres south of Bastia and some 275 metres west of the Bastia-Biguglia-Ajaccio road, in the Commonwealth War Cemetery. There are now sixty Second World War casualties commemorated in this site.

We honour their memory.

*See also 11.8 *A Beeding Hero*

Bridges that Spanned the Adur

Back beyond memories and the known facts of history, which we call time immemorial, there have been crossings of the Adur. In earlier times there was only one way across on foot and that was by the old 'veteri ponte' at Botolphs. We know this because St. Botolphs was known before the Conquest as St. Peter de Veteri Ponte (St. Peter of the old bridge). Other ways across were by ferry of some sort. This old bridge or causeway fell into disrepair around the time the bridge at Bramber was erected just after 1066. By 1250 the 'Great Bridge of Bramber' had been rebuilt in stone 170 feet long with a chapel on its central pier. It endured after being rebuilt circa 1477, until sometime in the 17th century, by which time the river had receded.

Beeding Bridge, which has always spanned the main course of the river, was of timber up to 1785 when it was rebuilt by Magdalen College who were the owners from 1459. Bricks were used then, and again, when it was widened on the north side in 1845. The first footbridge was added in 1926.

The timber bridge known as the 'Old Shoreham Toll Bridge', was built in 1781 because the ferry, owned by the priory of Hardham, had become increasingly more dangerous. In 1787 the revenue was said to be £20 per annum. The Duke of Norfolk originally built the bridge, but it was rebuilt by the RAILWAY Co. in 1916 to the same dimensions as the original. Another bridge of the trestle type was built to the South of the toll bridge around 1845 to carry the London, Brighton and South Coast Railway to Worthing and beyond. This was replaced by the present one at the end of the 19th century. The supporting cylinders filled with concrete were sunk some 70 feet into the riverbed.

The first 'Norfolk' bridge was opened on May Day 1833. It was a suspension bridge designed by Tierney Clarke the architect of Hammersmith and Marlow Bridges. There was some influence from Captain Samuel Brown, the builder of the Brighton 'Chain Pier' 1822/3. One of the tollgates from this first bridge can be seen at the entrance to Sele Priory. The cantilever bridge which, replaced the first one, was built in 1924 and, owing to the growing congestion, tolls were finally abolished in 1927. This structure was again replaced recently using earlier supporting piers to give a new wider concrete deck.

In our Parish alone four bridges now span the Adur; the Southdowns Way Bridge, the Bypass Bridge, Beeding Bridge, and the Old Foot-Bridge to Kings Barnes, built originally in 1724 but replaced in 1905 and known locally as the 'White Bridge'. During recorded history there have been, or still exist, 22 across the Adur south of Henfield.

KN-B introduced the theme of bridges in 5.7

Emergency

Established in the 'Cold War' era, Upper Beeding's Emergency Committee was composed of Councillors and volunteer residents. When first formed, the prime area of responsibility was nuclear attack the village had a machine to give 4 minutes warning of a missile launch (just time to boil an egg!); the warning machine still exists, but is now switched off. There is still danger from nuclear contamination from French nuclear power stations in Normandy and the north noast of France; should there be a terrorist attack on them, the fall-out would be with us in a few hours as we are only some 80 miles down wind.

At the end of the 'cold war' the Emergency Committee turned its thoughts to other potential accidents: what to do if a plane crashed on to the village area? Or if a petrol tanker should catch fire at the garage? We are still prepared in a small way to offer help and assistance, with plans in place for the evacuation of affected residents, and supply of their needs such as food and blankets.

Another facet of the activities of the Committee is the very real threat of flooding in the area. We have stocks of sand bags at two locations within the area of Beeding and have acquired a petrol driven water pump to assist any who have their house at risk of immediate inundation. Priority will be given to the disabled and elderly; and we urge that those who have experienced flooding in the past acquire their own stocks of sandbags.

A National Government would issue warnings on our own Citizens' Band if there were any danger of terrorist threat to poison our water supply; it would then be our own responsibility to guard our two deep wells at the 'Waterworks Corner', and the reservoir at the Bostel. Firearms would be issued in an emergency by the police, who would be entitled to confiscate shotguns and the like.

One of the duties of the Emergency Committee is the distribution of food. We have in the past issued large amounts of butter, cheese, tinned steak and other surplus supplies to the unemployed and pensioners.

Numismatics

The oxen of biblical times, when mentioned in the context of transactions, were not always beasts. In the Middle East copper ingots have been excavated and historians agree that these may have been the equivalent value of an ox and could have been mediums of exchange in those early times. The Greek civilisation produced the first coins with properly engraved dies. The Owl of Athens was one of the first motifs along with portraits of Greek heroes and leaders like Alexander the Great and his father Philip. Dolphins were also popular devices.

The Romans followed Greece in producing finely made coins, using gold, silver, bronze, and 'electrum', a natural alloy of gold and silver. They were so prolific with their minting that even today some Roman coins are available to young collectors for a few pence

In Britain, when the Romans withdrew their legions in the early part of 5th century, local tribes cast their own coins, which were very crude; other coinage known as 'hammered' was in use from the Viking period and endured until the 17th century. 'Hammered' was a term for using two dies and hammering them together on a metal disc by hand. 'Milled' coins, struck by machine, were first in use in the reign of Elizabeth I.

Platinum was discovered, by mining, in Russia in the 19th century. This new metal was viewed with suspicion, and was first minted into coin in the regal Russian currency, replacing silver. This coinage is now much sought after and fetches large sums at auction.

At the time of the Industrial Revolution there was a dearth of regal coins and many private issues were made, especially for the colonies (America & Canada); commerce could not function without small change. Unlike the man with 'The Million Pound Note', a man with a shilling could not buy an article for a halfpenny if the trader didn't have the eleven pence halfpenny change.

Archaeologists are delighted to discover coins as they help to 'date' dig sites. As the founding chairman of the local Burial Board I was involved in the excavations at Botolphs burial ground prior to it being commissioned. I remember the discovery of a coin of the Roman, Hadrian [AD 117-38] and another, a silver penny of Henry III.

KN-B dealt with this subject in 3 .5

Two Decades

It is twenty years this month since *The Villager* came into being; before that time the Parish Magazine had been known by various names over the years, and was called *The Christian* for the last few years immediately before the birth of *The Villager*.

In March 1983 a committee of editors was formed for the re-birth of the magazine under the title *The Villager*. I was invited by the editors to write a monthly article on aspects of the history of the three villages; the inaugural editors were June Kennard, Francis Fyfe, Stuart Faires, Beth Tanner and Andrew Knights; Vera Finding organised and reported on the churchwomen's meetings and 'Uncle John' (Horsley) for the youngsters.

Over these last twenty years (which seem like only yesterday) I have covered the history of many local institutions and locations, among them the churches, The Towers, the schools (founded by the Church) and delved into the reasons why the prefixes 'Upper' and 'Lower' apply to Beeding. Residents have asked questions of me about the villages and I have tried to research and answer those enquires presented as articles each month, in return I have learned much from villagers about the past in the Adur Valley.

Earlier historians, in the main, overlooked the commonplace and did not record the customs and practices of the residents which were not regarded as of any great interest, kings and queens and national events being seen as more important. There were a few exceptions, diarist Thomas Turner and William Cobbett (*Rural Rides*) being two such recorders.

Valuable information on the commonplace customs can be gleaned from outsiders who visit a place and then relate these strange happenings to others by letter. I have many such letters and accounts of life in our area; as an example a letter from the West Country remarks that when the local housewife cuts bread she held the loaf (4lb quartern) under one arm to cut two slices! I can vaguely remember this. Before World War II recycling was a must, nobody would throw string away, parcels were unwrapped with care and the string was kept in a special box or joined up to make a large ball, this was then used mainly by the gardener for tying bean poles etc. Builders when finishing a building used to place a coin in their work – one such coin can be seen at St. Peter's above the window in the east end of the south aisle. Many children thought it was a gold sovereign, but on close inspection from a ladder, when I cleared the guttering some years ago, I found it was a farthing (just as well!). This coin was placed there by the father of Miss Olive Elms during restoration work.

There is a national trend these days to rubbish the past, and history is not taught with as much pride in our country as when I was at school (early 1930s). Without knowledge of past happenings many of the awful mistakes of earlier generations will be carried into the future.

Picture Gallery

Further illustrations of interest

1. Bramber Water or Beeding River?

Early morning mists in the Adur Valley give an impression
of the former sea estuary. Earlier names include Sore or Saore, Weald Ditch, Bramber
Water and Beeding River. [2.8,7.2]
(Photograph by courtesy of Anne Ketteman)

2. Bramber in the early 19th century

Old Bramber Street with St. Mary's c1821 [4.1]

Steel engraving of St. Nicholas Church by J. Rouse [7.9]

3. Bramber Refreshments

The Bun Shop c1900 [15.9]

Rose Tea Gardens c1920, one of eight tea-gardens in Bramber [15.5]

4. Searching for the Past

Archaeologist Hilda Holden with the 12C tile she discovered under the floor in the Monks' Parlour at St. Mary's during excavations in 1985 [10.1]

Vincent Camilleri during the exploration of the reputed underground chapel at St. Mary's [10.1]

5. Lords of the Manor

Sir Thomas Seymour, 1st Baron Sudeley, Lord of the Manor of Beeding [2.7]
Married the dowager Queen Catherine Parr on 4th April 1547.

George, Lord Edgcumbe (later the 1st Earl) 1720 – 1795, by George Chalmers
Distinguished Admiral with the Plymouth Command.   Extensive estates in Devon,
Sussex and the West Indies. Lord of the Manor of Kings Barnes [1.5]
(*Photograph by kind permission of the Mount Edgcumbe Collection*)

6. Honourable Members for Bramber

Nicholas Barbon, christened Nicholas-If-Jesus-Christ-Had-Not-Died-For-Thee-Thou-Hadst-Been-Damned Barebon. Son of the Puritan Praise-God Barebone. Purchased St. Mary's as a 'burgage' and was elected Member of Parliament for Bramber in 1690 and 1695. He was a ruthless developer of London, buying up great swathes of land after the Great Fire of 1666. He invented the terrace house and made a fortune by introducing fire-insurance and mortgage schemes, but came to a bad end, being reduced to bankruptcy through outrageous speculative schemes. [See. 9.7]

Sir Richard Gough Member of Parliament for Bramber 1714-1727. Of an entrepreneurial nature, he purchased St. Mary's Bramber as a 'burgage'', thus giving him the right to obtain parliamentary privileges. He was proprietor of the East India Company. His son, Sir Henry Gough-Calthorpe succeeded him. [See 9.7]

7. St. Mary's from 1984

Renée Linton with Peter Thorogood in the Library at St. Mary's, c1989. She was able, jointly with Mary Thorogood, to purchase Orchard Lodge, the house in the garden of St. Mary's, built by Miss Dorothy Ellis for her retirement [10.10]

Peter Thorogood and his sister, Mary, and Roger Linton in the garden at St. Mary's c1997. Roger succeeded in saving the Victorian walled gardens, together with the former head-gardener's cottage [10.10]

8. Beeding Celebrations

A convivial gathering of Beeding lads c1920
with Mr and Mrs Harry Woolgar (far right) [3.9]

Beeding Court: Preparing for the local procession marking the coronation
of King Edward VII 1902 [4.8]
(by courtesy of the Cross family)

9. Bramber and Beeding Schoolchildren

Beeding schoolchildren 1919

Beeding and Bramber schoolchildren open their new school.
Keith, as Chairman of Beeding Parish Council with, on his left, Gill fox, Chairman of
Bramber Parish Council, next to Peter Thorogood of St. Mary's House [page 14]
(*by courtesy of the Adur Herald*)

10. Bramber Events and Recreations

Competitors struggle to regain control in one of the first Bath Tub Races, pictured here at Bramber causeway, their original site, during the annual floods [15.8]

Regular excursion trains brought tourists to Bramber to enjoy the delights of the eight tea gardens, Potter's Museum of Curiosities, Bramber Castle amusements, and pleasant river walks [4.7, 15.5]

11. Beeding Games and Recreations

Saturday fun with the 'buns and treacle' contest.
2nd Annual Welfare Sports, Beeding, August 2 and 3, 1926 [14.2]

Sunday boating on the Adur [10.9, 15.9]

12. The Bridge Between

Beeding   Bramber

Interesting drawing of Beeding Bridge with coal barge in 1887,
at a time when the Adur was a busy working river. [5.5, 11.2]

The Adur was still navigable in the early 1900s [5.5]

13. Beeding and Bramber Local History Society

The History Society Tent at the Stuart Fayre in 1988.
Pam Chalmers-Dixon (centre under tent) with Martin Toomey and Alison Noble (right)

Millennium Photograph by Ken Scott of Members of the Society in 2000.
Front row: James Panton, Cecily Moorhouse, Lily Holden, Alison Noble, Phyllis Fretwell,
Pat Nightingale, Sheila Holdstock, Margaret and Keith Nethercoate-Bryant.
Back row: Michael Moorhouse, Graham Cooper, Alan Barwick, Dawn and David Burrage,
Dave Nightingale, Jane Schrouder. *Far back*: Allan Shaw.
The Society continues to foster an interest in the history of the three villages of Beeding,
Bramber and Botolphs, holding regular meetings throughout the year, a summer walk to a
place of local historical interest, and a Christmas Party.

APPENDIX ONE

Articles from
The New Adur Herald

The Dead of Bramber

Even the briefest glance at parish registers can provide many fascinating discoveries, and a very real glimpse into the past of a community. Here in Bramber we have some very old burial records.

The name Woolgar (in several spellings) appears more often than any other. Perhaps the saddest entry in this name relates to the burial on 26th September 1826 of two baby boys, Stephen and William Wolgar, who had both died aged just eleven days. Sadly the records are full of details of child deaths: on 17th March 1938, just before the last war, John Cobby was buried – he was the 3-year old son of Bramber's Station Master.

The first recorded burial of ashes in Bramber took place on 5th January 1948, being the cremated remains of William Cecil Hammond-Williams, aged 53. Interestingly, there are no recorded burials of soldiers lost in either world war; all of Bramber's fallen apparently being buried overseas where they died.

Walter Potter, owner and curator of Bramber's famous 'Potter's Museum' was buried on 25th May 1918, aged 82. He was buried by Laurence Hamerton, then the parish priest, who is himself buried in Beeding.

On 9th October 1920, a burial took place at Bramber. The service was conducted by the Assistant Curate, Father Parkin, and the deceased is recorded as'An unknown man found dead in the river Adur, aged about 60.

Early 1922 was a bad time to live in the Railway Cottages at Bramber. George Dance, aged 64, from one cottage, died and was buried in February that year. Two months later his neighbour, Henry Mitchell, aged 58, also died and was buried at Bramber Churchyard.

William House, who died and was buried in Lambeth Hospital, aged 77, in June 1929, was brought back to Bramber and buried at St. Nicholas' Church on 4th July. He made this last journey home as he had formerly been resident at the Tollgate in Bramber Street.

Interestingly, the burial registers also record several persons of no fixed abode. These are not tramps or vagrants, but rather members of the travelling community who have long shared with local residents a sense of Bramber and Beeding as 'home'.

Many of the burials recorded in the register for St. Nicholas' Church were conducted by the Revd. Thomas Green DD, who was Rector of Bramber and Botolphs for 47 years. He died on 31st August 1830, aged 88. The same register which bears his signature so many times then records his own burial on 7th September 1830. Dr. Green had known his share of sadness in life, and was buried in a vault under St. Nicholas' Church, which had already contained the remains of his wife, Ann (died aged 37) and their eldest daughter, also named Ann, who died aged 40.

Another former parish priest, the Revd. Thomas Granthan BD, died on 18th April after 33 years as Rector. He is buried under thr nave floor, where a simple stone is marked with his initials and the year of his burial. Memorials of both priests may be seen on the chancel wall of St. Nicholas' Church.

St. Nicholas Church, Bramber by R. S. Nibbs

Farewell to the Parish Magazine

It is sad to be writing these words, but they DO say that "all good things must come to an end". This is the final edition of our Parish Magazine, which has been published every month with church and community news since at least 1898.

Nobody is really sure when the magazine started! However, the earliest edition in our archives is January 1898, and as Beeding and Bramber with Botolphs were first united to share a single incumbent (Parish Priest) in 1897, it seems that the origin of the magazine is about then.

Over the greatest part of its life (1898 to 1973) it was simply entitled *The Parish Magazine*. It was re-launched in January 1974 with a new title, *Christian*. It was during 1983 that the editors again changed the title, this time to *The Villager*. Finally, following merger at the end of 2005, the title became The *New Adur Herald*.

The earliest editions were more like a newspaper in style. There were few illustrations, and no front covers. The front page, like the inside, was just a mass of type, full of news. It was after the Second World War that the front cover became illustrated with pictures of the church buildings. The drawings changed over the years, but five worship centres were depicted - St Peter's (Beeding), St Nicholas* (Bramber), St Botolph's (Botolphs), the Church Centre (Small Dole), and the Mission Hall (Dacre Gardens). In the 1970s the church pictures were replaced with three coats-of-arms, one for each of our three main patron saints. Later Dacre Gardens closed and Small Dole was transferred to Henfield, so that in the 1980s when the cover returned to depicting church buildings, just our two main churches in Beeding and Bramber were shown; however, by the late 1980s St Botolph's had re-appeared on the cover again. In the 1990s a stylised cross took the cover position. Finally, just before the new millennium, we reached the age of monthly cover illustrations, and since then a range of cartoons, drawings and phtoographs has graced the front cover.

Now all this has come to an end. Elsewhere in this magazine you can read about the reasons why publication must now cease. Here, however, we will content ourselves with sitting back and letting the magazine talk for itself. What follows are several randomly selected extracts from copies of this magazine across the years.

January 1898

The new Rector, Henry Meyrick, urged parishioners to attend the Eucharist at Bramber when he was to be instituted as the incumbent (He also introduced the new Assistant Curate John Tennent). "It would be a cause of great thankfulness to me if as many communicants as possible will join in receiving the 'Bread of Life' from the hands of our Diocesan, and thus unite themselves by this most sacred link to their Bishop, to their Parish Priest, and to one another".

"The Rev. J. Paget Davies has inspected Beeding School in Religious Knowledge, and has sent the following satisfactory report:- The improvement noted last year is fully maintained. I am glad to find the older children able to find places readily in their Prayer Books. Their singing is in good tune. The infant class (37 present) has been admirably taught in all respects'. We heartily congratulate Miss Bloyd, Miss Hubble, and the scholars on so good an account of their work. The Vicar conducted an examination in Religious Knowledge at the Small Dole School, and was pleased to find the results quite satisfactory."

April 1898

"At Evensong on Sunday, March 20th, the two new Bells were dedicated at Beeding Church." The following notes listed the clergy present and the names of parishioners who contributed to the costs. There is an account of the sermon delivered by the Headmaster of Lancing College, the Revd. Ambrose J. Wilson, DD.

"Miss Cann, of Annington, has kindly undertaken to play the Harmonium on Sunday afternoons at St Botolph's Church, and she has also succeeded in getting together a small choir; her help is greatly appreciated."

December 1904

"The Venerable the Archdeacon of Lewes hopes to pay an official visit to Upper Beeding on Monday, December 12th. The Archdeacon preserves a specially warm corner in his heart for our parish, as fifty years ago he was an inmate of Beeding Priory, being a pupil of the Rev. R. Lewis Browne." Does anyone know of this school at Beeding Priory?

"The Vicar is very glad to give his official sanction and his warm personal approval to the kind labours of Miss Witts, Miss Parker, and Miss Holland among the growing community which is situated near the Cement Works. These labours are the outcome of a deep love for souls, and can only be productive of good in our midst" What were these ladies doing?

June 1907

This bumper edition reports the ordination of the Vicar's son (Cyril Meyrick), a confirmation, and a visitation. The origins of the Dacre Gardens Mission Hall are revealed. A certain Mrs Dunlop bought the Mission Hall at Oreham Common and had it moved to Beeding and "considerably extended". She had previously been Miss Alice Robertson. Her father was Prebendary David Robertson, Vicar of Henfield, and her husband (Mr Dunlop) was also the Vicar of Henfield, in his time! She was yet another person who had lived at The Priory as a child - it was clearly a busy place! We also learn the fascinating news that in the 1850s Beeding had no Vicar, but instead a Curate-in-Charge, subject to the Rector of Bramber - early preparation for the coming union of the parishes in 1897.

July 1910

It was reported that on St Peter's Day the Vicar had hosted the annual school treat in his garden, which was attended by 200 children and 200 adults. There were prizes, followed by tea (children served first), and then games and races on the lawns. Finally all 400 people crammed into St Peter's Church for a short service. We'd like to observe the faces of the Wardens today if 400 people turned up at St Peter's for worship!

August 1961

We note that Mrs Betty Parker was on brass cleaning duty! Despite there being 24 advertisements for local businesses, the editors were appealing for more advertising to help keep the magazine going – how ironic! The adverts printed included no fewer than three tearooms, and two general stores all situated in The Street, Bramber. The Vicar hoped soon to revive an old English custom: "In olden days, Mid-Lent was called Mothering Sunday. Children brought presents to their mothers to show their love. It was a day when the whole family shewed special kindness to mother, in return for all the kindness that she had shown to them. This is one of the old customs that is well worth reviving." We can assure him that it has been duly revived.

So after 110 years of publication we say: "Farewell to the Parish Magazine."

The End of the Road

After 110 years (at least!) of publication in our community, the united Parish Magazine of Beeding and Bramber with Botolphs has come to the end of the road, and this will be the very final issue. It is always sad when something reaches the end of its life, especially something old and venerable and familiar to us all. However, we must be realistic, and sadly our magazine is no longer viable.

Over recent years the number of subscribers has fallen away drastically. As people have died or moved away we have not managed to sell new subscriptions to keep up the numbers. It seems that there are fewer and fewer people for whom a Parish Magazine is important. Our estimated number of readers per issue has now sunk to around 300, which is simply not viable as a return on the costs of production - both financial costs, and costs in terms of manpower and commitment of resources.

There has been, however, another and more serious problem that has arisen over the past 5 or 6 years. The number of staff working for this magazine has fallen off even more drastically, and despite repeated appeals we have been unable to secure replacements. The most serious gaps in staffing have been for a Treasurer, a General Editor, and an Advertising Manager.

Without a Treasurer, there has been nobody to keep the accounts, bank the subscriptions, and regulate the advertising rates.

Without a General Editor the key decisions about covers, photos, content, and so on have had to be taken on an ad hoc basis by the parish's general Office staff, and by the Rector and the pastoral team. This is not their job, and they have appealed over and over again for someone to come forward with some commitment to the magazine to take the reigns - but nobody has come! It is a far cry from the parish where Father Timothy worked in the mid 1990s in Suffolk, where so many people wanted to edit the parish magazine that annual elections had to be held for the editorial board, to which five people were elected each year! Everyone wanted the job, and they produced a monthly 40-page magazine!

Without an Advertising Manager, we have not had sufficient income to cover our costs. The last Advertising Manager (Frances) retired from the post some 5 years ago. Since then the Rector has pursued one or two regular advertisers and so produced enough advertising revenue to keep our heads above water - but it has been a holding operation until we had someone wilting to do the job properly, but nobody has materialised.

To those of you who have stayed with us to the end, we thank you for your support. 110 years of history is an accomplishment in itself! We still hope that if an Advertising Manager can be found we may be able to bring a free Christmas magazine to every home in the parish on an annual basis, but this is the end of the monthly magazine. Goodbye.

APPENDIX TWO

Reference Section

1. Articles repeated in later issues of *The Villager*

No articles by KN-B appeared in 22.11, 22.12, 23.1, 23.2, 23.4, 23.5, 23.6

2. Select bibliography
List of works mentioned in the text

Albery, W. *Parliamentary History of Horsham 1298-1885.* Longmans Green 1926

Allcroft, Hadrian, *The Waters of Arun* 1855 1.2

Anglo-Saxon Chronicle, The (See G.N Garmonsway)1.1, 2.1, 3.11, 4.2, 8.12, 12.2, 18.1
(1), 18.1 (2), 18.2, 19.3,

Anon *Beowulf* Late 10thC poem in Old English 2.1, 8.12

Anon *Englands Remarque.* Printed for Langley Curtis in Goat Court at
Ludgate-hill. 1678

Anon *Guide to Steyning, Bramber, Beeding, Wiston, Ashurst and district.* Batemans.
1902

Anon *Poynings, a tale of the Revolution.* J. Masters. 1847

Arnold, Revd. H. E. B.: 'Parish Magazine' articles (1930s) 1.1, 2.3, 3.1, 6.11, 9.11, 9.12,
12.1, 12.2, 13.7, 15.3

Bede, The Venerable, *An Ecclesiastical History of the English People* 2.1

Bible, The 1.1

Bishop, Lucie, *Henfield in Battledress* Ditchling Press 1947

Blaker, Nathaniel P., *Sussex in Bygone Days.* Combridges, Hove (1906) 6.6, 8.8

Bloxam, Revd. Dr. John Rouse, 'Rough Notices of Beeding Parish Church and Priory'
[1888] 1.1, 1.3, 5.2, 6.4, 10.7, 11.5 (See also in Index 3 - Village People)

Bloxam, Revd. Dr. John Rouse, *New Houses at Nell* [Knell, called 'Castletown'] 1.3

Boyne, *17th Century Tokens* (1891)

Branwell, F., godfather to KN-B, author of *The History of Windmills of Brighton* 10.12

Brocklehurst, G., *Tithes and Tithe Rentcharge.* Bale, Kent. 1911

Burke, John, *Sussex* Batsford 1974 10.11

Burrell, Timothy *The Journal of Timothy Burrell* 11.12

Camden, W., *Magna Britannia.* Guilielmum Blaeu, Amsterdam 1629. 2.8

Camp, John 12.7 (bell-ringing)

Candole, H. de, *The Story of Henfield.* Combridges, Hove. 1947. 10.6

Cartwright, E., *History of the Western Division of Sussex,* Vol II, part 2:.
B. Nichols, *Rape of Bramber.* Dalloway and Cartwright. (1830) 12.2, 18.8

Chartulary of Sele Priory (See under Salzman)

Chaucer, Geoffrey, *The Canterbury Tales* 6.2

Cheal, Henry, *The Ships and Mariners of Shoreham.* F. M. Blame.1909. 9.10, 11.4

Cheal, H, junr., *The Story of Shoreham.* Combridges, Hove. 1947 11.4

Cheynell (mentioned in name only) 6.3

Christian, The, first parish magazine 3.11, 6.3

Clerkenwell document (Templar), St. John's Gate 4.1

Clifford, Lady Ann, *TheDiary of the Lady Ann Clifford.* William Heinemann (1923)

Cobbett, William, *Rural Rides* 1830 21.4

Colquhoun, Edward and K. T. Nethercoate-Bryant, *Shoreham-by-Sea: Past and Present*
(*Britain in Old Photographs* series). Sutton Publishing Limited. 1997. 10.1

Cooke, A.S., *Off the Beaten Track in Sussex.* E. Jenkins 1923

Dallaway, James, and Cartwright, Edward, *History of the Western Division of Sussex.*
Vol II 12.2

Davies, Edward (engraver to publisher Edmund Cartwright 1830) 6.5, 18.8

Davy, Allen, *Henfield Folk 55 Years Ago: Gleanings about Henfield, by an Old Henfielder.* 1896. 8.11

Delany, M. C., *Wealden Iron Industry.* Benn Bros. 1921

Dengate, Revd.W. A., *Slaugham, a Parish in Sussex.* Razell, Watson & Viney. 1929.

Domesday Book, The 1.1, 1.2, 4.2, 5.1, 6.6, 8.12, 15.10, 18.1 (1), 18.1 (2), 19.3

Drayton, Michael, *Polyolbion.* 1612. 2.8, 14.9/10

Dunning, James, *The Roman Road to Portslade.* 14.4

Durden, Diana, *A Glimpse into the Past: One hundred years of Baptist Worship in Upper Beeding.* 2005. [Published subsequent to K-N-B's reference in 4.8]

Ellis, C. H., *The London Brighton and South Coast Railway.* Ian Allen re-print. 1971

Ellis, W. H., *Parks and Forests of Sussex.* H. Wolff, Lewes. 1885

Erridge H. E., *History of Bramber Castle.* Crowhurst, Brighton. 1860

Evans, Colonel, local historian (research on Bramber Causeway) c.1930

Fea, A., *The Flight of the King.* Bodley Head. 1897

G. N. Garmonsway (translator). See *Anglo-Saxon Chronicle.* Editor, W.D.Parish. J. M. Dent 1953

Garratt, John G., *Bramber and Steyning, with notes on Beeding, Coombes and St.Botolphs.* Privately published. 1949. Reprinted 1973

Gildas, *De Excidio e Conquestu Britannicae* (AD571) 19.3n

Godfrey, Walter, *Sussex Archaeological Society* (S.A.C. lxxxvi)

Gotham, John, Map (1627) 2.1, 2.8, 4.11, 5.8. 12.8, 18.8

Grose, F., *Antiquities of England and Wales* c.1761. 7.9

Haines, Richard, *Memoir of Richard Haines (1633-1685) Henfield and Small Dole,* 1899. Harrison and Sons. Privately printed.

Hall, *Dictionary of Sussex Dialect* 1.3

Hall, M., *Smocks.* Shire Publications. 8.5

Historia Ecclesiastica Gentis Anglorum (Bede)

History of the County of Sussex Vols. II to VI (*Victoria County Histories*)

Holden, E.W., FSA. & T. P. Hudson M.A. Ph.D., *Sussex Archaeological Collections* Vol. 119 (on salterns) 2.4n, 12.2, 12.3

Hopkins, Thurston, S*ussex Rendezvous* (1928) 2.6, 11.10

Horsefield, T. V., *History of Sussex.* Two vols. Lewes 1835

Horsham District Council, *Steyning, Bramber and Upper Beeding Local Plan 1978-88.* 1978

Howe, F.A., *A Chronicle of Edburton and Fulking.* Hubners, Crawley. 1958   6.6

Hubbard, A. J. and Geo.Hubbard, *Neolithic Dew-Ponds and Cattle-Ways.* Longmans Green 1905

Hudson, D., P*otter's Museum.* Salmon. Sevenoaks.

Hudson, Professor T. P., Assistant Editor, *The Victoria County History* 1.2. 10.12

Kelly's *Directories of Sussex* 1906-15

King, M. E., *Round and About a Brighton Coach Office.* John Lane. Bodley Head. 1896

Laud Chronicle, The, 18.1(2)

Lewis-Smith, Ann, Welsh poet, (honeymoon at St. Mary's Bramber) 10.1

Lowe-Warren, J, compiled list of Sussex tokens. 1888. 3.6

Lucas, E.V., *Highways and Byways in Sussex.* Macmillan (1907) (See 'Sir Thomas Lawrence) 3.2

Magdalen Studies 7.12

Magna Carta (1215) 8.8

Manor Court Book of Beeding 4.4

Manor Rolls, The 3.4

Mason, J., *The Land of Snelling* 1733

Meresmen Report Books

Nethercoate-Bryant, Keith, *Some of the Lesser Known Facts of Beeding and Bramber, from 'The Villager' Magazine'.* Unpublished manuscript.

Nethercoate-Bryant, Keith, *The Villager* Beeding and Bramber with Botolphs Parish Magazine 12.2

Parish Magazine (See Revd. Arnold) 3.11, 8.7

Parish Registers (transcribed by Revd. Dr. Bloxam) 1.1

Parish, Revd. W.D., vicar of Selmeston, *Dictionary of the Sussex Dialect.* Farncombe, Lewes. 1875. Updated by Helena Hall, 1957.

Parish W (Ed.)., *Domesday Book: Sussex.* Printed in Lewes for Sussex Archaeological Studies by H. Wolfe

Parker Chronicle 18.1 (2) (quoted)

Pawson, E., *Transport and Economy, Turnpike Roads of the 18ᵗʰ century.* Academic Press 1977

Penny Illustrated Paper 9.2

Pictorial Times, The

Purefoy, Henry, *The Purefoy Letters* 1741. 8.5

Rand, Cater (drainage engineer), *Map drainage: Recommendation for the Rape of Bramber* (1806) 11.11

Rede, Bishop Robert, *Register (1409)* 9.9

Rees, Arthur J., *Old Sussex and Her Diarists.* John Lane The Bodley Head. 1929

Roberts, R. G., *The Place Names of Sussex.* Cambridge University Press. 1914

Salmon E. F. & Pilmore, A., *The Two Shorehams...by two inhabitants.* Emery & Sons. 1902

Salzman, L. F. (Ed.), *Chartulary of the Priory of St. Peter at Sele.* W. Heffer, Cambridge 1923.Covers Beeding and Bramber history from Jan 1080 to the last entry. Dec.1304. 1.1, 1.2, 2.1, 3.12, 5.8, 5.10, 10.10, 12.2, 13.1, 15.3, 17.11, 18,11

Scott, Sir Walter, (quoted) 14.9/10

Simpson, S*ussex Folklore* 9.8

Simpson, J., *The Turning Year* 10.4

Smith, W. C. (Ed), *Sussex Smugglers.* King, Brighton. 1850

Stedman, Fabian Cambridge printer, author of book on bell-ringing

Stevenson, R. L., T*reasure Island* (1883) 3.5

Stukely, Revd. William, 18.7 (researched Roman sites for artefacts)

Sussex Archaeological Society Collections (SAS). 2.4, 4.1, 12.2

Sussex Notes and Queries

Sussex Weekly Advertiser 11 December 1775

Tanner, T., *Notitia Monastica.* The Theater, Oxford, 'sold by A & J Churchill at the sign of the Black Swan in Pater-noster-row. London 1695

Telephone Directory, The (as a source of information used for research) 5.5

Tennyson, Alfred Lord, *Rizpah* 13.3

Trenqualéon, Max de, *West Grinstead et les Caryll.* Two vols. Burns & Oates. 1893. 12.4, 13.4

Trory, E., P*ostal History of Brighton 1673-1783.* Crabtree Press. 1953

Tyssen, A. D., *The Church Bells of Sussex.* Farncombe, Lewes. 1915

Underwood, R., Ransome (unpublished family history) 6.12

Victoria County History, ed. Dr. T. P. Hudson 1.1, 1.2, 2.1

Walton, Isaac, *The Compleat Angler* (1653) 8.10, 17.9

Warner, Revd.John, *The Seaboard and the Downs* (Vol. 1) Rivingtons. 1860. 4.12   See Woodman T.C.

West Sussex *Local Plan – Protection Against Flooding* (*1978-1988*) 12.8

Widsith, (poem in Old English about a minstrel) 2.1

Wolseley, Viscountess, *Sussex in the Past.* Medici Society. 1928

Woodford, Cecile, *Portrait of Sussex.* Robert Hale 1972 10.11

Woodman, T. C. *The Seaboard and the Downs* (Vol. 2) R. & C. Treacher, Brighton. 1902   (See Revd. John Warner) 14.9/10

3. Index of village people mentioned in the text

Convent Sisters, arrived from France 1903 1.5

Cook, Madge, founder of the Adur Players 8.6

Cross, Thomas Daniel, farmer of Beeding Court 4.8 (founder of Baptist movement in Beeding), from Crewkerne 7.7, 8.3 (trustee of Beeding Village Hall). See Hobbs, Fowler and Hatton

Cruley, Jack, the gambling miller of Beeding 14.8

Curling, Richard, gatekeeper to Sele Priory 7.5

Dacre, Sir Thomas 7.4

Dance, George, of Railway Cottages, died aged 64. See *The Dead of Bramber* (2001)

Dunford, Thomas, 'a sturdy vagrant' 5.2

Edgecombe, Lord, Lord of the Manor of Beeding 1.5

Edwards, Mr. (shoe-maker and church flute-player) 9.11

Edwards (thatcher) 8.11

Ellis, Miss Dorothy, owner of St. Mary's House Bramber (See Introduction p 18) 10.1

Elms, Frederick 3.10, 21.4

Elms, Olive 21.4

Evans, Colonel, local historian, field research on causeway south of Beeding Court (1930s) 1.2, 10.10

Faires, Stuart, inaugural editor of *The Villager*. See Fyfe, Finding, Kennard, Knight

Finding, Vera, inaugural churchwomen's editor of *The Villager*. See Faires, Fyfe, Kennard,

Fowler, Thomas Horatio, trustee, Beeding Village Hall 1930, 8.3. See also Hatton, Cross and Hobbs.

Frenssh, John 7.4

Fretwell, William and Phyllis (owners of Beeding Court) 4.8

Fyfe, Francis, inaugural editor of *The Villager*. See Faires, Finding, Kennard, Knight 21.4

Gaston, Frank Edward, Beeding hero 19.9

Gates, John, yeoman, of Horton Manor 3.4

Goddard, Mr., ironmonger, Beeding Stores, 3.8, 3.9, 14.12 (Parish Chairman)

Goddard, Richard, schoolmaster (1841) 1.6, 9.2, 13.3, 14.12

Goddard 9.2 (killed by falling tree in storm. Aged 66)

Goffe, Revd. Stephen, Rector of Bramber-cum-Botolph's, regicide 7.3

Gough, Matthew 7.4, 22.1

Gravenor, Miss 1.3

Green, Dr., restorations of St. Peter's, Beeding (1785)

Green, Revd. Thomas, Rector of Bramber and Botolph's for 47 years, died 31 August 1830, aged 88. See *The Dead of Bramber* (2001)

Gregory, Frank, wheelwright 10.12

Grinyer, Councillor 16.8

Haines, Thomas, of Barrowhill Farm 11.9

Hammond-Williams, William Cecil, died 5th January 1948, aged 53. See *The Dead of Bramber* (2001)

Hatton, G. Sugden, trustee, Beeding Village Hall 1930, 8.3. See also Fowler, Cross and Hobbs

Hayward (farm supervisor) 6.1

Hobbs. George Thomas, trustee, Beeding Village Hall, 8.3. See Cross, Fowler and Hatton.

Holden, Eric, FSA, 5.9, 5.10, 12.3, 13.1, 15.10 (Roman finds) (See *Sussex Archaeological Collections*)

Holden, Hilda 13.1, PG4

Hollyman, George, bookseller 14.4

Horsey, John, Lord of the Manor of Horton 3.4

Horsley, John, inaugural young people's editor of *The Villager*. See Faires, Fyfe, Finding, Knight, Tanner, Kennard

Hutchinson, Revd. Thomas, Vicar of Beeding and Bramber (See 'The Priory') 2.11, 9.12 (removed ruined parts of St. Peter's without permission)

House, William, buried Lambeth Hospital, died June 1929, aged 77. Resident at the Tollgate. See *The Dead of Bramber* (2001)

Jay, Richard, of Bewbush (part of Upper Beeding), benefactor. 12.4 (gift to restore Bramber Bridge and Chapel 1466/7. Gift of alms to St. Mary Magdalen Hospital, Bidlington)

Kennard, June, inaugural editor of *The Villager* 21.4 See Fyfe, Faires, Tanner, Knight, Finding, Horsley

Keymer, Walter, owner of 'The Towers' (1897), 1.5. Leased to Arthur Payne.

Kidd, Hugh and Thomas, owned Beeding Mill. Hucksters 8.8

Kidd, John, carpenter, Horton Manor 3.4

Kidd, Richard, miller 14.8

Knight, Andrew, inaugural editor of *The Villager*. See Faires, Finding, Fyfe, Kennard, Tanner,

Kidd, Sarah, landlady of Ann Boler

Lancaster, Ann, 'of Beeding at Seale' (lent money to Thomas Haines, farmer) 3.9, 11.9

Laud, Archbishop 9.12

L'Estrange, Revd. Father Timothy 16.11

Lewes, William of Sele

Local residents 7.11, 7.12

Long, Mr 17.9

Lucas family, Beeding groceries and provisions, 3.8

Lucas, Douglas 3.8 (succeeded his father, Frank, at Beeding Stores)

Lucas, Frank, grocer, Beeding Stores 3.8 (succeeded Obadiah, 1923), churchwarden, parish councillor) 3.8, 14.2 (organist at St. Peter's). See 'Memorial Playing Fields'.

Lucas, Keith, organiser of 'Beeding in Bloom' 16.8

Lucas, Obadiah (groceries and provisions) 3.8

Luckin, William, wheelwright (1841) 8.4

McCarthy, John and Morag, Tinker's Court, Bramber 15.7

Marcellin, Father, Assumptionist, French priest accompanying the Sisters from France 1.4

Marshall, Henry, coachman, mentioned in Bloxam's census 1.5, 3.7 (landlord of The King's Head with wife Rebecca, victuallers, King's head inn-sign)

Mary Agnes, Sister (lessee of 'The Towers') 1.5 See Elizabeth Wyatt

Meyrick, Revd. H. D, provided allotments 4.4, 4.10 (attended village Coronation celebrations)

Middleton, Revd. Thomas, Rector of Beeding, donor of chalice 7.8

'Miles', Parish Clerk 4.12

Mills, William, District Inspector, meresman, tenant of Pond Farm) 3.9

Morgan, Revd. John, Vicar of Beeding 9.12

Morris, Joseph, of Beeding Court (District Inspector) 3.9, 14.12

Musgrave, Alfred, owner of St. Mary's House, Bramber 1899-1907

Nethercoate-Bryant, Keith 5.4 (autobiogrpahical), 5.6, 13.2, 14.3, 14.4, 21.4 (memories)

Newlin, Revd. Thomas, Vicar of Beeding and Bramber 2.11

'Nicholas the Harper' 15.3

Nicholas, Revd. Dr. 9.12

Noel, Sister Mary, came as a girl from France and became a Sister 1.4

Norris, Wally (Priory Field) Bonfire committee member 5.11

Oglethorpe, Owen, Vicar of Beeding (later Bishop of Carlisle. Crowned Queen Elizabeth I) 18.1 (2)

O'Shea, Matilda (Mattie), popular Beeding resident 9.6

Painter, William, vicar of Sele 18.11

Palmer, John 3.10 (mail-coaches) See Post Office

Parish, Revd., W. D., Vicar of Selmston, author of *A Dictionary of Sussex Dialect* 9.4

Patching, Henry, of Toddington Farm 3.9 (District Inspector)

Patching, Mr., KN-B's schoolmaster 13.2

Payne, Arthur, owner of 'The Towers' 1.5

Pocock, Isaac (fishing rights between Shoreham and Beeding) 8.10, 17.9

Potter, Walter, taxidermist (1835-1918) 4.7 (founder of Potter's Museum) 9.3. For funeral service, see Appendix One, *The Dead of Bramber* (2001)

Rand, Cater (teacher, educationist, and drainage engineer) 11.11

Ricardo, Harry (later 'Sir Harry') 9.6 (lived at Tottington Manor)

Rousell, Albert E., Beeding hero 11.8

St. Merry, Sister, the first Superior at 'The Towers' Convent 1.4

Sancto Audreoni, Ralph de, his 'salt pit at Anningedon' 13.1

Sanford, Len, district councillor. See illustrations 12.6 & 13.8

Sayer, Richard, of Nightingale Hall 8.11

Smith, George, builder of 'The Towers', resident at 'Wheelers', probably former house on 'The Towers' site. Leased site to Charles Bruton 1.5

Smith, S., probably brother of George Smith 1.5, 12.12

Snellying, John, disinterred 15.2

Sowton family, The 7.11

Stukeley, Revd. William 18.7

Tanner, Beth, inaugural editor of *The Villager*. See Faires, Finding, Fyfe, Kennard, Horsley

Tribe, Harry, blacksmith 6.8

Tufnell, Revd. J.G.F., Vicar of Edburton and Fulking 6.6, Tunnels 10.2

Turner, Revd. 8.4 ('a trusted accurate historian')

Upton, Harry, built first Beeding Garage 6.10

Upton, Obediah Henry, blacksmith, father of Harry 6.10

Ventris, Edward (quoted concerning hunger riots) 4.10

Ventris, Revd. James 2.11, 4.10 (hunger riots)

Vinall, Arthur 3.10 (Postmaster)

Warner, Charles, appointed teacher, aged only 15 (1841)

Welling Wheeler family 18.1

Wells, Harry, wheelwright (wheelwright, lived at The Malt House) 11.5

Wheeler, Jasper, coachman, inherited a rich widows fortune, sold to George Smith freehold of land 'The Towers' now stands on 1.5

Wheeler, Welling, and family 18.1 (1)

'William the Piper' 15.3

William Winter, apprentice 18.1 (1)

Winton, Thomas, pauper of the parish 18.1(1)

Wolgar, Stephen, died aged 11. See *The Dead of Bramber* (2001)

Wolgar, William, nicknamed 'Dead Horse' 8.11

Wolgar, William, died aged 11. See *The Dead of Bramber* (2001)

Woolgar, Bridger, Meresman 2.9

Woolgar, Charles, Meresman 2.9, 3.9 (Parish Council Chairman 1837) 6.5, 15.11, PG8

Woolgar, Harry with Mrs.PG 8

Woolgar, Mary 1.7 (illustration)

Wyatt, Elizabeth, lessee of 'The Towers', became Sister Mary Agnes 1.5

Wynch, Elizabeth Ann, later Sister Mary Agnes, leaseholder of 'The Towers' (1904). Purchased' 'The Towers' 1908). Left the house to the Sisters in her will (1918) 1.5

Young, Revd. de Mowbray, vicar of Beeding and parish councillor (c1939) 14.2

4. Index of Persons, Places and Pursuits

For many specific references to Beeding, Bramber, and Botolphs, see also under their separate headings. Local residents are listed in the Index of Village People. PG indicates a related illustration in the Picture Gallery.

A

B

Backshall/Backshell/Bagshall, John, copyholder of 'Knell' (1703), owner of 'Brooks', 'Clays' and 'Flaxlands' 1.3, 1.5, 2.2, lived at New House (1733) (later Valerie Manor) 1.5

Baptist movement in Beeding (See 'Thomas Daniel Cross' 4.8)

Barbon, Nicholas, (MP for Bramber) PG6 (cf. 9.7)

Barge, clay 5.5

Barge, coal PG12

Barge commodities 5.5, 11.11, 18.8

Barge families 4.6, 5.5

Barn, The (See 'King's Head') 3.7

Barrowhill Farm 11.9

Barter 9.1 (exchange in kind) 11.9. See 'millsoke' 13.1

Bath Tubs (annual race) 15.8, PG10 (original tubs)

Battle for Bramber 6.3

Baybridge Canal Company 2.8, 4.6, 11.2, 15.8

Beacons 12.6

Beating the Bounds 2.9, 15.11/12

Beeching, Dr. Alfred 4.8

Beddingham and Beding 19.3 (homes of Beida)

Bede, The Venerable (aka Baeda) 2.1

'Beding' (ancient spelling of 'Beeding' up to 19th century) 10.10, 16.2, 18.1(2)

Bedney 02.8, 4.6, 17.9 (fisheries)

Beeding Academy 1.6

'Beeding alias Sele' 3.4

Beeding and Bramber Local History Society. See introduction pp13 & 20, 9.5, PG13

Beeding Bridge 2.5 (timber), 5.7, 7.2, 12.10 ('turnpiked'), 15.4 (at risk from housing development)), 15.8, 16.8, 19.10 (rebuilt c1785 by Magdalen College – owners from 1459)

Beeding Cement Works 2.12, 7.1, 11.2

Beeding Court 1.2, 4.8, 7.1 (remains 13thC foundations), 12.3, 18.2, PG8 (Coronation 1902)

Beeding Court (See 'Court Leet' and 'Court Baron'. (See 'Vestry' 1.9)

Beeding dovecote (1326) 14.6

Beeding Forge 6.8, 9.1 (shoeing horses, oxen)

Beeding Garage (1920s) 6.10, 15.1 (excavations: mammoths, aurochs, woolly rhinoceros). See under 'Tribe'.

Beeding Hero 11.8

Beeding Higgler 14.5

Beeding High Street (built on Norman causeway) 10.11

Beeding Hill 2.3, 2.10, 3.10 (Royal Mail route), 9.8

Beeding Manor Court Book 1.9

Beeding Memorial Playing Fields 2.9, 4.4, 11.1 (50 years of)

Beeding milestone (resited from High Street) 11.3

Beeding Mill (c1724) (Destroyed in gale 1888) 2.10, 10.12

Beeding Mill roundhouse (ruin) 2.10

Beeding Millfield 14.7

Beeding mill pond 14.7

Bostel, The, 3.10 (Royal Mail route), 16.1 ('bost-hill' – secluded pathway up a hill), 18.7, 19.12 (See 'Hollow-way')

Botolphs (village) 7.1 (formerly called 'Old Bridge'), 10.10 (connection with St. Peter de Veteri Ponte), 19.3 (Saxon settlement). See more under 'St. Botolph's'

Bounds, beating of the, 2.9, 3.4 (Horton Manor)

Boundary Commission (1988) 19.4

Bowring, Sir John 17.5 (advocated decimal coinage)

Bramber, the Great Bridge of, 2.3, 2.6, 5.7, 5.9 (repairs of), 12.3, 19.10

Bramber, the great fire of (1286), 5.10

Bramber bridge (stone) 2.5, 5.7 (Chapel of St. Mary's), 12.4

Bramber bridge ((timber) 1.2 (early swing bridge) 1.11, 2.5, 5.7, 7.2, 10.10, (rediscovered 1829)

Bramber bypass (10th anniversary) 1.2, 9.7, 12.4

Bramber Castle 6.3 (Key-Keeper) (damaged or looted), 7.2 (ditches flooded at high tide until 11thC), 10.2 (tunnels, ghosts), 12.3, 12.10 (stones used for road-building), 14.4, 15.3 (minstrels), 19.3 (earlier Saxon settlement), 19.10 (chapel)

Bramber, Constable or Headborough of, 5.9, 13.8

Bramber Hoard (1981), 15.4

Bramber Mace 13.8

Bramber outings and excursions 4.7, PG10

Bramber regicide (See 'Stephen Goffe') 7.3

Bramber, 'rotten borough' 9.7

Bramber 'Serpent' 15.3

Bramber sewer trenches 12.3

Bramber shot contest 5.7, 15.7

Bramber station, 1.4, 2.8, 5.10, 9.3, 11.10, 15.5 (platform extension)

Bramber tea-rooms, 2.8, 15.5 (tea-gardens), PG3

Bramber token 3.6

Bramber toll house 2.3

Braose, John de, 8.10 (gift for mills and fisheries), 17.9 (John de Brawysa [sic] fisheries)

Braose Aanor de, (gift of land to Templars AD 1312) 4.1

Braose, William de, Governor, Bramber Castle 2.11, 4.8, 7.9 (built St. Nicholas c.1093), 12.3 (collector of tolls)

Braose, William de, (the Fifth), Lord of Bramber (c.AD1260) 4.2, 13.7 (his horses and hounds)

Bread and Ale, the Assize of, 8.8

Brembre, Sir Nicholas, Lord Mayor of London, local landowner 3.12, 17.11

Brembre, Philip de, 3.12

Brewing 8.8

Bridge, Beeding 2.5 (timber), 5.7, 7.2, 12.10 ('turnpiked'), 15.4 (at risk from housing development)), 19.10 (rebuilt c1785 by Magdalen College – owners from 1459)

Bridge, Bramber, Great of, ((timber) 1.2 (early swing bridge) 1.11, 2.3, 2.5 (stone) 2.6, 5.7 (Chapel of St. Mary's) , 5.9 (repairs of), 7.2, 10.10, (rediscovered 1829), 12.3

Bridges 5.7 (over the Adur) and numerous references under 'Beeding' and 'Bramber'

British Portland Cement Works 2.12

Broadsheets, posters, auction notices 11.7

Bronze Age 4.5, 4.9 (St. Botolph excavation finds), 6.7, 15.4 (Clay's Hill and Fever's Fields)

Bruce, Robert the, (Scottish version of Braose) 13.4

Bun Shop, The (Bramber) PG3
Bubs abd Treacle Contest PG11
Buncton Church 7.9 (Sele Priory windows)
Bungalow Town, Shoreham Beach 7.11
Burbeach 'Hundred' 1.9, 3.11, 4.2, 6.9, 12.11, 13.3
Burial Board 21.3
Burial ground, St. Botolph's 4.9
Burletts, temporary billet for Artillery (four 25-pounders lodged there) 12.6
Burrell, Sir Charles 2.6
Burrell, Timothy, local author of journal (See bibliography) 11.12
Bus services, local 11.10
Butcher's Fields 4.11
Bypass 9.7

C

Cade, Jack 2.7, 2.4, 5.2, 7.4
Calhoun, Revd, Thomas (started Beeding School) 1.6, 9.11
Calculations, 8.9 See under 'Coinage'
Camden, John (*Magna Britannia* 1586) 2.8, 12.8
Camilleri, Vincent PG4
Canadian Regina Rifles 12.6 (part of 3rd Division, billeted at Sele Court until March 1944).
Canals 4.6
Canterbury Tales, The Geoffrey Chaucer
Carmelite Friars of Shoreham (AD 1493) 2.11 (rebuilding of Priory), 5.4, 5.6, 6.4
Carters 16.1 (care of their horses) 16.1
Caryll, Sir Edward, owner of Kings Barnes 2.7, 5.3, 12.4 (cadet branch of de Braose family), 13.4, 17.10
Castle, Bramber, see under 'Bramber'
Castletown 1.3, 3.10, 7.1 (Saxon origins), 12.6 (ammunition stockpiled) 18.7
Cater Rand (teacher and drainage engineer) 11.11
Causeway 1.2, 2.8, 5.9, PG
Caxton, William (printer) 6.2
Cement 2.12, (See Beeding Cement Works 11.2)
Census (*Domesday* AD1085) 4.2
Census 1801, 6.1
Census 1811, 16.1
Census 1841, 1.6, 3.7
Census1851, 1.6, 3.7
Census (church attendances 1851) 9.11, 11.5 (communicants and residents)
Census 1871-1883 (Bloxam's) 1.5
Census returns 11.7
Chain Pier, Brighton 19.10
Chalk pits 2.12, 11.2
Chancel Arch, (underpinning at St. Peter's) 15.10
Chapel of St. Mary, Bramber Bridge 2.6, 6.2 (See 'de Sens' inventory), 10.1, 12.3, 12.4, 19.10
Chapel House (St. Mary's, Bramber) 5.9, 12.3 (residence of bridge wardens)

Charcoal 17.10

Charity (Poor Laws) 7.12, 17.12

Charles I, 3.10 (founded the Royal Mail), 7.3

Charles II, 1.3, 2.2, 3.7, 4.5, 10.1, 15.8

Chequer-board method of counting 8.9

Child benefit 17.12

Children's games 5.5, 5.6, 10.4

Chimney boys 11.6

Chimneys 11.6 (wood fires) (See 'Fire places')

Christmas 5.12, 11.12, 17.12

Church calendar 10.4

Church music 15.3

Church mysteries 13.12

Church rate 18.1

Church repairs 9.11

Cissbury 6.7 (See *Flint Tools*), 12.5, 13.8 (flint mines)

Clay barges 5.5

Clay's Hill 12.6

Cliff House (1890s) 7.1

Coach wall 12.10 (made higher to prevent passengers from peering over)

Coaching days 12.10, 14.8 (staging-posts). (See 'Inns'), 11.3 (milestones)

Coal barge PG12

Coal wharf (Beeding Bridge) 11.2

Cobbett, William, (author of *Rural Rides*)

Coins 3.5, 3.6 (tokens), 8.9 (Philip and Mary shilling), 13.6, 11.9, 17.5, 18.6.
    (See 20.3 *Numismatics*)

Coinage 3.8, 8.9 (calculations), 11.9, 13.8, 14.11, 16.3, 17.5, 18.6

Coleuile, William de, Prior of Sele 18.11 (his salt-pit)

Colquhoun, Eddie, antiques dealer 10.1 (cellars at St. Mary's Bramber)

Colvile, Walter de, Prior of Sele 13.7

Conquest, Norman 4.9

Constable or Headborough of Bramber, see under 'Bramber'

Convent of the Blessed Sacrament (See *The Towers*) 1.4, 1.5

Convent Sisters 1.5

Coppicing 5.12

Copyhold 4.4

Corona, at St. Peter's 17.2

Coronation 1902 PG8

Coronation Day (1935) 1.8

Cornish quarries (coal, slate, lime from) (See 'Canals') 4.6

Court Baron 1.9

Court Book, Beeding Manor 1.9

Court Leet 1.9

Country pursuits 5.6

Crime and Punishment 3.9, 9.8, 10.6, 13.3, 18.1 (1)

Cromwell, Oliver 7.3, 15.2 (abolished playing of church organs)

Cromwell, Thomas

Crusades 2.6, 4.1, 15.3

Customs, local, 10.4

D

E

Ethelwulf, King of England 4.11, 5.1
Elizabeth, Queen 5.10
Emergency (nuclear attack/flooding) 19.12
Enaghdun, Bishop 6.11
Entertainment (village theatricals) 5.6, 7.11, 8.6
Erringham 3.10 (mail robbery), 8.2 (See *Beeding Cement Works*, *Erringham Chalk Pit*)
      11.2 (as coal-yard), 13.3
Erringham (chalk-pits) 2.12, 11.2
Ethelwulf, King 4.11, 5.1
Excavations 2.6 (Bramber sewers c.1957), 2.11 (Sele Priory 1966), 4.9, 10.1,
      15.10 (St.Peter's 1983), PG4 (cellars at St. Mary's)
Excursions, 4.7

F

Fagge, Sir John 6.3 (Bramber Castle 'damage' theory), 22.5
Fairies 9.8
Farming 4.4 (enclosures), 8.2 (primitive methods),10.3, 14.8 (See under 'Agriculture')
'Felons' Associations' 13.3
Ferry 1.2
Field names 4.11, 11.1
Fields 10.11 (patterns in the soil), 11.1 (measurements), 12.3
Film and stage celebrities at Shoreham Beach 7.11
Fire, Bramber (1286) 5.10
Fire places 11.5, 13.12 (See 'Hearths')
Fire ships 5.10
Fishing 8.10
Fishing rights (see *The Adur River* 2.8), 8.10
Flax and linseed oil 4.5
Flax 8.5, 9.4
Flaxlands 1.3, 4.5, 4.11, 8.5
Flint tools 6.7, 12.5
Floods 7.2, 12.8, 15.8, 18.11
Flying bombs 1.7
Flying days at Shoreham 7.10
Flying Fortress bomber 13.5
'Foldsoke' 4.4
Follies, The (See 'Dawn Close', #Dawn Crescent') 7.1
Food preservation 2.4
Footbridge from Kings Barnes 19.10 (See 'White Bridge')
Fords 5.8
Forests, destruction of, 5.3
Forge, Beeding, 6.8, 9.1 (shoeing horses, oxen)
Fox, Geoff, councillor, Bramber Parish Council 13.8 (illustration)
Fox, George (Quaker meeting in Beeding 1655) 10.8
Fox, Gill, Chairman, Bramber Parish Council 13.8 (illustration), PG9
Fox-hunting 13.7
Frankpledge (See *The Parish Council*) 1.9, 3.9, 12.11, 13.3
Fraud 14.11

Fry, Elizabeth, social reformer 10.8

G

'Galile' 9.12n (the term explained)
Games 5.6, 11.1, 11.10
Garage, Beeding (See *The Blacksmith* Part 2.   Also under 'Tribe') 6.10), 15.1
    (excavations: mammoths, aurochs, woolly rhinoceros)
Gardiner, Mark, field officer, Institute of Archaeology 4.9
Gas 5.12, 10.7
George V (Jubilee) 1.8
Gibbet ('Hangman's Acre') 13.3
Glebeland 4.11, 12.9
Gnomonics (time and time-keeping) 8.1
Godfrey, Walter 4.1
Goffe, Revd. Stephen, rector of Bramber-cum-Botolph's) 7.3 (son William, the
    regicide) (See 'Temple')
'Gooding Day' 7.12 (the poor of the parish)
Goring, Sir Harry, of Highden 11.12
Gotham, John, map-maker 18.8 (See Bibliography)
Gough, Si Richard PG6
Gough-Calthorpe, Sir Henry, of Elvetham Hall, Hampshire 9.7 (See 'Elections')
Gounter, Captain, author of narrative of Charles II's escape 2.2
Great Bridge of Bramber, see under 'Bramber'
Greystone Wealden marble 2.6
Gunpowder Plot 5.11
Guide Books and Diaries (See *Earlier Views of the County)* 13.2
Guthrum (Danish king) 15.3
Gypsy Lane 2.2, 10.8

H

Hammer ponds 17.10
'Hangman's Acre' (on Tenantry Down) 13.3
Hearth tax 6.1
Hearths 11.6 (See 'Chimneys')
Hedge (See *Woodland and Hedge)* 8.2, 5.12
Henry III, 5.3, 5.9. 17.10. 20.3
Henry VIII 7.8 (jewel-keeper)
Hero, Beeding 11.8 (See also *Beeding's Heroes* 19.9
Hide, or hyde, defined 4.2
Higgler 6.1 (See *The Beeding Higgler* 14.5)
History (KN-B's view of) 1.1, 10.3
Hoard, Bramber 1981 (See *A Bronze Age Hoard)* 15.4
Hollar, Wenceslas, painter 6.3, 7.9 (St. Nicholas)
'Hollow-ways' 2.3, 6.6
Holly Cottage 3.10
Horses and Horse-power 8.2, 16.1
Horton clay-pit 2.12

Horton Farm 8.11

Horton Hall (farmhouse) 2.6 (See *The Great Bridge of Bramber*), 3.5

Horton Manor 14.1

Hospital, Bidlington 12.4

Hounds, Lord of Bramber's 13.7

House names 11.1

Huckster 6.1, 8.8

Hundred Court 3.7

Hunter-gatherers 15.1

Hunting with hounds 13.7

Hutchinson, Revd. Thomas, Vicar of Beeding and Bramber (See '*The Priory of Sele*' 2.11) 9.12 (removed ruined parts of St. Peter's without permission 1974)

Hyde (area of land that could be ploughed in a season). (See note 8.5) 4.2, 6.9, 17.6 ('husbandland' cf. husbandry)

Hyde Farm estate 7.1

Hyde Street 19.3

I

Ice storage 7.7 (ice-wells) 14.6 (ice-pits)

Immigrant tribes a threat 18.2

Individual houses by name 7.1

Industrial Revolution 1.6, 5.3, 12.5 (early parallel with)

Industry (local) 5.3, 17.10

Industry (domestic) 4.5

Ine, King of Wessex 18.1 (2)

Ing 11.1 (measurement) (See *Beida's Ing* 18.2)

Inns 3.7

Inns and alehouses:

The Rising Sun (formerly 'The Star') 1.9, 8.3, 14.8 (toll booth on south side/ Vestry Meetings at inn)

The King's Head: (See 'hundred court') 1.9, 3.7 (the only Beeding inn on coaching map), 3.9, 3.10, 6.10, 8.3, 12.11, 14.8, 14.12

The Sussex Pad 4.12 (smuggling trade)

Internal combustion engine (I.C.E.) 6.10, 7.10

Investment (land) 11.9

Iron industry in Sussex 5.3, 17.10

J

James I 3.6

John, King of England 13.4 (visit to Knepp, AD 1202)

Jordan, Mrs., actress 3.2 (portrait by Sir Thomas Lawrence)

K

Key Keeper, Bramber Castle (custodian) 6.3

Kings Barnes (river crossing to Sele Priory) 2.7

Kings Barnes (Royal residence of Saxon kings) 2.7, 4.12, 14.1 (removed from Bramber parish)
King's Head, The, (See 'Inns'), 15.11/12
Kings of Wessex 4.9 (reigned over Sele Priory estates) 5.1
Knepp Castle 13.4 (raised to the ground)
Knepp Castle ruins 2.5 (See 'Caryll')
Knights Templar (Bramber) 2.6, 4.1, 6.11
Knights of St. John (Hospitallers) 3.12, 4.1, 6.11

L

Lancaster, educationist.1.6 (See Raikes, Bell)
Lancing Carriage Works 7.11
Land drainage and reclamation 11.11 (See Cater Rand)
Land investment 11.9
Land Measures (See *Hyde*) 17.6
Landscape, changes in, 5.6
Law and order 5.2
Law and order (deterrents) 13.3
Lawrence, Sir Thomas, painter (See *The Picture*) 3.2, 9.5, 17.2
Le Chapelier, Isabel (pursuit of) 9.10
Lechepole, Andrew de, (unpopular Steward of Bramber Castle) 5.10
Legend, the importance of , 10.2
Leper hospital, Bramber
Lime-burning 2.12. 11.2
Limestone (for causeway)
Linton, Renée, of Orchard Lodge, Bramber PG7
Linton, Roger, Curator, St. Mary's House, Bramber PG7
Livestock farming 14.5
Local customs 10.4
Local legends 10.2
Locks 4.6
Lollards (followers of John Wycliffe) 5.2
Lord of the Manor 2.10 (Beeding), 4.4 (role, rules and customs)
Lost settlements 10.11
Lower Beeding   See under 'Beedings'

M

Macabre cure 9.8
Mace (Bramber) 13.8
Magdalen College, Oxford 1.7, 2.5, 2.11, 6.4, 7.2, 7.9 (armorial bearings at St. Nicholas), 9.12, 12.4 (acquired Priory of Sele. See Waynflete), 16.8, 17.9
Magna Carta 8.8 (standard measures for wine and ale)
Mail coaches 3.7, 3.10 (See 'Turnpike' and 'Inns')
Mail robberies 19.7 (Erringham)
Maines Farm Road 2.3, 4.3
Mammoths   (See *Inhabitants* 15.1)
Manor of Horton 3.4

Manorial Court 2.10, 8.3
Manors of Sussex 4.2
Map of Bramber 18.8
Manorial system 4.2, 4.4
Maps 18.8
Margaret, St. (dedication of bell) 5.8
Mary Agnes, Sister (lessee of 'The Towers') 1.5
Maubank, Sir Philip, of Dorset, Lord of the Manor of Horton 3.4
Maundy Money 14.11
Measurements 6.9, 11.1, 17.7
Medal 5.10
Medicine, medieval 6.12
Memorial Playing Fields, Beeding 2.9, 4.4, 11.1 (50 years of), 14.2
Mercator, Gerhardus (Flemish cartographer) 18.8
Meresman   2.9, 6.1, 6.5 (looked after parish bounderies)
Merestones (markers of parish boundary) 6.1
Mesolithic period (Middle Stone Age) 12.5
Milestones 11.3 (decline with railways). (See 'Coaching days'))
Millennium Map 18.8
Millennium Meeting, Beeding Parish Council PG13
Mill pond 14.7
Mills 2.10, 10.12, 14.7
'Millsoke' 11.9 (percentage of corn ground for villagers) (See 'Barter')
Miners 5.3
Mission Hall 8.6 (Dacre Gardens - Sunday School, magic lantern shows)
Moated Site 5.10, 12.3
Mock Bridge 11.11
Monaco, Princess Charlotte of, pupil at 'The Towers' 1.4
Monaco, Prince Louis of, visited his daughter, Princess Charlotte 1.4
Money-lending 11.9 (investing in land)
Monks of Sele (Benedictine AD1083-c.1480) 5.4, 12.1, 12.4 (reprimanded for neglect of
        St.Mary's Chapel)
Monks of Sele (Carmelite AD c1480-c1536) 5.4, 12.1
Moral Economy (fair prices) 4.10
Motor cars 6.10, 9.6
Mummers' plays 8.6
Murder, Beeding (See *Sanctuary*) 9.10
Music, in church 13.8
Mysteries, Medieval (village disappearances) (See 'Black Death') 4.3, 13.8

N

Names 5.5 (barge families) 6.1, 8.11 (nick-names), 11.8, 17.10 (history of), 18.7
Napoleonic Wars (1795-1832) (effect on Sussex) 4.10
National Savings in wartime 10.3
National Society (promotion of education) 1.7
Naval operations (WWII) 12.6
Navigation (see *Cater Rand*) 11.11
Navigation Act 1807, 2.8, 11.11, 18.8

Neale, John Mason (composer of 'Good King Wenceslas') 17.11

Nell (new houses at) 18.7

Neolithic period 12.5 (New Stone Age c1800 BC), 13.7 (weapons and tools), 15.1

New House (later Valerie Manor) 1.5, 2.2,

Newman, Cardinal Henry (friend of Dr. Bloxam) 9.11, 17.2, 18.1(2) (stayed at Priory of Sele before leaving for Rome)

Nicknames 8.11

Norfolk, Duke of, 5.8 (Gotham map in his library), 7.9 (armorial bearings at St. Nicholas), 8.9 (fishing rights), 17.9 (fishing grants),

Norfolk suspension bridge 5.7, 19.10 (opened 1833)

Normans 12.3

Nuclear attack 19.12 (preparations for)

Numerals 8.9

Numismatics 8.9 (Philip and Mary shilling discovery), 20.3

Nuns 1.4

O

Occupations (local) 6.1

Oglethorpe, Owen, Vicar of Beeding (later Bishop of Carlisle. Crowned Queen Elizabeth I) 18.1(2)

Old Beeding (south of Beeding court - conjectural) 5.9

Old Shoreham Toll Bridge (timber) 19.10 (See also Shoreham Toll Bridge)

Ordnance Survey (1791) 18.8

Outings and excursions, 4.7

Overseers of the Poor 1.9, 12.11

Owling (i.e. smuggling) 4.12, 11.4

Ox-bow 2.8, 4.6 (loop from Bedney round to Kings Barnes), 11.11

Oxen 9.1, 19.3, 20.3

Oxford Movement (See Newman) 9.11, 14.9/10, 17.2, 18.1(2)

P

Paleolithic period (dawn of history) 12.5, 13.8

Parish Council (law and order) 1.9, 10.5 (control of water supply), 12.11, PG13

Parish Magazine *The Christian* (precursor of *The Villager*) 1.1, 3.11, 8.7 (See Appendix One for ceasing publication)

Parish Records 3.9, 6.1 (Parish 'sure-coffer')

Partridge Green (See 'Locks') 4.6

Patterns in the fields 10.11, 12.3, 12.9 (crop patterns)

Peasants' Revolt (See *Jack Cade*) 3.12, 7.4, 9.9, 17.11

Peel, Robert 14.12 (founding of first police force – 'bobbies' or 'peelers')

Penn Cottage, Steyning 3.1 (Quaker meeting in Beeding)

Penny Blacks 6.6

Penny Post 3.10

Pepperscombe Farm 10.8

Peppersgate 10.8

Pepys, Samuel, diarist 2.2

Perambulations of the Bounds 3.4

Philip, King of Spain 8.9

Pieces of eight 3.5

Pig, A tale of a, 9.8

Piles, Bramber Bridge 2.6 (sewer excavations), 4.1

Pinder 6.1 (pound manager)

Pipe Rolls 12.10

Playing-fields 14.2 ('The Ham') See 'Memorial Playing Fields'

Pocock, Isaac (fishing rights) 8.10, 17.9

Police (1856) (See *The Early Years* 18.1) 3.9, 14.11 (the village policeman)

Policeman, Beeding's first 13.3

Poll tax 5.2

Polyalbion (1610) (See Michael Drayton) 2.8

Pond Farm 2.9, 3.7 (19th century barn)

Ponds (for fish-stocks) 8.10

Poor, The 5.2, 7.12, 8.2

Poor Law 4.4

Poor rate 1.4, 18.1(1)

Population, Beeding's 18.1(1)

'Porringer' (chalice), St. Botolph's 7.8

Port, father of Beida and Maegla 18.1 (Landed AD 501 at 'Portsmuda' - Portsmouth)

Portrait (see Sir Thomas Lawrence) 3.2, 15.6 (repeat)

Portus Adurni 2.8

Postcards of Bramber and Beeding 7.2 (floods)

Post Office, Beeding 3.10

Post-war austerity 10.3

Potter, Walter, taxidermist (1835-1918) 4.7 (founder of Potter's Museum), 9.3

Potter's Museum 4.7, 9.3, 15.2

Pound (animal enclosure) 6.1

Pound (coinage) 18.6

Pound House Cottage 3.1

Poverty in the countryside 4.10

Praty, Bishop 12.4 (reprimanded monks 1440, for neglect of St. Mary's Chapel)

Princess Royal, The 16.11

Printing 6.2

Priory Church (building of, before AD1096) 2.1

Priory Field (post WWII) 7.1

Priory of Sele, founded by William de Braose. (See also 'Sele Priory') 2.10, 2.11 (refurbished 1724/5), rebuilt 1788-1790. (See *Revd. Thomas Hutchinson*. See also under 'Revd. Thomas Newlin'), 6.2 (Stephen de Sens inventory), 6.4 (origins), 9.12, 12.4 (decline and fall from neglect (1459), Priory of Sele (Carmelite rebuilding c.1480), 12.4 (given to Magdalen College, Oxford as endowment c.1490), 13.7 (horses and hounds lodged with monks), 14.7 (watermill) 2.11, 9.11

Prisoners 7.5

Properties, Beeding (names of) 1.3

Pugin, Augustus Welby Northmore, architect and designer 17.2 (corona at St. Peter's)

Punishment of vagabonds (cruelty of) 5.2

Q

R

S

St. Cuthman's port 1.2, 2.6

St. Leonard's Forest 3.11, 5.3 (iron industry), 6.9, 13.4, 17.10, 18.1(2) (dragons recorded)

St. Mary Magdalen 12.4 (hospital in Bidlington)

St. Mary's House, Bramber 2.6, 4.1(Templar settlement), 5.9, 6.11 (Richard II, departure for Crusades), 10.1 (secret passages), PG2

St. Mary's House, Bramber, Headquarters, for Commanding Officer 12.6

St. Mary's House, Bramber 6.11, 8.9 (Philip and Mary shilling discovery)

St. Mary's House, Bramber 12.3 (ref. previous buildings on site) 12.3

St. Mary's House, Bramber 5.9, 12.3 (ref. 'wardens' residence)

St. Nicholas 6.11 (Templar Maltese cross), 7.9 (c AD 1093, rebuilt 1790) PG2, 7.9 (Hollar's picture, c1640), 7.9 (new chancel), 7.9 (armorials), 13.8 (the Mace)

St. Peter's, Beeding 2.1, 5.5 (barge families), 5.8 (comparison with St. Peter's at Manningford Bruce), 6.2

St. Peter's 12.7 (bells), 14.9 (yew avenue), 9.5 (extra-mural cemetery)

St. Peter's, erection of 'gallile' [gallery] 1790/1) 9.12

St. Peter's (old-style music/ harmonium, flute-player) 9.11 (See Edwards)

St. Peter's (repairs/new south aisle 1852) 9.11

St. Peter's rood screen and old gallery removed 9.11, 13.12

St. Peter's War Memorial tablet 11.8

St. Peter de Veteri (St. Peter of the Old Bridge) 4.3

St. Wilfrid 2.1, 10.11, 12.9, 19.3 (arrived in Sussex c.681)

Salt 2.4 (see also *Sussex Archaeological Collections*), 5.9, 11.6 (salt rack/shelf), (See Eric Holden), salt-cotes 12.3 ('shed-like structures'), 12.8 (16thC wall-painting at St. Mary's), 18.11

Salt mounds 12.3 (in Adur valley)

Salt pits in the Adur valley 13.1, 18.11

Salt trade in Sussex 13.1, 18.11

Salterns (food preservation) 2.4, 12.3, 12.8

Saltings Field (salt-workings) 12.8

Saltings Way (1960s) 7.1 (gap formed to make way for)

Salzman, L.F. (ed.) *The Chartulary of Sele Priory,* 2.1, 5.8, 5.10, 10.10, 13.1, 13.7, 15.3 (minstrels, Nicholas the Harper, William the Piper), 17.11

Sanctuary (seeking refuge in churches) 9.10

Saumur 7.5

Saxons (See *Beeding's Dark Age*) 4.9, 8.12 (settlement), 12.11 (administration), 19.3

School House (house of Len Acton) 1.6

School outings and excursions 4.7

Schools 1.6, 1.7, 1.8, 9.3 (visits)

Scott, Sir Walter (quoted) 14.9/10

Scottish regiment 12.6 (15th division, billeted at Sele Court until D-Day)

Screen (rood screen fragment) 9.1

Script (Phoenician onwards) 9.4

Sea floods 9.2

Sele (or Sela) 2.1 'hamlet of Sele' (See *Chartulary of Sele*), 3.4 ('Beeding alias Sele'), (See also 'Priory of Sele') 5.4, 5.8, 8.12, 14.1 (origins of name 'Sele'), 15.10 (excavations), 18.2 ('happy/hall')

Sele (Sale) Croft (place for fattening sheep and cattle)

Sele 8.12 (Saxon settlement), 12.9 (first Christian church 11thC)

Sele Court 12.6 (now part of 'The Towers')
Sele Field (site for Beeding School) 1.7, 11.1
Sele Gardens (1920s) 7.1
Sele Priory 1.6 (as a school), 2.10 (watermill), 2.11 (cloisters), 4.3 settlement), (See 6.4
    Windows into the Pas)t, 7.5, 7.8 (silver plate), 7.9 (windows at Buncton Church),
    9.5 (vicarage), 12.3, 12.9 (Chapel of St. John), 17.9 (fishing rights)
Sele Vicarage House survey (1787) 9.12
Sele village 12.3
Sele's 'two churches' 12.9
Semaphore 14.4, 18.7 (Roman signal station). (See 'Truleigh Hill' 22.2
Sennis (aka de Sens) Stephen 6.2
Serpent, The Bramber, 15.3
Service Station, Beeding 6.10
Sewers for the Rape of Bramber (1807), Commissioners of, 4.6, 11.11
Sewers in Bramber (1957) 2.6
Seymour, Sir Thomas, of Sudeley, Lord of the Manor of King's Barns (1547) 2.7, PG5
Sheep-farming 8.2
Shoreham Airport 7.10 (See *Buzzing Over Beeding*)
Shoreham Custom House 11.4
Shoreham Road (1930s) 7.1
Shoreham toll bridge 2.5, 19.10 (See also 'Old Shoreham Toll Bridge')
Shot contest, Bramber 5.7, 6.3 (cannon), 15.7
Siamese Twin (Edburton) 6.6
Small Dole 23.3 (formerly 'Dole Green' in Elizabethan times)
Small Dole Board School 1.8
Smith, George, builder of 'The Towers' 1.5
Smock 8.5 labourer's (linen garment/ Sunday smocks), 18.7
Smuggling 11.4 (tobacco), (See *Owling*)
Snellings (See 'Mason') 1.3
Soare (or Sore), (old name for the Adur river) 1.2, 2.8, 7.2
Soil (See *Answers in the Soil* 10.11)
South Downs Way 1.2
Speed, John (map-maker) 18.8
Spelling 9.4
Spender, Stephen (poet) (quoted) 11.8
Sports 11.1 (See 'Memorial Playing Fields')
Stage-coach 3.10
Station, Bramber 1.4, 2.8, 5.10, 9.3, 15.5 (platform extension)
'Statute of Labourers' (1351) 5.2 (See *The Poor. Medieval Mysteries)* 7.4
Statute of Winchester (1285) 13.3 (parish to keep its own law and order)
Steyning and District Waterworks Company 10.5, 17.6
Steyning Electric Light Company 6.10,
Steyning, nearest market town 7.1
Stone Age finds (Botolph's) 4.9, 15.1
Stone Age periods: See Paleolithic (dawn of history), Mesolithic (Middle Stone Age),
    Neolithic (New Stone Age) 12.5, 13.8
Steyning bypass, see under 'Bramber'
Stirton, John, corporal in the Royal Engineers, Ordnance Survey Department 2.9
Stores, Beeding (See *Village Stores*) 3.8

Storms 9.2 (storm damage)
Streatham, Manor of, 9.9
Stuart Fayre 1988 PG13
Superstitions 9.8
Sure-coffer, keeper of register of births, marriages and deaths, 6.1
Sussex 19.3 (origin of name)
Sussex marble (winklestone) 2.6
Sussex Pad (see *Inns*)
Sussex Portland Cement Company 2.12 (See Beeding Cement Works, Also *Chalk-pit*)
Swing bridge 1.2
Swiss Gardens 15.5
Symons, Mrs. Ursula (sister of Capt. Gounter) 2.2

T

Tattersall (See Tettersal)
Tax and duty on wool 9.9
Taxes 5.1, 6.1, 9.9
Tea-gardens 15.5 (Bramber), (Shoreham 'Swiss Gardens')
Templar Maltese Cross at St. Nicholas 6.11
Templar settlements (Adur Valley), 4.1 (St. Mary's House, Bramber), 10.1, PG4
Temple, James, Colonel (Governor, Bramber Castle), regicide 6.3
Temple, Knights of the, 2.8, 6.11, 10.1, 13.4
Tenantry Down 13.3
Terrier (land ownership map) 1.3, 1.6, 12.8
Tettersal (Tattersal) family 11.5, 18.5 (helped Charles II in his escape to France)
Thatched cottages 5.10
Thorogood, Mary, of Orchard Lodge, Bramber PG7
Thorogood, Peter, St. Mary's House, Bramber PG7
Thundersbarrow (near Shoreham A27 Tunnel) 14.1 (iron age fort), 18.2
Tidemills 2.10
Timber conservation 11.2
Tinder Box 16.2, 16.2 (Potter's Museum exhibit)
Tithes 5.1, 9.9 (Tithe Act 1925)
Token, Bramber, 3.6
Toll Bridge, Old Shoreham 5.7, 18.8
Toll bridges 5.7
Toll gate, Beeding 12.12
Toll gates 2.2, 2.3, 3.10, 5.7
Toll house, Bramber 2.3 See also front cover illustration
Toll-keeper 3.10
Tolls 2.2, 3.10
Tools of our ancestors 6.7
Tottington Manor sale notice (May 1832) 11.7
Towers, The, 1.3, 1.4, 1.5 (built by George Smith), 8.6 (plays & charity events), 18.7
Trades (running in families) 11.7, 14.5
Trade tokens 3.6, (See 'Boyne' and 'J. Lowe-Warren), Transport (local) 11.10, 13.6
Travelling players 8.6
Trestle bridge to carry South Coast railway) 19.10 (replaced in 1890s)

Trevithick, Robert 4.2 (inventor of first locomotive)
Truleigh Hill 6.7 (See *Flint Tools*), 18.7 (site of motte and bailey c1066 approached by a 'bostel')
Tub race (See 'Bath Tub Race')
Turner, Thomas, diarist 21.4
Turnpike roads 2.3, 2.5, 3.7, 5.3, 12.12
Turnpike Act 1807 14.8 (for new turnpike road on eastern side of Adur River)
Turnpike Acts 2.3, 2.12, 3.5 (See 'Mail coaches'), 12.10 (bad state of roads), 2.12 (tolls)
Twin Aid and Third World 9.1, 16.11
Tyler, Wat (Peasant's Revolt') 17.11

U

Unemployment (during Napoleonic Wars) 4.10, 12.11 ('the idle'), 18.1(1) (Vestry Minutes report)
'Upper' and 'Lower' Beeding 3.11, 5.1, 10.9 (See *Beedings*. Also 'Rape of Bramber')

V

Vagrants 5.2
Valerie Manor (formerly 'New House'. Rrenamed by later owner, Valerie Samuels) 1.5
Vandalism 15.3
V E Day (See *Forget it Not!*) 13.5
Vertical sundial (St. Botolph's) 8.1 (see *Gnomonics*)
Vestry Minute books 3.9, 8.2 (See *The Early Years*)
Vestry used as court 1.9
Veteri Ponte (Roman bridge) 1.1, 1.2, 2.3, 4.8, 5.7, 10.8 (possible Quaker crossing point for Peppersgate), 10.10 (pontoon style), 12.3, 14.1, 18.2, 19.10
Vikings, 5.1
Village Hall (Beeding and Bramber) 8.3 (new hall, 1930)
Village occupations 6.1
Village people 8.4 (for complete list see Index of Village People)
Village Signs 16.8
Village Stores 3.8
Village theatricals (See *Entertainments*) 8.6
Villager, The, See Preface, PT's introduction, KN-B's 'Introduction' 1.1. See azticles in Appendix One and 'List of Village People' ('Faires' etc.) in Appendix Two – 'Faires' etc.
Villages, 4.3 (See *Medieval Mysteries*), 4.8, 5.2, 12.9 (deserted), 14.1 (Boundary Commission), 16.8 (Black Death)

W

Wages 5.2 (See *The Riots at Beeding* 4.10)
'Walled Garden' 1.5 ('New house'. See Backshall))
Walton, Izaak, author of T*he Compleat Angler* 17.9
Wandering Minstrel 15.3

War (bombing) 1.7
War Effort 10.3 (rationing)
War memorials 12.6 11.8 (St. Peter's War Memorial tablet)
Water carts 8.6
Watermill, Beeding 2.10, 10.12
Watermill (Millfield) 2.5, 2.10
Watermills 12.9, 14.7, 18.11
Water Supply 10.5, 17.5
Water transport 4.6 (See 'Ox-bow'. Also 'Locks')
Wartime Beeding (1942) 5.6, 10.3 (National Savings)
Waynflete, Bishop of Winchester 5.9 (repairs to Bramber bridge),
        2.4 (acquired Priory of Sele 1459), 12.9
Weald, The 6.1, 9.1
Weathervanes 14.3 (The Pope's Decree)
Wells 7.7 (See *Psalm 54 v.10*), 10.5, 17.6 (well-digging)
West Grinstead (See *Locks*) 4.6
Wharves at St. Mary's, Bramber 2.6, 4.1 (discovered by Eric Holden)
Wheelwright 8.4
'White Bridge' 2.3, 5.8, 10.10, 11.11 (indicated as 'New Bridge'), 12.3, 19.10
Widsith (Anglo-Saxon poem) 2.1
Wild animals 10.11 (St. Leonard's Forest), 11.4 (Wild Beast Show)
William of Waynflete, Bishop of Winchester 5.9, 12.4
William I, the 'Conqueror' 12.4, 14.11
Winchester (Ethelwulf re-interred there) 2.7
Windmill Hill 2.3, 2.10, 10.12, 13.3
Windmills 10.12, 18.11
Window tax 6.1
Windpower 2.10
Windpumps 2.10
Wood and peat fires 11.6
Woodland and hedge 5.12
Wool trade (duty on it in Henry III's reign) 4.5
World War I, 1.1, 14.2
World War II, 10.3, 10.4, 11.12 (heroes), 13.5 (air-raids), 13.11, 19.2, 19.9
        (See *Beeding's Heroes*)
Worthing Museum 15.4
Wycliffe, John 5.2

Y

Yew, The 14.9 (St. Peter's yew avenue)
Yobe 15.7, 16.11 (See *Twin Aid*)

5. Alphabetical index of titles

Other books about Beeding and Bramber

See Bibliography for list of authors and titles mentioned in the text

Bygone Steyning, Bramber and Beeding
Aylwin Guilmant. Phillimore. 1988

Bramber – Glimpses of a Village
Beeding and Bramber Local History Society. 1996

The Adur Valley – Bramber and Beeding (1997)
The Adur Valley – South from Beeding (1998)
Graham Keane and Tony Ketteman. Sussex History Walks.
    Steyning Museum

St. Mary's Bramber: A Sussex House and its Gardens
Peter Thorogood   Bramber Press. 1998

The Parish and Priory Church of St. Peter
Parish of Beeding and Bramber with Botolphs. 1999

Beeding Millennium Map
Beeding and Bramber Local History Society. 2001

Bramber Millennium Map
Bramber Parish Council. 2001

A Glimpse into the Past:One Hundred Years of Baptist Worship in Beeding
Diana Durden. Upper Beeding Baptist Church. 2005

The Towers Convent – The First Hundred Years or So
Sister Mary Andrew. The Towers Convent. 2006

Beeding and Bramber.Two Sussex Villages. A Study of the Probate Inventories, Wills and Accounts 1613-1775
Beeding and Bramber Local History Society. 2007

Beeding: History of a Village.
Beeding and Bramber Local History Society. Revised edition 2010

PETER THOROGOOD

Born in Essex in 1927, Peter Thorogood was educated at Brentwood School (1937-1946) and Trinity College, Dublin (1948-52). On graduation, whilst waiting to take up an appointment with the Bristish School of Milan, he spent a year as a resident assistant master at Seaford College junior school, which was, at that time, situated in Mill Road, Worthing. In October 1953 he was appointed Director of Studies (and later Vice-Principal) of the British School of Milan, at the same time taking up the post of Lector in English Studies at the State University of Milan (1953-59).

On his return to England, he was appointed Lecturer in English Literature and Phonetics, British Council (1959-63), and Senior Lecturer in English, Polytechnic Central London (1963-84). As a social and literary historian, he has made a lifetime study of the poetry and comic verse of the 19thC Victorian poet, Thomas Hood. In 1966-7 he served as critic for 'The Spoken Word' column of the BBC weekly magazine, *The Listener*, and published his articles in book form under the title *Could I Hear That Again Please* (Bramber Press 2007).

In 1959 the family moved to Sussex, settling at Hurstpierpoint, which gave Peter the opportunity to enjoy long weekend walks on the South Downs and to acquaint himself with the heritage of the county. In 1984, he joined forces with designer and conservator, Roger Linton, with the purpose of restoring the medieval St. Mary's House in Bramber, Sussex, which, from 1987, has received many thousands of visitors to view the beautiful house and gardens.

For over a quarter of a century Peter has carried on research into the history of St. Mary's from its medieval origins to the present day and has, over the years, succeeded in establishing an important archive on the history of the house and its environs. For ten years he held the position of 'Key-Keeper' of Bramber Castle on behalf of English Heritage.

From 1960 onwards, Peter Thorogood began his researches into the life and work of the Victorian poet, Thomas Hood, and began to gather together a unique collection of first and later editions of Hood's poetry and prose, as well as original pen-and-ink sketches, watercolours and autograph letters. He published his best-selling *Thomas Hood: Poems Comic and Serious* in 2002.

Besides collating and editing *A Portrait of Village Life* by Keith Nethercoate-Bryant, Peter has also edited the work of several other writers, including the poems of the Sussex poet, Diana Dykes (*Late Flowerings*), the poems of the twin sisters, Margaret and Brenda Carpenter (*Two Hearts That Would Be True)*, and an 'upside-down' book for children by Garnet Durham (*The Tale of Septimus Jones*).

Peter has, for over fifty years, been a Fellow of the Royal Society of Arts. He is a Fellow of the Society of Antiquaries and a member of the Society of Authors. In 2006, Peter was, jointly with Roger Linton, awarded the MBE for 'Services to Conservation and the Arts' in the Queen's 80th Birthday Honours.

Books at Bramber Press

Poetry and Light Verse

Margaret and Brenda Carpenter: *Two Hearts that Would Be True.* Edited
    and introduced by Peter Thorogood. 2010
Garnet Durham: *The Tale of Septimus Jones.*
    An 'Upside-Down' Book. Edited by Peter Thorogood. 2005
Diana Dykes: *Late Flowerings.* Edited and introduced by
    Peter Thorogood. 2002
Thomas Hood: *Poems Comic and Serious,* edited with introduction and
    notes by Peter Thorogood. First published 1995, revised 2005
Peter Thorogood: *In These Places...At These Times. Selected Poems
    1950-1975.* 1997
Peter Thorogood: *The Complete Comic and Curious Verse of
    Peter Thorogood.* 2002

Fiction

Peter Thorogood: *South of the River: A Novel of the Fifties.* 2005

Criticism

Peter Thorogood: *Thomas Hood: A Chronology of his Life and Times* 2006
Peter Thorogood: *Could I Hear That Again, Please?* Articles from the BBC
    magazine, *The Listener,* 1966-1967. 2006

Non-Fiction

Ron Balaam: *The Royal Russell School 1980-1996.* 2009
Keith Nethercoate-Bryant: *Portrait of Village Life.* Collated and edited,
    with an introduction by Peter Thorogood. 2011
Tony Ketteman: *Return to Splendour: The Saving of a Country House.*
    Original photographs by Roger Linton. 2005
Peter Thorogood: *St. Mary's Bramber: A Sussex House and its Gardens.*
    1998
Peter Thorogood: *St. Mary's Bramber: A Pictorial Souvenir.* 1998